The Pocket Guide to
COMMERCIAL AIRCRAFT
and AIRLINE MARKINGS

AUTHOR'S NOTE:

The airline world had already entered a financially difficult time before the terrorist attacks against the USA on 11 September 2001, which have radically compounded the problem. Passenger markets have slumped, causing many airlines to cut the number of their employees and ground many of their aircraft, while the decrease in demand for new aircraft has led many manufacturers to lay off personnel and to slow production. These facts could not be introduced into 'The Pocket Guide to Commercial Aircraft and Airlines', which was already in production at the time of the terrorist attack, but the reader should be aware of the fact, and that a number of operators, such as Ansett, Sabena and Swissair, have collapsed as a result of these and other factors, but may possibly be revived.

First published in Great Britain in 2002
by Hamlyn, a division of Octopus Publishing Group Ltd

This edition published in 2003 by Bounty Books,
a division of Octopus Publishing Group Ltd
2–4 Heron Quays, London E14 4JP

ISBN 0 7537 0820 5

A CIP catalogue record for this book is available from the British Library
Printed and bound in China

The Pocket Guide to
COMMERCIAL AIRCRAFT
and AIRLINE MARKINGS

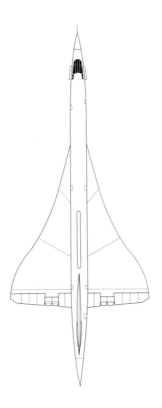

CONTENTS: Airliners section

AIRBUS INDUSTRIE A300

At much the same time that Boeing was finalizing the design of the world's first wide-body commercial transport, the Model 747, discussions had started in Europe to consider the design and manufacture of a large-capacity transport aircraft for short/medium-range services. On 28 May 1969, France and West Germany decided to go ahead with development of a European 'airbus' as the A300. Construction of the first machine began in September 1969, although it was December 1970 before Airbus Industrie was formally established for the 220- to 336-seat A300.

The first of two A300A1 aircraft made the type's maiden flight on 28 October 1972, and the first of two A300B2 machines, representing the basic production version, flew on 28 June 1973. The A300B2 entered service with Air France on 30 May 1974. Despite the excellent showing of the new airliner, orders were slow to materialize, but there was a major change of fortune in 1979 when Eastern Air Lines bought four A300B4 machines and then ordered 34 more.

Sales of the A300 amounted to 580 aircraft to the end of 2001 in variants that include the A300B2-100, with the fuselage lengthened by 8 ft 8 in (2.65 m); A300B2-200, with improved field performance; A300B2-220, with JT9D-59A turbofans; A300B2-320, an improved A300B2-220 with higher weights; A300B4-100, with more fuel; A300B4-120, an improved A300B4-100 with JT9D turbofans; A300B4-200, with structural strength-ening and extra fuel in the rear cargo hold; A300B4-200FF, with a two-crew flight deck; A300C4, convertible passenger/freight variant with a large port-side door; and A300-600, with greater passenger and freight capacity due to the addition of the rear fuselage of the A310 with the pressure bulkhead moved farther back, and a two-crew forward-facing flight deck with Electronic Flight Instrumentation System and new digital avionics.

Specification: Airbus Industrie A300-600 (Improved Version)
Origin: International
Type: two-crew short/medium-range wide-body transport
Powerplant: two General Electric CF6-80C2A1 turbofan engines each rated at 59,000 lb st (262.45 kN) dry
Performance: cruising speed, maximum 557 mph (897 km/h) at 30,000 ft (9145 m) and economical 543 mph (875 km/h) at 31,000 ft (9450 m); maximum operating altitude 40,000 ft (12190 m); range 4,297 miles (6852 km) with 266 passengers
Weights: empty operating 198,665 lb (90115 kg); maximum take-off 363,755 lb (165000 kg)
Dimensions: span 147 ft 1 in (44.84 m); length 177 ft 5 in (54.08 m); height 54 ft 3 in (16.53 m); wing area 2,798.71 sq ft (260.00 m²)
Payload: between 266 and 375 passengers within the context of an 87,391-lb (39885-kg) maximum payload

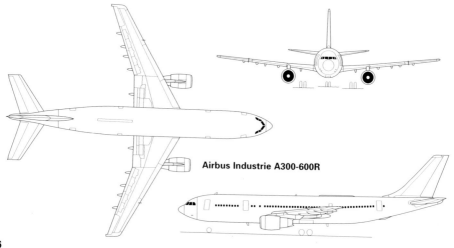

Airbus Industrie A300-600R

AIRBUS INDUSTRIE A310

It was in July 1978 that Airbus finalized the design and layout of the A310 as a smaller-capacity derivative of the A300, and decided to proceed with its development. The design was optimized for maximum commonality of components (structure and systems) between the A300 and the A310, for the latter is basically a variant of the former with the fuselage shortened by 13 frames. Although structurally similar that of the A300, the wing of the A310 differs aerodynamically and provides a higher lift coefficient. The wing is more efficient and combines with optimum utilization of cabin space to give the A310 exceptional 'fuel per seat' economy. The A310 made its maiden flight on 3 April 1982, received French and West German certification in March 1983, and entered service with Lufthansa and Swissair in the following month.

The A310 had originally been planned in short- and medium-range forms, but the former was cancelled and the latter became the A310-200, with the maximum weight of 266,755 lb (121000 kg) later increased to 305,555 lb (138600 kg) standard and 313,050 lb (142000 kg) optional with additional fuel capacity. The A310-200 was initially powered by two 50,000 lb st (222.41 kN) General Electric CF6-80A3 or 48,000 lb st (213.51 kN) Pratt & Whitney JT9D-7R4D1 turbofans, later options including CF6-80C2, PW4152 and PW4156A rated at up to 59,000 lb st (262.45 kN).

Further development of the airliner resulted in the A310-300 extended-range variant delivered from April 1986. This introduced the small triangular wing-tip fences and a basic maximum weight raised to 330,695 lb (150000 kg) to allow an increase in fuel capacity by the addition of tankage in the tailplane. Provision was also made for two additional fuel tanks in the wing's centre section.

By the end of 2001, Airbus had received orders for 260 aircraft.

Specification: Airbus Industrie A310-300
Origin: International
Type: two-crew short/medium-range wide-body transport
Powerplant: two Pratt & Whitney PW4156A turbofan engines each rated at 56,000 lb st (249.10 kN) dry
Performance: economical cruising speed 528 mph (850 km/h) at between 31,000 and 41,000 ft; range with 220 passengers and reserves for a 230-mile (370-km) diversion, 5,005 miles (8056 km); or, with additional fuel and take-off weight of 346,125 lb (157000 kg), 5,523 miles (8889 km); or, with additional fuel and take-off weight of 361,560 lb (164000 kg), 5,984 miles (9630 km)
Weights: empty operating between 177,130 and 178,135 lb (80344 and 80801 kg); maximum take-off between 330,675 and 361,550 lb (150000 and 164000 kg)
Dimensions: span 144 ft 0 in (43.89 m); length 153 ft 1 in (46.66 m); height 51 ft 10 in (15.80 m); wing area 2,357.37 sq ft (219.00 m²)
Payload: between 191 and 280 passengers with the context of a maximum payload of between 70,805 and 70,896 lb (32117 and 32158 kg)

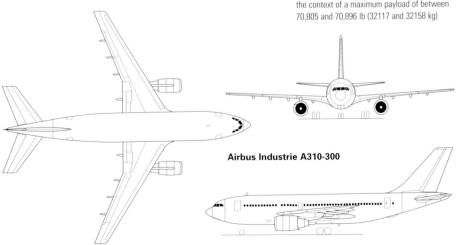

Airbus Industrie A310-300

AIRBUS INDUSTRIE A318 AND A319

It was with the launch of the 150-seat A320 in March 1984 that Airbus Industrie entered the market for single-aisle airliners with seating for under 200 passengers. The two longer-fuselage models are the A320 and A321, while the complementary pair of shorter-fuselage models are the 124-passenger A319 and the 100-passenger A318. The A319 programme was launched in June 1993 and the type entered service in May 1996. To August 2000, orders for the A319 totalled 712 machines, of which 367 had been delivered. In its A319-100 baseline form with CFM56-5A/B or IAE V2500-A5 turbofans rated at between 22,000 and 23,500 lb st (97.90 and 104.575 kN), the type can carry 124 passengers in a two-class arrangement over a typical range of 2,921 miles (4700 km) or an optional range of 4,225 miles (6800 km). In 1999 there began deliveries of the corporate jet version of the A319, and with up to seven auxiliary tanks, this can deliver a payload of 10 passengers over 7,208 miles (11600 km).

After considering an all-new 80/100-passenger AE31X family to be developed and manufactured in association with Chinese or Singaporean interests, Airbus Industrie then opted to proceed on its own with the creation of the A318 as a 100-passenger derivative of the A320. The first A318 is scheduled to make its maiden flight early in 2002 with deliveries starting about 12 months later. The A318 is in effect the A320 with its fuselage shortened by 4.5 frames (1.5 frames ahead of the wing and 3 frames behind the wing) and the powerplant options centred on the CFM56-5B and PW6000 turbofans. As a result of the shorter moment arm to the rear of the centre of gravity, the vertical tail is increased in area by adding some 2 ft 7.5 in (0.80 m) to its height. Orders for the A318-100 baseline model total 136 machines.

Specification: Airbus Industrie A318-100 (estimated)
Origin: International
Type: two/three-crew short-range narrow-body transport
Powerplant: two CFM56-5B/P or Pratt & Whitney PW6000 turbofan engines each rated at between 20,000 and 23,000 lb st (89.00 and 102.35 kN) dry
Performance: cruising speed, maximum 541 mph (871 km/h) at optimum altitude and economical 515 mph (829 km/h) at optimum altitude; certificated ceiling 39,000 ft (11885 m); range 1,724 miles (2775 km) with 107 passengers standard or 3,275 miles (5270 km) with 107 passengers optional
Weights: empty operating 87,015 lb (39470 kg); maximum take-off 130,071 lb (59000 kg) standard and 145,503 lb (66000 kg) optional
Dimensions: span 111 ft 10.5 in (34.10 m); length 103 ft 1.75 in (31.44 m); height 41 ft 2.5 in (12.56 m); area 1,319.70 sq ft (122.60 m²)
Payload: between 107 and 114 passengers within the context of a 29,813-lb (13523-kg) maximum payload

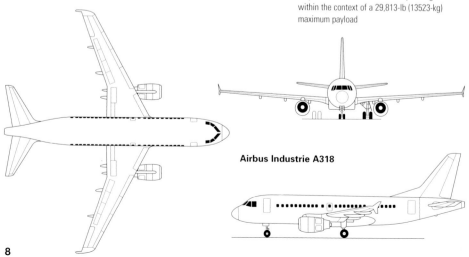

Airbus Industrie A318

It was in June 1981, after about ten years of initial consideration, that Airbus Industrie decided to go ahead with the A320 as a new 150-passenger short/medium-range airliner. Although it bears a very strong family relationship to the preceding A300 and A310 in terms of its basic layout, the A320 was a completely new design that nonetheless made full use of the structural and aerodynamic ideas that had proved so successful in the A300 and A310, and also of their systems and equipment. The A320 was also the world's first airliner with a quadruplex fly-by-wire control system operated with sidestick controllers.

The first A320 recorded the type's maiden flight on 22 February 1987, and European certification for the A320-100 was granted in February 1988 with deliveries following from March of the same year. Certification of the A320-200 followed in November 1988, and both of these variants were initially delivered with the powerplant of two CFM56-5A1 turbofans each rated at 23,500 lb st (104.53 kN). Aircraft with the revised powerplant of two V2500-A1 turbofans, each rated at 25,000 lb st (111.21 kN), followed after certification in April 1989. American certifications of the variants with the CFM and IAE engines were granted in December 1988 and July 1989 respectively.

Production of the A320-100 baseline model totalled only 21 aircraft, and with the end of this model's production the A320-200 became just the A320. This is otherwise differentiated from the A320-100 by the delta-shaped fences at its wing tips, tankage in the wing's centre section for an additional 1,763 Imp gal (8016 litres) of fuel, and a higher maximum take-off weight. By August 2001, Airbus Industrie had received orders for 1,539 A320-200 (or A320) aircraft, later machines with uprated engine options, and deliveries amounted to 962 aircraft.

Specification: Airbus Industrie A320-200 (highest-weight option)
Origin: International
Type: two-crew short/medium-range narrow-body transport
Powerplant: two CFM International CFM56-5B4 turbofan engines each rated at 26,500 lb st (117.88 kN) or two IAE V2525-A5 turbofan engines each rated at 25,000 lb st (111.21 kN) dry
Performance: cruising speed, maximum 561 mph (903 km/h) at 39,000 ft (11885 m) and economical 518 mph (834 km/h) at 39,000 ft (11885 m); certificated ceiling 39,000 ft (11885 m); range 3,395 miles (5463 km) with 150 passengers and reserves for a 230-mile (370-km) diversion
Weights: empty operating between 92,113 and 92,746 lb (41782 and 42069 kg); maximum take-off between 162,040 and 169,755 lb (73500 and 77000 kg)
Dimensions: span 113 ft 3 in (33.91 m); length 123 ft 3 in (37.57 m); height 38 ft 8.5 in (11.80 m); area 1,317.55 sq ft (122.40 m²)
Payload: between 150 and 179 passengers within the context of a maximum payload of between 41,735 and 42,372 lb (18931 and 19220 kg) in the highest- and lowest-weight options respectively

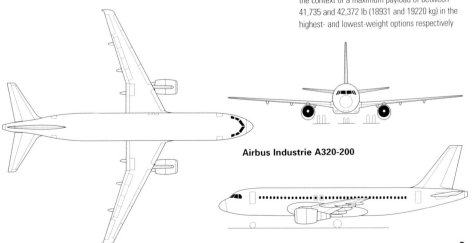

Airbus Industrie A320-200

AIRBUS INDUSTRIE A321

The success of the A320 was instrumental in persuading Airbus Industrie that there was sense in developing versions with shorter and longer fuselages. The A321 long-fuselage model was the first of the derivatives, its programme being launched in November 1989. The primary change from the A320 is a lengthening of 22 ft 9 in (6.94 m) to boost passenger accommodation to between 185 and 200. Other changes included structural strengthening and extension of the wing's trailing edge with doubled-slotted flaps for improved field performance. In overall terms, therefore, the A321 is very closely related to the preceding A320 and following A319/A318, which offers the attractive feature of a common pilot rating for all four members of the A320 family.

The first of four development aircraft recorded the type's maiden flight on 11 March 1993 with two IAE V2530-A5 turbofans each rated at 30,000 lb st (133.45 kN). The second followed in May 1993 with two identically rated CFM56-5B turbofans. The A321 received European certification with these different powerplants in December 1993 and February 1994 respectively, the first revenue-earning services starting in March 1994.

The baseline A321-100 has a maximum take-off weight of 105,495 lb (47852 kg), and has been complemented by the A321-200 extended-range version, which was launched in April 1995 for the holiday charter type of operation as well as North American domestic services with changes including a reinforced structure, higher-thrust versions of the same two basic engine options, and additional fuel tankage. The first A321-200 was delivered in March 1997, and Airbus has now offered developments of this model with weight increased to 205,025 lb (93000 kg) and still further enlargement of the fuel capacity for a range of up to 3,417 miles (5500 km). By August 2001, orders had been placed for 401 A321 aircraft, of which 207 had been delivered.

Specification: Airbus Industrie A321-100
Origin: International
Type: two-crew short/medium-range narrow-body transport
Powerplant: two CFM International CFM56-5B1 or IAE V2530-A5 turbofan engines each rated at 30,000 lb st (133.45 kN) dry
Performance: cruising speed, maximum 561 mph (903 km/h) at 39,000 ft (11885 m) and economical 522 mph (840 km/h) at 39,000 ft (11885 m); certificated ceiling 39,000 ft (11885 m); range 2,646 miles (4259 km) with maximum payload and reserves for a 230-mile (370-km) diversion
Weights: empty operating 105,495 lb (47852 kg); maximum take-off 182,980 lb (83000 kg)
Dimensions: span 111 ft 10 in (34.09 m); length 146 ft 10 in (44.51 m); height 38 ft 9 in (11.81 m); area 1,317.55 sq ft (122.40 m²)
Payload: between 185 and 220 passengers within the context of a 47,725-lb (21648-kg) maximum payload

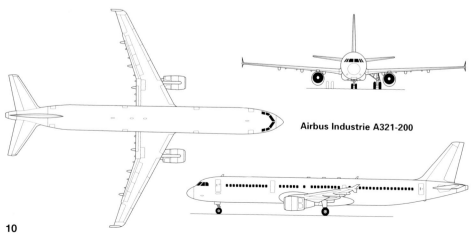

Airbus Industrie A321-200

On 5 June 1987, Airbus decided to proceed with the two-engined A330 and four-engined A340 as a pair of advanced airliners able to compete in technical and cost terms with the latest American airliners such as the Boeing Models 767 and 777. The two types share the same fuselage, tail unit, landing gear and flight deck, and the same basic wing is differentiated only by the number of pylons as well as insignificant changes to the structure and leading-edge slats.

The first A330 flew on 2 November 1992 with 67,500 lb st (300.25 kN) General Electric CF6-80E1A2 turbofans, and of the two alternative powerplants, the first to fly on the A330 was the identically rated Rolls-Royce Trent 768/772, followed by the 68,000 lb st (302.48 kN) Pratt & Whitney PW4164/4168. The A330 was certificated in October 1993 and entered revenue-earning service in January 1994.

The A330 is currently offered in two variants as the initial A330-300 and, despite its lower designation number, the following A330-200. The A330-300 is the basic version of this medium-range wide-body transport with two CF6-80E1, PW4164/4168 or 71,100 lb st (316.3 kN) Trent 768/772 turbofans. The A330-200 first flew on 13 August 1997 for service from April 1998, and is a reduced-capacity/longer-range version of the A330-300 with its fuselage shortened by 17 ft 6 in (5.33 m) and a strengthened wing derived from that of the A340-300 for the delivery of a maximum 380 passengers over a range of more than 6,215 miles (10000 km), or 253 passengers over a range of more than 7,455 miles (12000 km) after take-off at a maximum weight of 507,055 lb (230000 kg). By August 2001, orders for the A330 had reached 409 aircraft, of which 196 had been delivered.

Specification: Airbus Industrie A330-300
Origin: International
Type: two-crew medium/long-range wide-body airliner
Powerplant: two General Electric CF6-80E1A2 turbofan engines each rated at 67,500 lb st (300.25 kN), or Pratt & Whitney PW4164/4168 turbofan engines each rated at 68,000 lb st (302.48 kN), or Rolls-Royce Trent 768/772 turbofan engines each rated at up to 71,100 lb st (316.27 kN)
Performance: cruising speed, maximum 576 mph (927 km/h) at 41,000 ft (12495 m) and economical 535 mph (862 km/h) at 39,000 ft (11885 m); service ceiling 41,000 ft (12495 m); range with 335 passengers and reserves for a 230-mile (370-km) diversion 5,178 miles (8334 km)
Weights: empty operating between 264,575 and 266,245 lb (120012 and 120851 kg); maximum take-off 467,375 lb (212000 kg)
Dimensions: span 197 ft 10 in (60.30 m); length 208 ft 10 in (63.65 m); height 54 ft 11 in (16.74 m); area 3,908.50 sq ft (363.10 m²)
Payload: between 335 and 440 passengers within the context of a maximum payload of between 101,740 and 103,390 lb (46149 and 46988 kg)

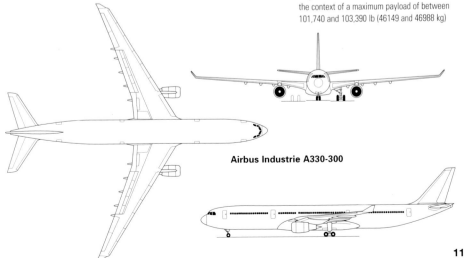

Airbus Industrie A330-300

AIRBUS INDUSTRIE A340

The A340 is the long-range counterpart of the A330 with a four- rather than two-engined powerplant. The two types have basically the same airframe with the exception of the limited modifications to the A340's wing structure and leading-edge slats required for the carriage of four engines. The longer of the two models planned from the outset, the A340-300 made its first flight on 25 October 1991. This machine was the first of six development aircraft built as four A330-300 and two shorter-fuselage A330-200 machines. Both variants entered service in March 1993.

In typical two-class layout, the A340-300 accommodates between 375 and 440 passengers. Intended for longer-range operations, the A340-200 does not require the A340-300's two-wheel auxiliary main landing gear unit under the fuselage, and has its fuselage shortened by some two frames to 194 ft 10 in (59.39 m) for three-class carriage of between 263 and 303 passengers. The A340-300 and A340-200 were both powered initially by four 31,200-lb st (138.78-kN) CFM56-5C2 turbofans, but later options are the more powerful CFM56-5C3 and CFM56-5C4 engines.

In April 1996, there entered service the A340-300 High Gross Weight variant intended for longer-range services. This has strengthened landing gear units and wing structure, CFM56-5C4 turbofans and additional fuel capacity for the carriage of 295 passengers over 8,228 miles (13242 km). The A340-200 HGW features increased fuel capacity, greater weights and the same powerplant as the A340-300 HGW, and is a very long-range model with 232-seat accommodation for a range of 9,195 miles (14800 km).

The latest developments are two models with the Rolls-Royce Trent 500 turbofan, the very long-range A340-500 carrying 313 passengers and the long-range A340-600 lifting 380 passengers.

Specification: Airbus Industrie A340-300
Origin: International
Type: two/three-crew medium/long-range wide-body transport
Powerplant: four CFM International CFM56-5C2 turbofan engines each rated at 31,200 lb st (138.78 kN), or CFM56-5C3 turbofan engines each rated at 32,500 lb st (144.57 kN), or CFM56-5C4 turbofans each rated at 34,000 lb st (151.24 kN)
Performance: cruising speed, maximum 569 mph (915 km/h) at 41,000 ft (12495 m) and economical 537 mph (864 km/h) at 39,000 ft (11885 m); certificated ceiling 41,000 ft (12495 m); range 7,710 miles (12416 km) with 295 passengers and reserves for a 230-mile (370-km) diversion
Weights: empty operating 279,700 lb (126873 kg); maximum take-off between 566,575 and 573,200 lb (257000 and 260000 kg)
Dimensions: span 197 ft 10 in (60.30 m); length 208 ft 10 in (63.65 m); height 54 ft 11 in (16.74 m); area 3,908.50 sq ft (363.10 m²)
Payload: between 295 and 440 passengers within the context of a 103,900-lb (47127-kg) maximum payload

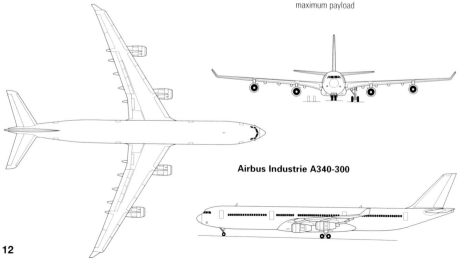

Airbus Industrie A340-300

AIRTECH CN-235

Given their success with the C-212 Aviocar utility light transport, it seemed sensible for CASA of Spain and IPTN of Indonesia to collaborate as Airtech for the design and development of a larger and more efficient, pressurized transport. Work on the resulting CN-235 began in 1980, and prototypes were manufactured simultaneously in Indonesia and Spain for first flights during 1983, on 30 December and 11 November respectively. Deliveries from the Indonesian and Spanish production lines began in December 1986 and February 1987 respectively. Since that time, the CN-235 has secured useful commercial success.

The main variants of the CN-235 civil series up to 2001 have been the CN-235-10 initial model, with two 1,700-shp (1268-kW) CT7-7A turboprops; the Spanish-built CN-235-100 and Indonesian-built CN-235-110 improved model, with CT7-9C turboprops, flat-rated at 1,750 shp (1305 kW), in new nacelles of composite construction; the CN-235-200 and CN-235-220, with structural strengthening; and the CN-235-300, with uprated engines for improved 'hot-and-high' take-off.

The civil variants typically carry up to 44 passengers or 13,227 lb (6600 kg) of freight. In overall terms, the CN-325, of which the last civil models were delivered in 1993, is of typical stressed-skin construction, mainly of light alloy with composite materials in a limited number of areas. It is of 'standard' airlifter configuration with its fuselage ending in an upswept section incorporating a ventral ramp/door arrangement and carrying the cantilever tail unit, a high-set cantilever wing, tricycle landing gear with the single-wheel nose unit retracting into the underside of the forward fuselage and the tandem-wheel main units semi-retracting into external sponsons whose use leaves the cabin unobstructed for payload, and two turboprops in nacelles on the outboard ends of the flat centre section's leading edge.

Specification: Airtech CN-235-300
Origin: International
Type: two-crew regional narrow-body transport
Powerplant: two General Electric CT7-9C3 turboprop engines each flat-rated at 1,750 shp (1305 kW) without automatic power reserve or 1,870 shp (1394.5 kW) with automatic power reserve
Performance: cruising speed, maximum and economical 283 mph (456 km/h) at 15,000 ft (4570 m); certificated ceiling 30,000 ft (9145 m); range 2,706 miles (4355 km) with a 7,936-lb (3600-kg) payload or 932 miles (1501 km) with maximum payload
Weights: operating empty 20,459 lb (9280 kg); maximum take-off 34,832 lb (15800 kg)
Dimensions: span 84 ft 8 in (25.81 m); length 70 ft 0.75 in (21.353 m); height 26 ft 10 in (8.177 m); area 636.17 sq ft (59.10 m²)
Payload: up to 44 passengers or 10,648 lb (4830 kg) of freight

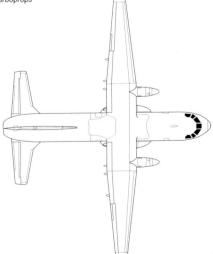

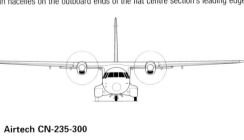

Airtech CN-235-300

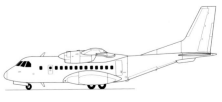

ANTONOV An-26 'CURL'

Although derived from the An-24, the An-26 (NATO reporting designation 'Curl') light transport was a new Soviet design from what is now the Ukraine with a host of improved features and additions. The most obvious of these changes is a new rear loading ramp, which forms the underside of the upswept rear fuselage when closed, allows the straight-in loading of items such as light vehicles when opened so that its rear edge rests on the ground, but which can be slid forward along tracks on each side of the underside of the fuselage to lie directly under the cabin, clear of the open hatch.

First seen in 1969, the An-26 'Curl-A' is fitted with a Tumanskii RU-19A-300 booster turbojet in the rear of the starboard engine nacelle. As well as acting as an APU, this can be used as a take-off booster and for increasing performance at other times. Less obvious are the facts that the An-26 has a pressurized cargo hold and that on all but the earliest aircraft the belly has been toughened to withstand the erosion and abrasion which go hand-in-hand with rough field operation. Other improvements adopted at the same time included more powerful AI-24T engines driving constant-speed four-blade propellers of the fully feathering type with the enlarged diameter of 12 ft 9.5 in (3.90 m), but since 1980, many engines have been upgraded to the AI-24VT standard.

Internally the An-26 features an electrically or manually operated conveyor flush with the cabin floor, while the An-26B, introduced in 1981, has roller gangs that can be swung up against the cabin walls when not in use. In all An-26 versions the interior can be reconfigured within 30 minutes as a transport with tip-up seats along the cabin sides to seat 38–40 passengers. Production ended in 1985 after the completion of some 1,410 aircraft, all but 425 of them for military operators.

Specification: Antonov An-26B 'Curl-A'
Origin: USSR
Type: five-crew regional narrow-body transport
Powerplant: two ZMDB Progress (Ivchyenko) AI-24VT turboprop engines each rated at 2,820 ehp (2103 kW) and one Soyuz (Tumanskii) RU-19A-300 turbojet engine rated at 1,765 lb st (7.85 kN) dry
Performance: cruising speed 273 mph (440 km/h) at 19,685 ft (6000 m); service ceiling 24,605 ft (7500 m); range 1,585 miles (2550 km) with maximum fuel and 683 miles (1100 km) with maximum payload
Weights: empty 33,950 lb (15400 kg); normal take-off 50,705 lb (23000 kg); maximum take-off 53,790 lb (24400 kg)
Dimensions: span 95 ft 9.5 (29.20 m); length 78 ft 1 in (23.80 m); height 28 ft 1.5 in (8.575 m); wing area 807.10 sq ft (74.98 m²)
Payload: up to 40 passengers or 12,125 lb (5500 kg) of freight

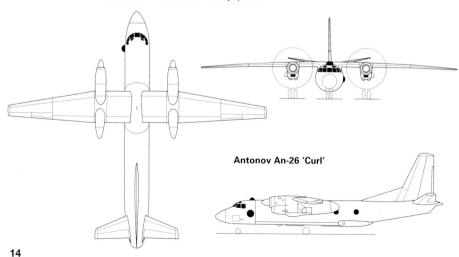

Antonov An-26 'Curl'

AVIONS DE TRANSPORT RÉGIONAL ATR-42

Avions de Transport Régional was established in February 1982 for the development, production and marketing of the ATR-42 regional airliner, launched three months earlier as a collaborative venture between Aérospatiale of France and Aeritalia of Italy. Stemming from a convergence of wholly national AS.35 and AIT 320 designs, this aeroplane needed careful consideration in terms of its capacity, eventually fixed at 42 passengers in an airframe of typical turboprop-powered regional transport layout with a high-set wing and a T-tail over an upswept rear fuselage.

The first of two ATR-42 prototypes made its maiden flight on 16 August 1984. French and Italian certification followed in September 1985, and the ATR-42 was delivered from December of the same year for a start to revenue-earning service in the same month. The ATR 42-100 and ATR 42-200 designations had initially been used for planned versions with maximum take-off weights of 32,848 lb (14900 kg) and 34,722 lb (15750 kg) respectively, the latter with a redesigned cabin permitting an increase in seating to 50. The ATR 42-200 then became the basis of the initial production model, namely the ATR 42-300 with still higher weights and delivered in two subvariants as the ATR 42-310 with 2,000-shp (1491-kW) Pratt & Whitney Canada PW120 turboprops and the ATR 42-320 with 2,100-shp (1567-kW) PW121 turboprops.

Further variants have included the ATR 42-400, first flown on 12 July 1995, with PW121A engines driving six- rather than four-blade propellers; the ATR 42-500, first flown on 16 September 1994, with 2,400-shp (1789-kW) PW127E engines and a new-look cabin; and the ATR-42 Cargo quick-change development, with provision for the carriage of up to 8,818 lb (4000 kg) of freight in nine containers.

By August 2001, sales of the ATR-42 had reached 366 aircraft, of which 363 had been delivered.

Specification: Avions de Transport Régional ATR-42-310
Origin: International
Type: two/three-crew regional narrow-body transport
Powerplant: two Pratt & Whitney Canada PW120 turboprop engines each rated at 2,000 shp (1491 kW)
Performance: maximum cruising speed 305 mph (490 km/h) at 17,000 ft (5180 m); certificated ceiling 25,000 ft (7620 m); range 1,208 miles (1944 km) with 46 passengers
Weights: empty 22,674 lb (10285 kg); maximum take-off 36,817 lb (16700 kg)
Dimensions: span 80 ft 7.5 in (24.57 m); length 74 ft 4.5 in (22.67 m); height 24 ft 10.75 in (7.59 m); area 586.65 sq ft (54.50 m²)
Payload: between 42 and 50 passengers within the context of a 10,835-lb (4915-kg) maximum payload

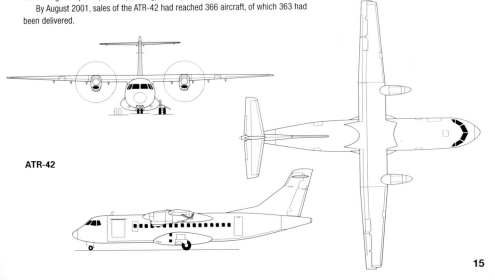

ATR-42

AVIONS DE TRANSPORT RÉGIONAL ATR-72

Announced at the Paris Air Show of 1985 and launched in January of the following year, the ATR-72 had been schemed as a higher-capacity development of the ATR-42 with higher-rated engines, greater fuel capacity and increased overall dimensions in which the fuselage was lengthened proportionally more than the wing was widened in span. The cabin, with a length of 63 ft 0.25 in (19.21 m), compared with the ATR-42 cabin's length of 48 ft 1.25 in (14.66 m), has the same cross section.

The programme started with the construction of three development aircraft, the first of which made the type's maiden flight on 27 October 1988. The ATR-72 received French and US certification in September and November 1989 respectively, and the first deliveries were made in October of the same year for a virtually immediate start of revenue-earning services. By August 2001, ATR had secured orders for 288 examples of the ATR-72 and delivered 264 aircraft. Planned variants include the ATR-52C freighter model, with a ventral ramp/door arrangement for the civil as well as military markets, and the ATR-82 stretched version of the ATR-72, with accommodation for up to 80 passengers. A development on the most recent examples of the ATR-72 and indeed ATR-42 families is a carbon-fibre composite tail to reduce weight.

Variants of this regional airliner have included the ATR-72-200 initial production model; the ATR 72-210, delivered from December 1992 with better 'hot-and-high' performance derived from the installation of an uprated powerplant of two 2,480 shp (1849 kW) Pratt & Whitney Canada PW127 turboprop engines driving improved propellers with composite blades on steel hubs; and the ATR 72-210A, certificated in January 1997 and later redesignated ATR 72-500 as a development of the ATR 72-210 with six- rather than four-blade propellers, higher weights and a new-look cabin.

Specification: Avions de Transport Régional ATR-72-200
Origin: International
Type: two/three-crew regional narrow-body transport
Powerplant: two Pratt & Whitney Canada PW124B turboprop engines each rated at 2,400 shp (1789 kW)
Performance: maximum cruising speed 327 mph (526 km/h) at 15,000 ft (4570 m); service ceiling 25,000 ft (7620 m); range 1,381 miles (2222 km) with 66 passengers
Weights: empty 27,558 lb (12500 kg); maximum take-off 47,399 lb (21500 kg)
Dimensions: span 88 ft 9 in (27.05 m); length 89 ft 1.5 in (27.17 m); height 25 ft 1.25 in (7.65 m); wing area 656.62 sq ft (61.00 m²)
Payload: between 64 and 74 passengers within the context of a 15,873-lb (7200-kg) maximum payload

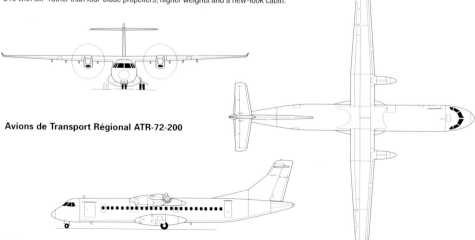

Avions de Transport Régional ATR-72-200

The Avro RJ is the current incarnation of a type that was first schemed as the Hawker Siddeley HS.146 and then initially built as the British Aerospace 146 with four Lycoming ALF502R turbofans. Some 219 aircraft were delivered up to 1993 for service from May 1983 as the BAe 146-100, -200 and -300, with maximum accommodation for 94, 112 and 128 passengers respectively.

By 1993, work was already well advanced on the RJ (Regional Jetliner) as a successor. The RJ is an updated version of the BAe 146 with features such as the more economical AlliedSignal (now Honeywell) LF507 turbofan, strengthening of the wing, fuselage and landing gear, and all-digital avionics.

The RJ is offered in a number of variants with fuselages of different lengths and basic passenger capacity indicated by the numerical suffix in the designation. The RJ-70 offers accommodation for between 70 and 94 passengers in a fuselage 85 ft 11.5 in (26.20 m) long, and has a maximum take-off weight of 95,000 lb (43092 kg); the RJ-85 seats between 85 and 112 passengers in a fuselage lengthened to 93 ft 10 in (28.60 m), and has a maximum take-off weight of 97,000 lb (43999 kg); the RJ-100 seats between 100 and 125 passengers in a fuselage lengthened to 101 ft 8.25 in (30.99 m); and the RJ-115 is an RJ-100 derivative with additional emergency exits and other changes to seat between 116 and 128 passengers in a six-abreast arrangement.

The RJX is a further updated model with Honeywell AS977 turbofans for 17 per cent more range and 15 per cent lower fuel consumption as well as a 20% reduction in engine maintenance costs. The variant is offered in RJX-70, RJX-85 and RJX-100 subvariants. The first of the new series flew on 23 March 1992 and secured certification on 1 October 1993. By August 2001, orders had been placed for 180 aircraft, of which 162 had been delivered.

Specification: BAE Systems Avro RJ-100ER
Origin: UK
Type: two-crew regional narrow-body transport
Powerplant: four Honeywell LF507-1F turbofan engines, each rated at 6,990 lb st (31.11 kN) dry
Performance: cruising speed, maximum 492 mph (791 km/h) at 29,000 ft (8840 m) and economical 351 mph (565 km/h) at 29,000 ft (8840 m); certificated ceiling 35,000 ft (10670 m); range 2,075 miles (3340 km) with 100 passengers
Weights: empty operating 56,481 lb (25620 kg); maximum take-off 97,498 lb (44225 kg)
Dimensions: span 86 ft 5 in (26.34 m); length 101 ft 8.5 in (31.00 m); height 28 ft 3 in (8.61 m); wing area 832.00 sq ft (77.29 m²)
Payload: between 100 and 125 passengers within the context of a 26,015-lb (11801-kg) maximum payload

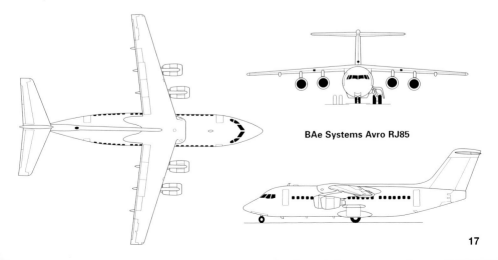

BAe Systems Avro RJ85

BOEING (McDD) MODEL 717

By the early 1990s, McDonnell Douglas felt that the time was more than ripe for it to offer a successor to the DC-9-30 based on a new powerplant, modern avionics and the combination of aerodynamic and structural improvements. The engine selected was the BMW Rolls-Royce (now Rolls-Royce) BR715 turbofan, rated at 18,500 lb st (82.29 kN) with an option for uprating to 20,000 lb st (88.97 kN) in the higher-weight MD-95-30ER that was being planned as an extended-range derivative with greater fuel capacity. Among this new engine's attractions were a high power/weight ratio, very good fuel economy, low noise and a thrust reverser that would allow the MD-95 to use comparatively short runways.

The company formally launched the MD-95 in October 1995 following the receipt of an initial order from ValuJet (now AirTran) for 50 aircraft. As work on the MD-95 was proceeding, McDonnell Douglas merged with Boeing in August 1997 and lost its separate identity. In January 1998, Boeing redesigned the MD-95 as the Model 717, at the same time confirming that it intended to proceed with the programme, as it saw the Model 717 as a type to fill the gap in its product line in the capacity bracket below that of the Model 737-600, which was then its smallest-capacity airliner.

The first Model 717-200 was rolled out on 10 June 1998, but the start of flight trials was delayed by final development problems with the BR715 engine. The Model 717-200 first flew on 2 September 1998, and the Model 717-200 entered revenue-earning service in September 2000. Boeing at one time proposed a shortened Model 717-100X for the carriage of 75 to 80 passengers and a Model 717-100X 'Lite' for 70 to 75 passengers. Another possibility remains the lengthened Model 717-300X for up to 130 passengers.

By August 2001, sales had reached 136, of which 68 had been delivered.

Specification: Boeing Model 717-200
Origin: USA
Type: two-crew regional narrow-body airliner
Powerplant: two Rolls-Royce BR715 turbofan engines, each rated at 18,500 lb st (82.29 kN) dry
Performance: cruising speed, maximum and economical 504 mph (811 km/h) at high altitude; certificated ceiling 37,000 ft (11280 m); range 1,680 miles (2704 km) with maximum payload
Weights: empty operating 67,493 lb (30615 kg); maximum take-off 110,200 lb (49987 kg)
Dimensions: span 93 ft 3.5 in (28.44 m); length 119 ft 3.5 in (36.36 m); height 28 ft 2.5 in (8.60 m); area 1,000.70 sq ft (92.97 m²)
Payload: up to 106 passengers within the context of a 26,940-lb (12220-kg) maximum payload

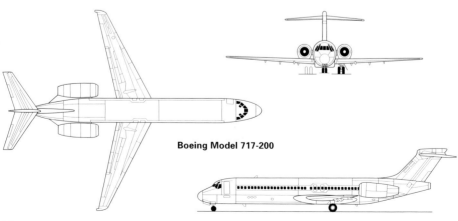

Boeing Model 717-200

The Model 727 was created as the short/medium-range counterpart of the epoch-making Model 707 long-range airliner. After United Airlines and Eastern Air Lines had indicated orders for 40 aircraft each, Boeing decided in August 1960 to go ahead, and the first Model 727 flew on 9 February 1963. Both initial operators began services with the new Model 727-100 in February 1964, but though the Model 727 revealed excellent reliability and operating economics, sales were sluggish. Boeing decided that the cause was a shortfall in capacity, and this paved the way for the Model 727-200 that was announced in August 1965. Its fuselage was lengthened by 20 ft 0 in (6.10 m), with equal-size 'plugs' fore and aft of the main wheels to increase capacity from 125 to 189 passengers.

The Model 727-200 was certificated on 29 November 1967 and entered revenue-earning service in December of the same year. By then, orders for the Model 727 orders had risen to more than 500. Sales of the Model 727-100 eventually reached almost 500, but those of the Model 727-200 variants reached nearly 1,300 within an overall production total of 1,832 aircraft delivered by September 1984.

The primary variants were the baseline Model 727-100; the Model 727-100C convertible passenger/freight variant; the Model 727-100QC quick-change convertible variant; the lengthened Model 727-200, with standard and maximum passenger capacities of 163 and 189 respectively, and a standard powerplant of three JT8D-9 turbofan engines each rated at 14,500 lb st (64.50 kN) but with an option of engines of up to 15,500 lb st (68.95 kN) available; and the Advanced Model 727-200 final production variant, which was generally similar to the Model 727-200 but with advanced features such as a performance data computer system to enhance economy and safety of operation, improved cabin interiors and equipment, and optional powerplants including the JT8D-17R, with automatic performance reserve (APR).

Specification: Boeing Advanced Model 727-200
Origin: USA
Type: three-crew short/medium-range narrow-body transport
Powerplant: typically three Pratt & Whitney JT8D-9A turbofan engines each rated at 14,500 lb st (64.50 kN)
Performance: maximum speed 621 mph (999 km/h) at 20,500 ft (6250 m); cruising speed 570 mph (917 km/h) at 24,700 ft (7530 m); certificated ceiling 33,000 ft (10060 m); range 2,487 miles (4002 km) with maximum payload
Weights: empty 102,900 lb (46675 kg); maximum take-off 209,500 lb (45027 kg)
Dimensions: span 108 ft 0 in (32.92 m); length 153 ft 2 in (46.69 m); height 34 ft 0 in (10.36 m); area 1,700.00 sq ft (157.93 m²)
Payload: up to 189 passengers or 41,000 lb (18598 kg) of freight

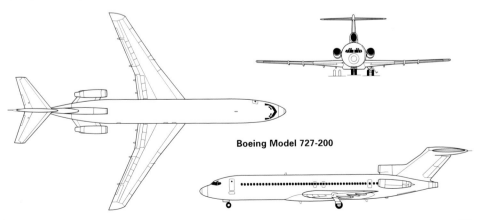

Boeing Model 727-200

BOEING MODEL 737

To complete the family of airliners also comprising the long-range Model 707 and medium-range Model 727, Boeing developed the short-range Model 737.

The first Model 737-100 made its maiden flight on 9 April 1967, and Lufthansa inaugurated its first services with this 100-passenger type on 10 February 1968. Only 30 Model 737-100 aircraft were built, the first major variant being the 130-seat Model 737-200, which entered service in April 1968. With more than 4,800 ordered, the Model 737 has since become the most prolific jet-powered airliner of all time, its popularity and sales success having been assured by a number of steadily improved variants.

The Model 737-200C is a convertible passenger/freight variant and the Model 737-200QC is a quick-change convertible passenger/freight variant. The Advanced Model 737-200 was the final production standard for the original Model 727-200 variant, with 130-seat accommodation, ability to operate at an optional maximum weight of 117,000 lb (53071 kg), and options for engines such as the JT8D-15, JT8D-17 or JT8D-17R, rated at 15,500, 16,000 or 17,000 lb st (68.95, 71.17 or 75.62 kN) respectively. The Advanced Model 737-200C and -200QC are convertible and quick-change convertible versions. The Advanced Model 737-200 High Gross Weight Structure is generally similar to Advanced Model 737-200 but available in two maximum-weight options with modifications including a strengthened wing and landing gear, new tyres, wheels and brakes, and installation of an auxiliary fuel tank. Introducing the 'Classic' series, the Model 737-300 has a fuselage stretched by 8 ft 6 in (2.59 m) to accommodate 128 passengers; the Model 737-400 has a further 10 ft 0 in (3.05 m) increase for between 146 and 168 passengers; and the 108-passenger Model 737-500 is similar in size to the Model 737-200 but with the improvements of the Model 737-300. The 'Next Generation' introduced an increase in span to 112 ft 7 in (34.31 m), a new flight deck of the 'glass' type, and a powerplant of two CFM56-7 turbofans each rated at 22,000, 24,000 and 26,200 lb st (97.86, 106.76 and 116.54 kN) in the Model 737-600, -700 and -800 that replaced the Model 737-500, -300 and -400 respectively. The Model 737-900 is Boeing's counterpart to the Airbus A321 and offers 177-passenger accommodation.

Specification: Boeing Advanced Model 737-200
Origin: USA
Type: two-crew regional and short-range narrow-body transport
Powerplant: two Pratt & Whitney JT8D-15 turbofan engines each rated at 15,500 lb st (68.95 kN) dry
Performance: cruising speed 576 mph (927 km/h) at 22,600 ft (6890 m); certificated ceiling 35,000 ft (10670 m); range 2,648 miles (4262 km) with maximum payload
Weights: empty 61,050 lb (27692 kg); maximum take-off 117,000 lb (53071 kg)
Dimensions: span 93 ft 0 in (28.35 m); length 100 ft 2 in (30.53 m); height 37 ft 0 in (11.28 m); area 980.00 sq ft (91.04 m²)
Payload: up to 130 passengers within the context of a 34,790-lb (15781-kg) maximum payload

Boeing Model 737-700

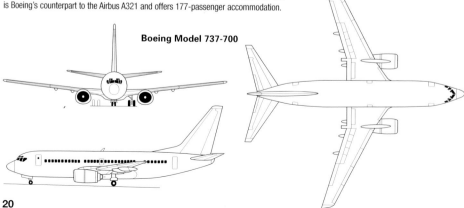

The Boeing Model 747 introduced the concept of the 'jumbo' wide-body airliner, and the first machine was a production aeroplane that recorded the type's maiden flight on 9 February 1969 and, powered by four 43,000-lb st (192.27-kN) Pratt & Whitney JT9D-3 turbofans, the Model 747-100 entered service with Pan Am in January 1970.

Sales have since passed 1,350 in a large number of steadily improved variants with alternative General Electric and Rolls-Royce engines. The Model 747-100B was strengthened. The Model 747-200B Convertible is equipped for all-passenger or all-freight use. The Model 747-200F Freighter is a freight version with the fuselage nose opening forwards and upwards for straight-in loading. The Model 747SP is a lighter-weight Special Performance long-range version with the fuselage length reduced by 47 ft 1 in (14.35 m) and a new tail unit of greater area. The Model 747SR is a short-range version with structural modifications for a higher frequency of take-off and landing operations. The Model 747SUD is the Stretched Upper Deck variant, available optionally on -100B, -200B, -200B Combi and Model 747SR types, providing economy-class seating for 69 passengers on the lengthened upper deck. The Model 747-300 was the first variant built with the extended upper deck, with its rear moved 23 ft 4 in (7.11 m) closer to the tail. The Model 747-400 retains the fuselage of the -300, but has a wing 12 ft 0 in (3.66 m) greater in span and terminating in drag-reducing winglets, a two-crew EFIS flight deck, numerous aerodynamic enhancements, and extensive use of composite materials for a significant reduction in empty weight. The -400 is available in subvariants such as the -400 Combi, -400F freighter, -400D (Domestic) for short routes in the Japanese domestic market with up to 568 passengers, and -400PIP (Performance Improvement Package) for options such as greater weight, a longer dorsal fin of composite construction and slower transfer of the fuel from the tailplane to reduce trim drag. Boeing has also considered a number of other improved versions.

Specification: Boeing Model 747-200B
Origin: USA
Type: three-crew long-range wide-body transport
Powerplant: four General Electric CF6-50E2 turbofan engines each rated at 52,500 lb st (233.53 kN) dry, or Pratt & Whitney JT9D-7R4G2 turbofan engines each rated at 54,750 lb st (243.54 kN) dry, or Rolls-Royce RB.211-524D4 turbofan engines each rated at 53,110 lb st (236.24 kN) dry
Performance: cruising speed 584 mph (940 km/h) at 35,000 ft (10670 m); certificated ceiling 45,000 ft (13715 m); range 7,082 miles (11397 km) with maximum passenger payload
Weights: empty 375,170 lb (170177 kg); maximum take-off 833,000 lb (377849 kg)
Dimensions: span 195 ft 8 in (59.64 m); length 231 ft 10 in (70.66 m); height 63 ft 5 in (19.33 m); area 5,500.00 sq ft (510.95 m²)
Payload: up to 516 passengers within the context of a 151,500-lb (68720-kg) maximum payload

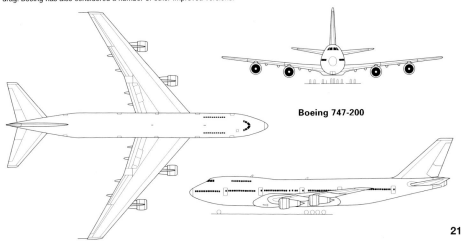

Boeing 747-200

BOEING MODEL 757

In the early months of 1978, Boeing announced its intention of developing a new family of twin-engined advanced-technology aircraft as the Models 757, 767 and 777, the first of the three differing most significantly from the last two in retaining the same narrow-body fuselage as the Model 727. A short/medium-range airliner with a typical capacity of between 178 and 239 passengers, the Model 757 was intended to provide new standards of fuel efficiency with powerplant options that were to have comprised the General Electric CF6-32 and Rolls-Royce RB.211-535 turbofans, but the former was abandoned in the development stage and replaced in Boeing's plans by the Pratt & Whitney PW2000 turbofan, initially in its PW2037 form but eventually in its higher-rated PW2040 form.

Featuring a forward fuselage revised from its originally planed configuration to allow the incorporation of a flight deck identical with that of the wide-body Model 767 and thus permit a common rating for the crews of the two types, the Model 757 recorded its maiden flight on 19 February 1982 and entered service in January 1983. By August 2001, orders stood at 1,047 aircraft, of which 968 had been delivered. Variants of this important airliner include the Model 757-200 initial variant; the Model 757-200PF specialized Package Freighter variant; the Model 757-200M Combi mixed passenger/freight variant; the Model 757-200F freighter variant; and the Model 757-300 variant, with strengthening of the wing and landing gear as well as the lengthening of the fuselage by 23 ft 3 in (7.09 m) for between 243 and 280 passengers. It is probable that in the near future, variants will be introduced with structural strengthening and additional fuel capacity for still further range.

Specification: Boeing Model 757-200
Origin: USA
Type: two/three-crew short/medium-range narrow-body transport
Powerplant: two Rolls-Royce RB.211-535C or -535E4 turbofan engines each rated at 37,400 or 40,100 lb st (166.36 or 178.37 kN) dry, or two Pratt & Whitney PW2037 or PW2040 turbofan engines each rated at 38,200 or 41,625 lb st (169.92 or 185.16 kN) dry
Performance: cruising speed 582 mph (936 km/h) at 31,000 ft (9450 m); certificated ceiling 38,000 ft (11580 m); range 3,662 miles (5893 km) with maximum payload
Weights: empty 126,250 lb (57267 kg); maximum take-off 240,000 lb (108864 kg)
Dimensions: span 124 ft 10 in (38.05 m); length 155 ft 3 in (47.32 m); height 44 ft 6 in (13.56 m); area 1,994.00 sq ft (185.24 m²)
Payload: between 186 and 239 passengers within the context of a 57,530-lb (26096-kg) maximum payload

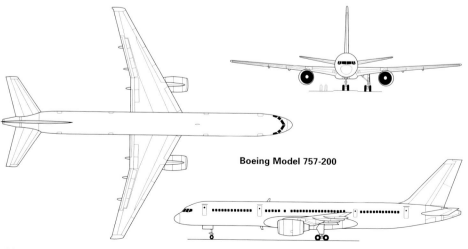

Boeing Model 757-200

Announced simultaneously with the Model 757, the Model 767 is Boeing's first twin-engined airliner of the wide-body type, and was projected in the early and mid-1970s to provide Boeing with an airliner to rival the Airbus A310 in the market for medium-range transports for between 250 and 300 passengers. The Model 767 introduced a completely new fuselage structure 4 ft 1 in (1.24 m) wider than that of the Model 757.

At first, Boeing planned two versions as the Model 767-100, with a shorter fuselage and accommodation for approximately 180 passengers, and the Model 767-200, described above. The company then dropped the Model 767-100 in preference for subvariants of the Model 767-200 with alternative maximum weights between 282,000 and 315,000 lb (127915 and 142884 kg) with different fuel weights. The first Model 767-200 flew on 26 September 1981, and the type entered service in December 1982.

The primary variants are the Model 767-200 baseline type; the Model 767-200ER extended-range development; the Model 767-300 development of the -200 with structural strengthening and the fuselage lengthened by 21 ft 1 in (6.43 m) for the carriage of up to 269 passengers over a range of between 4,603 and 4,902 miles (7408 and 7889 km); the Model 767-300ER extended-range development of the -300 with further increased centre-section fuel tankage for ranges of between 6,605 and 6,974 miles (10630 and 11223 km); the Model 767-300 Freighter dedicated freight derivative of the -300; and the Model 767-400ER version, lengthened by 21 ft 0 in (6.40 m) for a maximum of 303 passengers and fitted with a strengthened and aerodynamically modified wing of increased span with raked tip extensions, longer landing gear legs carrying Model 777 wheels and brakes, and a new flight deck based on that of the Model 737 'New Generation' series and the Model 777.

By August 2001, orders stood at 921 aircraft, including 830 delivered.

Specification: Boeing Model 767-200
Origin: USA
Type: two/three-crew medium-range wide-body transport
Powerplant: two General Electric CF6-80A or Pratt & Whitney JT9D-7R4D turbofan engines each rated at 48,000 lb st (213.51 kN) dry, or CF-80A2, JT9D-7R4E, JT9D-7R4E4 or PW4050 turbofan engines each rated at 50,000 lb st (222.41 kN) dry, or PW4052 turbofan engines each rated at 52,000 lb st (231.31 kN) dry, or CF6-80C2B4 turbofan engines each rated at 52,500 lb st (233.53 kN) dry
Performance: cruising speed 529 mph (851 km/h) at optimum altitude; certificated ceiling between 38,700 and 39,700 ft (11795 and 12100 m) depending on powerplant; range between 3,636 and 4,430 miles (5852 and 7129 km) depending on powerplant and version
Weights: empty 177,500 or 178,400 (80514 or 80922 kg) depending on powerplant and version; maximum take-off 300,000 or 315,000 lb (136080 or 142884 kg) depending on powerplant and version
Dimensions: span 156 ft 1 in (47.57 m); length 159 ft 2 in (48.51 m); height 52 ft 0 in (15.85 m); area 3,050.00 sq ft (283.35 m²)
Payload: up to 290 passengers within the context of a 44,100-lb (20004-kg) maximum payload

Boeing Model 767-200

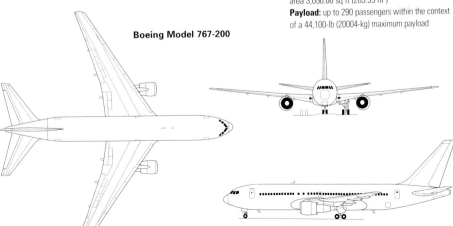

BOEING MODEL 777

Interest in a transport providing a passenger capacity between those of its Model 767-300 and Model 747-400 led Boeing at the end of 1986 to start work on a wide-body type to rival the Airbus A330 and A340. The project definition phase led to the launch of the Model 777 in October 1990, and after a first flight on 12 June 1994, the Model 777-200 entered service in June 1995. The fuselage diameter of 20 ft 4 in (6.20 m) provided a cabin wider than that of every other airliner except the Model 747, and accommodation is provided for between 328 and 440 passengers.

The Model 777-200 is offered in two primary versions with the same trio of engine options. The Model 777-200 has any of three maximum take-off weights between 506,000 and 535,000 lb (229522 and 242676 kg) for the carriage of 375 passengers over a range between 4,568 and 5,546 miles (7352 and 8926 km). The Model 777-200ER has greater fuel capacity, uprated engines and the option of three maximum take-off weights between 580,000 and 632,500 lb (263088 kg and 286902 kg) for the carriage of 305 passengers over a range between 6,939 and 8,493 miles (11168 and 13667 km). There is also to be a very long-range Model 777-200LR with 110,000-lb st (489.50-kN) General Electric GE90-110B1 engines for the carriage of 301 passengers over 10,194 miles (16,405 km).

Boeing is also producing the Model 777-300, with a strengthened airframe and the fuselage lengthened by 33 ft 3 in (10.13 m). This type made its maiden flight in October 1997 and provides accommodation for between 368 and 550 passengers at a maximum take-off weight of up to 660,000 lb (299376 kg) with engines each rated at up to some 98,000 lb st (436 kN). There is also to be a Model 777-300ER analogous to the -200ER but with 115,000-lb st (511.75-kN) GE90-115B engines. By August 2001, Boeing had received orders for 578 Model 777 airliners and delivered 349 machines.

Specification: Boeing Model 777-200
Origin: USA
Type: two/three-crew long-range wide-body transport
Powerplant: two Pratt & Whitney PW4074 turbofan engines each rated at 74,000 lb st (329.17 kN) dry
Performance: cruising speed 575 mph (925 km/h) at optimum altitude; certificated ceiling 43,100 ft (13135 m); range 4,840 miles (7785 km) with 363 passengers
Weights: empty 298,900 lb (135,581 kg); maximum take-off 515,000 lb (233604 kg)
Dimensions: span 199 ft 11 in (60.93 m); length 209 ft 1 in (63.73 m); height 60 ft 9 in (18.51 m); area 4,605.00 sq ft (427.8 m²)
Payload: up to 440 passengers within the context of a 121,100-lb (54931-kg) maximum payload

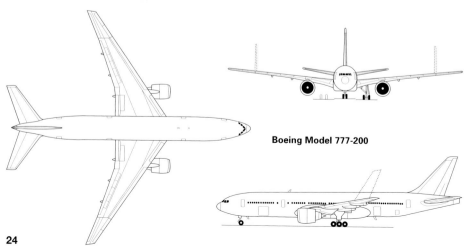

Boeing Model 777-200

BOEING (McDONNELL DOUGLAS) MD-11

McDonnell Douglas conceived the MD-11 as a development of its DC-10 wide-body airliner with increased passenger capacity in a restyled cabin, a revised wing with tip-mounted upper and lower winglets, a modified horizontal tail surface with an advanced cambered aerofoil, reduced leading-edge sweep and fuel tankage used mainly for longitudinal trimming in flight, a lengthened tail cone ending in a vertical chisel edge, new-generation engines, and a modern two-crew 'glass' digital flight deck of the EFIS (Electronic Flight Instrumentation System) type. McDonnell Douglas formally launched the programme in December 1986, and the first MD-11 flew on 10 January 1990. The test programme involved four aircraft with three 61,500-lb st (273.57-kN) General Electric CF6-80C2D1F turbofans and one with three 60,000-lb st (266.89-kN) Pratt & Whitney PW4460 turbofans.

The MD-11 entered service in December 1990, but sales were hindered by the need for the company to overcome drag and weight problems that adversely affected the performance that had been guaranteed. The company went on to produce the MD-11 in six subvariants. These were the MD-11 baseline model; the MD-11 PIP, resulting from the continuous Performance Improvement Program for greater range through drag reduction features and greater fuel capacity, as well as a 2,250-lb (1021-kg) reduction in structure weight; the MD-11 Combi mixed passenger/freight model; the MD-11CF convertible freighter; the MD-11F freighter; and MD-11ER extended-range subvariant with further increased fuel capacity for a maximum take-off weight of 630,500 lb (285995 kg) and an increment in range of 552 miles (889 km) or in payload of 6,000 lb (2722 kg).

When McDonnell Douglas merged with Boeing during August 1997, production of the MD-11 continued, but in June 1998 Boeing announced that production of the MD-11 series would end in 2000 with the completion of the 195th such machine.

Specification: Boeing (McDonnell Douglas) MD-11
Origin: USA
Type: two-crew medium/long-range wide-body transport
Powerplant: three General Electric CF6-80C2D1F turbofan engines each rated at 61,500 lb st (273.57 kN) dry, or Pratt & Whitney PW4460 turbofan engines each rated at 60,000 lb st (266.89 kN) dry
Performance: cruising speed, maximum and economical 588 mph (947 km/h) at high altitude; certificated ceiling 42,000 ft (12800 m); range 7,810 miles (12569 km) with 323 passengers
Weights: empty 288,880 lb (131036 kg); maximum take-off 625,500 lb (283727 kg)
Dimensions: span 169 ft 10 in (51.77 m); length 201 ft 4 in (61.37 m) with General Electric engines or 200 ft 11 in (61.24 m) with Pratt & Whitney engines; height 57 ft 9 in (17.60 m); area 3,648.00 sq ft (338.90 m²)
Payload: up to 410 passengers within the context of a 112,564-lb (51059-kg) maximum payload

Boeing (McDonnell Douglas) MD-11

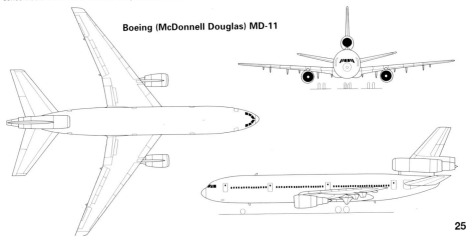

BOEING (McDONNELL DOUGLAS) MD-80

In 1977, McDonnell Douglas decided to produce a modernized DC-9 known as the DC-9 Super 80 (later DC-9-80), with a fuselage lengthened by 14 ft 3 in (4.34 m) over that of the current DC-9-50, two JT8D-209 engines, and other new features. This marked the beginning for a series that would prove to be the most successful of all DC-9 variants, with production eventually totalling 1,191. The DC-9 Super 80 first flew on 18 October 1979, and the company offered three variants with the same overall dimensions. These were the DC-9-81 baseline model; the DC-9-82, with 20,000-lb st (88.96-kN) JT8D-217 engines and the same fuel capacity as the DC-9-81; and the DC-9-83, with 21,000-lb st (93.41-kN) JT8D-219 engines and greater fuel capacity. During 1984, the three variants were redesignated as the MD-81, MD-82 and MD-83.

The DC-9-81/MD-81 entered service in October 1980 with accommodation for up to 135 passengers. The DC-9-82/MD-82 was the counterpart of the DC-9-81 for 'hot-and-high' operations, and entered service in August of the same year; in 1982 this variant spawned a subvariant with JT8D-217A engines and the maximum take-off weight raised to an optional 149,500 lb (67812 kg). The MD-83 was the longer-range counterpart of the first two variants, and entered service before the end of the same year.

During 1985, McDonnell Douglas announced a new variant as the MD-87, with its fuselage reduced in length by 16 ft 5 in (5.00 m) for a capacity of between 114 and 130 passengers, the fin heightened by 10 in (0.25 m) above the tailplane, and two 20,000-lb st (88.96-kN) JT8D-217B engines: the MD-87 entered service in November 1987. The fifth and last member of the MD-80 series was the MD-88, which was in effect an upgraded and updated version of the MD-82 with JT8D-217C engines, a maximum take-off weight of 160,000 lb (72575 kg), greater use of composite materials, and a redesigned cabin for 142 two-class passengers. The MD-88 entered service in January 1988.

Specification: Boeing (McDonnell Douglas) MD-81

Origin: USA

Type: two-crew short/medium-range narrow-body transport

Powerplant: two Pratt & Whitney JT8D-209 turbofan engines each rated at 18,500 lb st (82.29 kN) dry

Performance: cruising speed, maximum 574 mph (924 km/h) at 27,000 ft (8230 m) and economical 505 mph (813 km/h) at 35,000 ft (10670 m); certificated ceiling 37,000 ft (11280 m); range 1,800 miles (2896 km) with 155 passengers

Weights: empty 78,420 lb (35570 kg); maximum take-off 140,000 lb (63503 kg)

Dimensions: span 107 ft 10 in (32.87 m); length, 147 ft 10 in (45.06 m); height 29 ft 8 in (9.04 m); area 1,270.00 sq ft (117.98 m²)

Payload: up to 172 passengers within the context of a 39,579-lb (17953-kg) maximum payload

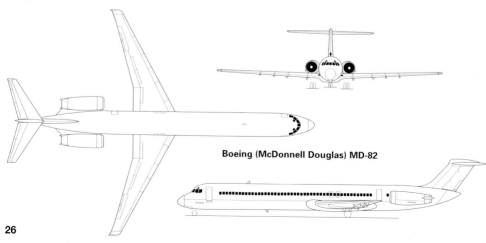

Boeing (McDonnell Douglas) MD-82

BOEING (McDONNELL DOUGLAS) MD-90

McDonnell Douglas schemed the McDonnell Douglas MD-90 in the second half of the 1980s as a modernized MD-80 with more modern engines, a redesigned and lengthened passenger cabin, carbon brakes, and an upgraded two-crew digital 'glass' flight deck of the EFIS (Electronic Flight Instrumentation System) type, a flight management system, a digital flight guidance system with an auxiliary control system, and an advanced inertial reference system with a ring laser gyro. The key to the company's thinking was the powerplant of two IAE V2500-D5 turbofan engines offering high reliability in combination with low noise, low emissions and low specific fuel consumption. The V2500-D5 is offered in two forms, with ratings of 25,000 and 28,000 lb st (111.21 and 124.55 kN) dry, and has a full-authority digital engine control system and a cascade-type thrust reverser.

The first MD-90 made its maiden flight on 22 February 1993, and the type entered service in March 1995. The first variant was the MD-90-30, derived directly from the MD-80, with the enlarged tail surfaces of the MD-87, powered elevators and the fuselage forward of the wing lengthened by 4 ft 9 in (1.45 m) to balance the greater weight of the new powerplant and at the same time provide two more seat rows for between 153 and 172 passengers. The second variant was the MD-90-30T TrunkLiner, essentially the MD-90-30 built in China by the Shanghai Aviation Industrial Corporation, which completed only two rather than the planned 20 aircraft.

Then, in August 1997, McDonnell Douglas merged with Boeing and lost its separate identity. Boeing decided in November 1998 that manufacture of the MD-90 would end in 2000 after the completion of the 113 aircraft then on order.

Specification: Boeing (McDonnell Douglas) MD-90-30
Origin: USA
Type: two-crew short/medium-range narrow-body transport
Powerplant: two IAE V2500-D5 turbofan engines each rated at 25,000 lb st (111.21 kN) dry
Performance: maximum cruising speed 503 mph (809 km/h) at 35,000 ft (10670 m); certificated ceiling 35,000 ft (10670 m); range 2,620 miles (4216 km) with 153 passengers
Weights: empty 88,000 lb (39916 kg); maximum take-off 156,000 lb (70760 kg)
Dimensions: span 107 ft 10 in (32.87 m); length 152 ft 7 in (46.51 m); height 30 ft 7.25 in (9.33 m); area 1,209.00 sq ft (112.32 m²)
Payload: up to 172 passengers within the context of a 38,250-lb (17350-kg) maximum payload

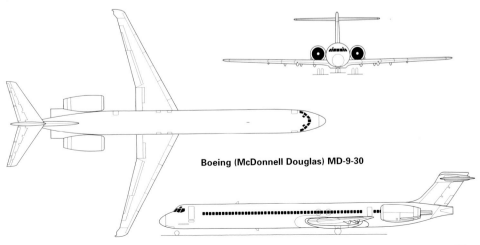

Boeing (McDonnell Douglas) MD-9-30

BOMBARDIER (CANADAIR) CRJ

The CRJ was planned by Canadair, then recently acquired by Bombardier Inc., as a regional airliner development of the Challenger 'bizjet'. Canadair was able to freeze the basic design in June 1988 as the Challenger, with its wing increased in span by 5 ft 3 in (1.60 m) and its fuselage lengthened by 19 ft 5 in (5.92 m) for the carriage of 50 passengers. Other changes included options for higher weights, more comprehensive digital avionics with provision for an HUD, and a higher certificated ceiling. The company launched the Regional Jet (otherwise the RJ or CRJ) at the end of April 1989, and the first of three development aircraft recorded its maiden flight on 10 May 1991. By the autumn of 2001, Canadair had received orders for 937 aircraft, of which 522 had been delivered.

Variants include the CRJ100 baseline model; the CRJ100ER extended-range development; the CRJ100LR long-range development, with still more fuel than the CRJ100ER, for the delivery of the maximum payload to a range of more than 2,267 miles (3648 km); the CRJ200 development of the CRJ100, with two CF34-3B1 turbofans possessing the same rating as the CF34-3A1 but maintained to a temperature of 86°F (30°C) and offered in standard, ER and LR subvariants.

Launched in January 1997, the CRJ700 is a 70-seat derivative of the CRJ100/200 to meet the increasing demand for larger aircraft with superior operating economies on regional airline routes. The type, of which 195 have been ordered, has 70- and 78-passenger models, and is offered in standard, ER and LR models, all with the span and length increased by 6 ft 0 in (1.83 m) and 19 ft 6 in (5.94 m) respectively, and with two 13,790-lb st (61.34-kN) CF34-8C1 turbofans. Launched in 1999 and the recipient of 30 orders, the CRJ900 has 14,500-lb st (64.53-kN) CF34-8CB turbofans and its fuselage further 'stretched' by 12 ft 6 in (3.81 m) to carry 86 passengers.

Specification: Canadair Regional Jet Series 100
Origin: Canada
Type: three/four-crew regional narrow-body transport
Powerplant: two General Electric CF34-3A1 turbofan engines each rated at 9,220 lb st (41.01 kN) dry
Performance: maximum cruising speed 529 mph (851 km/h) at 37,000 ft (11275 m); certificated ceiling 41,000 ft (12495 m); range 1,128 miles (1815 km) with maximum payload
Weights: empty 30,100 lb (13653 kg); maximum take-off 47,450 lb (21523 kg)
Dimensions: span 69 ft 7 in (21.21 m); length 87 ft 10 in (26.77 m); height 20 ft 5 in (6.22 m); area 587.10 sq ft (54.54 m²) excluding winglets
Payload: up to 52 passengers within the context of a 12,100-lb (5488-kg) maximum payload

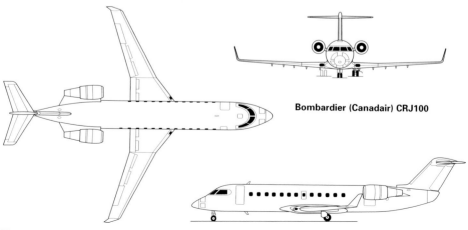

Bombardier (Canadair) CRJ100

BOMBARDIER DHC-7 DASH 7

Representing a courageous attempt to meet the requirements of third-level airlines for a medium-capacity transport offering the ability to operate into and out of small and sometimes difficult airports, and also very good operating economy, by exploiting the unrivalled practical experience of de Havilland Canada (now Bombardier) in the design, development and manufacture of STOL transports, the DHC-7 Dash 7 first flew on 27 March 1975 and was certificated some 25 months later.

In common with others of the company's STOL transport range, the Dash 7 has a high-set straight wing, in this instance carrying the powerplant of four PT6A-50 turboprop engines driving large-diameter propellers at low speed to produce slow blade-tip speeds and thus low noise levels. The high-aspect-ratio wing is equipped with large double-slotted flaps and includes a pair of inboard spoilers acting as lift-dumpers on landing and an outboard pair acting differentially in flight to assist aileron control, and the result is excellent STOL capability. Accommodation in the initial DHC-7 Series 100 is provided for up to 50 passengers in the cabin of the circular-section pressurized fuselage, while the DHC-7 Series 101 has provision for mixed freight and passengers. The only later variants before production ceased after the completion of a mere 113 aircraft were the DHC-7 Series 150 and DHC-7 Series 151, which were counterparts of the Series 100 and Series 101 variants with a greater fuel capacity and higher operating weights.

Specification: Bombardier (de Havilland Canada) DHC-7 Dash 7 Series 100
Origin: Canada
Type: two/three-crew STOL regional narrow-body transport
Powerplant: four Pratt & Whitney Canada PT6A-50 turboprop engines each flat-rated at 1,120 shp (835 kW)
Performance: maximum cruising speed 266 mph (428 km/h) at 8,000 ft (2440 m); service ceiling 21,000 ft (6400 m); range 795 miles (1279 km) with 50 passengers
Weights: empty 27,000 lb (12247 kg); maximum take-off 44,000 lb (19958 kg)
Dimensions: span 93 ft 0 in (28.35 m); length 80 ft 7.7 in (24.58 m); height 26 ft 2 in (7.98 m); area 860.00 sq ft (79.90 m²)
Payload: up to 50 passengers within the context of an 11,310-lb (5130-kg) maximum payload

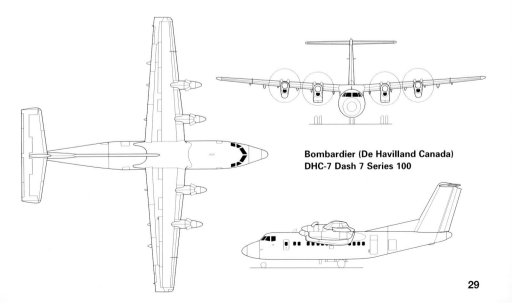

**Bombardier (De Havilland Canada)
DHC-7 Dash 7 Series 100**

BOMBARDIER DHC-8 DASH 8/Q

Created to fill the market gap between the company's 19-seat DHC-6 Twin Otter and 50-seat DHC-7 Dash 7, the 30/40-seat DHC-8 Dash 8 first flew on 20 June 1983 and entered service with PW120 turboprops driving constant-speed propellers with four reversible-pitch blades. The cabin can accommodate between 36 and 40 passengers, or mixed passenger/freight loads. The initial DHC-8 Series 100 was replaced in 1990 by the Series 100A, with PW120A or optional PW123 engines and a revised cabin with greater aisle headroom, and in 1992 there followed the further improved Series 100B with PW121 engines.

In 1992, the Series 200 introduced uprated PW123C engines, and there followed the Series 200A, with PW123C engines for improved payload/range performance, and the Series 200B, with PW123D engines offering full power at higher ambient temperatures. The Series 300 has its wing extended by 5 ft 0 in (1.52 m) and its fuselage lengthened by 11 ft 3 in (3.43 m) for up to 56 passengers. Subvariants include the Series 300A, with 2,380-shp (1775-kW) PW123A engines; the Series 300B, with 2,500-shp (1864-kW) PW123B engines; and the Series 300E, with improved 'hot-and-high' performance due to 2,380-shp (1775-kW) PW123E engines.

The Series 400 entered service early in 1999 with the wing increased in span to 92 ft 3 in (28.12 m), the fuselage lengthened to 103 ft 8 in (31.60 m) for up to 78 passengers, 5,067-shp (3778-kW) PW150A engines, and an active Ultra Electronics NVS (Noise and Vibration System) to reduce interior noise and vibration. Since 1998, the Dash 8 has been known as the Dash 8/Q to signify the incorporation of NVS. By the autumn of 2001, the manufacturer had received orders for 662 aircraft, of which 610 had been delivered.

Specification: Bombardier (De Havilland Canada) DHC-8 Dash 8 Series 100A
Origin: Canada
Type: three-crew regional narrow-body transport
Powerplant: two Pratt & Whitney Canada PW120A turboprop engines each rated at 2,000 shp (1491 kW)
Performance: maximum cruising speed 305 mph (491 km/h) at 15,000 ft (4570 m); certificated ceiling 25,000 ft (7620 m); range 960 miles (1546 km) with maximum passenger payload
Weights: empty 22,600 lb (10251 kg); maximum take-off 34,500 lb (15649 kg)
Dimensions: span 85 ft 0 in (25.91 m); length 73 ft 0 in (22.25 m); height 24 ft 7 in (7.49 m); wing area 585.00 sq ft (54.35 m²)
Payload: up to 39 passengers or freight within the context of an 8,400-lb (3810-kg) maximum payload

Bombardier DHC-8 Dash 8

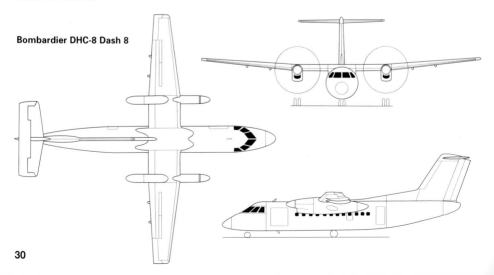

EADS/BAE SYSTEMS CONCORDE

In January 1996, the Concorde completed its first 20 years of operational service with Air France and British Airways, the only two airlines to have bought this supersonic airliner, one of only two such transports to have entered full service. Despite the fatal crash of one French aeroplane in 2000, requiring modification to the landing gear, fuel tanks and some of the wiring before a return to service in the autumn 2001, it is still the only one in such service after the early end of the Tupolev Tu-144's career.

From the mid-1950s, the British and French considered the development of increasingly similar supersonic airliners. Throughout these two separate design efforts, the British and French governments had became all too aware of the inevitably high cost that would be entailed, and the governments therefore decided on a single collaborative programme. The inter-governmental agreement of 29 November 1962 listed the principal airframe and powerplant elements as the British Aircraft Corporation (later British Aerospace and now BAE Systems) and Aérospatiale (now EADS), and Rolls-Royce and SNECMA respectively.

Flight trials and development were undertaken by the Concorde 001 and 002 prototypes and Concorde 101 and 102 pre-production aircraft, the prototypes recording their maiden flights on 2 March and 9 April 1969 respectively. The pre-production aircraft were completed to a standard closer to that fixed for production aircraft, and therefore possessed longer front and rear fuselages, revised nose visors, changes to the wing geometry, and an uprated powerplant. There followed just 16 production aircraft, Concorde 203 to 216, of which the first flew on 6 December 1973.

The Concorde made its first revenue-earning flights simultaneously on 21 January 1976 with Air France and British Airways, the supersonic transport's only two purchasers. Limited scheduled and charter services have been flown to many parts of the world, but the Concorde's staple in the transatlantic route, on which useful operating profits have been made.

Specification: EADS/BAE Systems (Aérospatiale/BAe) Concorde
Origin: International
Type: four-crew supersonic narrow-body airliner
Powerplant: four Rolls-Royce (Bristol Siddeley)/SNECMA Olympus 593 Mk 610 turbojet engines each rated at 38,050 lb st (169.25 kN) with afterburning
Weights: empty operating 173,500 lb (78700 kg); maximum take-off 408,000 lb (185069 kg)
Performance: maximum cruising speed 1,354 mph (2179 km/h) or Mach 2.05 at 51,300 ft (15635 m); initial climb rate 5,000 ft (1525 m) per minute; service ceiling about 60,000 ft (18290 m); range 3,870 miles (6228 km) at Mach 2.02 with maximum payload
Dimensions: span 83 ft 10 in (25.56 m); length 203 ft 9 in (62.10 m); height 37 ft 5 in (11.40 m); wing area 3,856.00 sq ft (358.25 m²)
Payload: between 100 and 144 passengers within the context of a 25,000-lb (11340-kg) typical payload

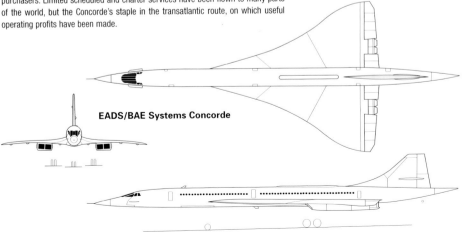

EADS/BAE Systems Concorde

EMBRAER RJ-145

At the Paris Air Show of June 1989, EMBRAER announced the development of a 45/48-seat turbofan-powered regional airliner based on its turboprop-powered EMB-120 Brasilia transport. A minimum-change design process led initially to the EMB-145 Amazon, in which a version of the EMB-120's airframe (with a lengthened fuselage) was combined with the powerplant of two 7,000-lb st (31.14-kN) Allison AE 3007 turbofan engines in nacelles over the wing roots. Wind-tunnel tests revealed several problems, however, and the design was reworked between October 1990 and March 1991 to implement changes, including a shorter and stiffer wing of supercritical section and swept at 22.3º, the engines in nacelles pylon-mounted under the wing, and the forward fuselage lengthened so that a longer nosewheel unit could be fitted. Further changes were announced in October 1991 after the engine installation had been altered to nacelles pylon-mounted on the sides of the rear fuselage, and the design was frozen in July 1992.

The prototype first flew on 11 August 1995, and the prototype and three production aircraft completed the test and certification programme by December 1996, when the EMB-145 entered service with Continental Express in the USA. In 1997, the EMB-145 was redesignated the RJ-145 (ERJ-145 when not prefixed by EMBRAER), and the type's main operators are two American airlines, Continental Express and AMR Eagle (now American Eagle), which between them have lodged orders and options for 274 aircraft. Firm orders stood at the figure of 552 aircraft by August 2001, by which time deliveries amounted to 362 machines.

The ERJ-145 has two subvariants in the form of the extended-range ERJ-145ER, with 7,040-lb st (31.32-kN) AE3007-A1 engines, and the long-range ERJ-145LR, with greater fuel capacity and AE3007-A3 engines flat-rated at 7,430 lb st (33.05 kN) for a maximum-payload range of 1,887 miles (3037 km).

Specification: EMBRAER RJ-145ER
Origin: Brazil
Type: two/three-crew regional narrow-body transport
Powerplant: two Rolls-Royce North America (Allison) AE 3007-A1 turbofan engines each rated at 7,040 lb st (31.32 kN) dry
Performance: cruising speed, maximum 511 mph (823 km/h) at 37,000 ft (11280 m) and economical 423 mph (680 km/h) at 32,000 ft (9755 m); initial climb rate 2,379 ft (725 m) per minute; service ceiling 37,000 ft (11280 m); range 975 miles (1569 km) with maximum payload
Weights: empty 25,772 lb (11690 kg); maximum take-off 42,328 lb (19200 kg)
Dimensions: span 65 ft 9 in (20.04 m); length 98 ft 0 in (29.87 m); height 22 ft 1.75 in (6.75 m); area 550.91 sq ft (51.18 m²)
Payload: up to 50 passengers within the context of an 11,926-lb (5410-kg) maximum payload

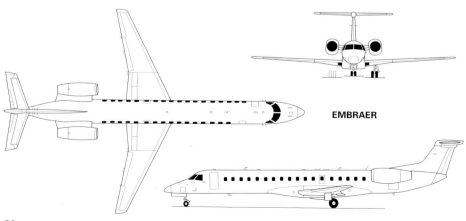

EMBRAER

FAIRCHILD DORNIER Do 328

After deciding in 1986 to develop a 30-seat regional transport under the designation Do 328, Dornier backed away from the project before returning to it during August 1988 with a decision to relaunch the programme for the Do 328, which is now more properly known as a Fairchild Dornier product after Fairchild's acquisition of Dornier in mid-1996. The Do 328 that emerged from this effort was conceived as an advanced development of the basic concept embodied in the Do 228, and combined essentially the same TNT advanced supercritical-section wing with a new T-tail and, for a high-altitude cruise capability, a pressurized circular-section fuselage derived from the lessons of the company's NRT (Neue Rumpf Technologien, or new fuselage technologies) programme.

Intended to provide field and climb performance in no way inferior to that of the Do 228 in concert with much improved speed and altitude performance, the Do 328 was schemed round a cabin providing standing headroom in the aisle and greater seat width than the Boeing Models 727 and 737. The Do 328 first flew on 6 December 1991, and was certificated in October 1993 respectively.

Standard accommodation in the Do 326-100 baseline model is for 30 to 33 passengers. Later additions were the Do 328-110, with the maximum weight increased to 30,843 lb (13990 kg) for a full-load range of 1,150 miles (1853 km); the Do 328-120, with thermodynamically enhanced 2,180-shp (1625-kW) PW119C engines driving slightly larger propellers for improved field performance; and the Do 328-130 development of the Do 328-120, with PW119C engines, a rudder-enhanced deflection system, and additional flap settings for further improved field performance.

By late 2001, sales had reached 104 aircraft, of which all had been delivered.

Specification: Dornier Do 328-110
Origin: Germany
Type: two-crew regional narrow-body transport
Powerplant: two Pratt & Whitney PW119B turboprop engines each rated at 2,180 shp (1625 kW)
Performance: maximum cruising speed 388 mph (620 km/h) at 20,000 ft (6095 m); certificated ceiling 25,000 ft (7620 m) normal and 31,000 ft (9450 m) optional; range 1,150 miles (1853 km) with 30 passengers
Weights: empty 19,665 lb (8920 kg); maximum take-off 30,842 lb (13990 kg)
Dimensions: span 68 ft 10 in (20.98 m); length 69 ft 9.75 in (21.28 m); height 23 ft 9 in (7.24 m); area 430.57 sq ft (40.00 m²)
Payload: up to 33 passengers within the context of an 8,135-lb (3690-kg) maximum payload

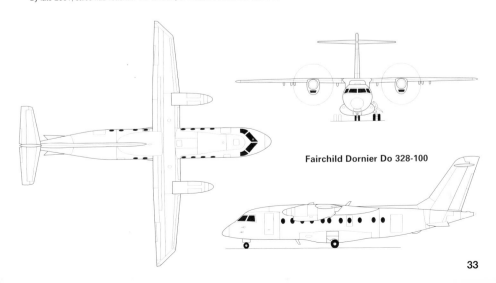

Fairchild Dornier Do 328-100

FAIRCHILD DORNIER Do 328JET

By the mid-1980s, the world's airline industry had come to the belief that one of the major markets of the near future would be regional transport of the type that would deliver passengers between outlying airports and the major hub airports served by high-capacity airliners of the medium- and long-range types. This anticipated growth attracted the interest of many manufacturers, especially in Brazil, Canada and Germany. Here smaller companies started to plan a new generation of regional transports based on airframes offering low operating costs and possessing considerable 'stretch' potential to allow increases in passenger capacity and installed power as the market evolved.

In Germany, Dornier decided that its current turboprop-powered Do 328 regional transport could form the basis of a more profitable type with fuel-efficient but quiet turbofan engines. However, the cost of the programme for what was initially known as the Do 328-300 but later as the Do 328JET was really beyond the capabilities of Dornier, whose parent organization then sold 80 per cent of Dornier to Fairchild. The company now known as Fairchild Dornier decided to proceed with the Do 328JET. The prototype was the second Do 328, revised with 6,075-lb st (27.02-kN) PW306/9 turbofans, and this first flew on 20 January 1998. The Do 328JET received certification in the first half of 1999 and entered service in the middle of the same year.

A corporate transport version with accommodation for a maximum of 19 passengers, but more typically between 12 and 14 passengers, is offered as the Envoy 3 (originally Do 328 Business Jet). By the autumn of 2001, Fairchild Dornier had taken orders for 137 aircraft, of which 69 had been delivered. Major developments of the Do 328JET concept include the larger 70-seat Do 728JET, due to enter service in 2003 with General Electric CF34-8D3 turbofans, and the 95/110-seat Do 928JET, also due to enter service in 2002, with a larger wing and higher-rated CF34-10D turbofans.

Specification: Fairchild Dornier Do 328JET
Origin: International
Type: two-crew regional narrow-body transport
Powerplant: two Pratt & Whitney Canada PW306B turbofan engines each rated at 6,050 lb st (26.91 kN) dry
Performance: maximum cruising speed 460 mph (741 km/h) at 25,000 ft (7620 m); certificated ceiling 31,000 ft (9450 m) with an option for 35,000 ft (10670 m); range 1,035 miles (1666 km) with 32 passengers
Weights: empty 20,282 lb (9200 kg); maximum take-off 33,047 lb (14990 kg) with an option for 33,510 lb (15200 kg)
Dimensions: span 68 ft 10 in (20.98 m); length 69 ft 9.75 in (21.28 m); height 23 ft 8.75 in (7.23 m); area 430.57 sq ft (40.00 m²)
Payload: up to 34 passengers within the context of a 7,518-lb (3410-kg) maximum payload

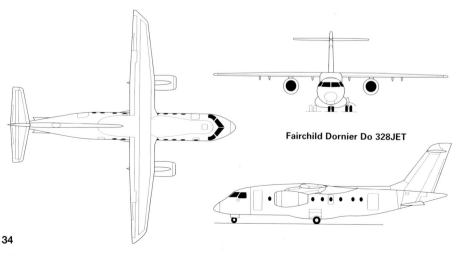

Fairchild Dornier Do 328JET

FAIRCHILD DORNIER METRO

The Swearingen Aviation Corporation became a wholly owned subsidiary of Fairchild Industries in 1979, and in 1964 began work on the Merlin IIA as a turboprop-powered eight-seat executive aeroplane that first flew on 13 April 1965 and scored useful sales. In August 1969, the company flew the first example of the SA 226TC Metro as the 19-seat commuterliner counterpart of the current Merlin III, with a longer fuselage, new surfaces and 840-shp (626-kW) TPE331-303G turboprops.

Merlin and Metro development continued apace, leading to the generally improved Metro II in 1975. By 1981, the versions available were the 8/11-seat Merlin IIIC executive transport, with 900-shp (671-kW) TPE331-10U-503G engines; the Merlin IVC 13/16-seat corporate aeroplane; and the generally similar Metro III 19-passenger commuter transport. A new version of this last was delivered from 1983 as the Metro IIIA, which differed from the Metro III primarily in its powerplant of two Pratt & Whitney Canada PT6A-45R turboprops each flat-rated at 1,100 shp (820 kW). On 10 March 1982, a Metro III was the 500th Swearingen turboprop aircraft to be delivered. Further development continued, and at the end of the 20th century the versions available were the SA 227CC and SA 227DC versions of what is now the Metro 23, with TPE331-11U-612G and TPE331-12-UAR-701G engines respectively; the Metro 23E, with an EFIS flight deck; the Merlin 23 business equivalent of the Metro 23; the Expediter I all-freight version, introduced in the mid-1980s, with a maximum payload of more than 5,000 lb (2268 kg); and the Expediter 23, introduced in 1991, with a maximum payload of 5,500 lb (2495 kg).

Production of the Merlin and Metro ended in March 2000 after the completion of 1,053 aircraft, including 607 examples of the Metro.

Specification: Fairchild Dornier Metro 23
Origin: USA
Type: two-crew commuterliner and short-range narrow-body transport
Powerplant: two Honeywell (originally Garrett and then AlliedSignal) TPE331-121UAR turboprop engines each rated at 1,119 shp (834 kW)
Performance: cruising speed, maximum 340 mph (546 km/h) at 15,000 ft (4570 m) and economical 290 mph (467 km/h) at 25,000 ft (7620 m); certificated ceiling 25,150 ft (7665 m); range 1,283 miles (2065 km) with maximum payload
Weights: empty operating 9,500 lb (4309 kg); maximum take-off 16,500 lb (7484 kg)
Dimensions: span 57 ft 0 in (17.37 m); length 59 ft 4.25 in (18.09 m); height 16 ft 8 in (5.08 m); area 309.00 sq ft (28.71 m²)
Payload: up to 19 passengers within the context of a 5,000-lb (2268-kg) maximum payload

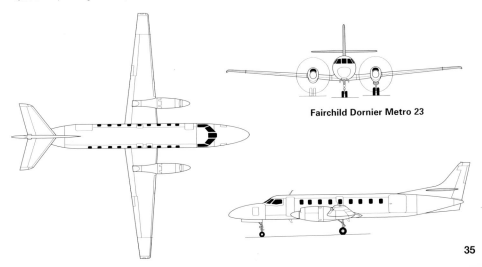

Fairchild Dornier Metro 23

FOKKER 50

The Fokker 50 is a comprehensively modernized version of the F.27 Friendship Mk 500 airliner, and after being announced in November 1983, first flew on 27 December 1985 as the precursor of a type marketed in passenger, freight and combi (mixed passenger/freight) variants. The F.50 was delivered from August 1987.

Until Fokker went into bankruptcy in March 1996, the type was offered on the civil market in two variants: the F.50 Series 100, with two PW125B turboprops and between 46 and 58 passengers in F.50-100 four-door and F.50-120 three-door subvariants; and the F.50 Series 300 (otherwise F.50 High Performance), for 'hot-and-high' operations, with two PW127B turboprop engines each flat-rated at 2,750 shp (2050 kW) and available in F.50-300 four-door and F.50-320 three-door subvariants. In the mid-1990s, Fokker was planning the F.50 Series 400 with its fuselage lengthened by 7 ft 10.5 in (2.40 m) for 68 passengers in F.50-400 four-door and F.50-420 three-door subvariants.

The F.50-100 baseline model is externally similar to the F.27, but features a host of structural and system improvements (the latter including digital avionics and an EFIS flight deck) as well as greater use of composite materials in the airframe, and is powered by PW125B turboprop engines each flat-rated at 2,500 shp (1864 kW), driving a six- rather than four-blade propeller and supplied with fuel from an internal weight of 9,090 lb (4023 kg) for the carriage of a maximum payload of 13,404 lb (6080 kg).

The last F.50 was delivered in May 1997, ending production of the F.50 series at 212 aircraft, including four examples of the F.60 utility transport derivative for the Royal Netherlands Air Force.

Specification: Fokker 50-100
Origin: Netherlands
Type: two/three-crew regional narrow-body transport
Powerplant: two Pratt & Whitney Canada PW125B turboprop engines each flat-rated at 2,500 shp (1864 kW)
Performance: cruising speed, maximum 325 mph (522 km/h) at optimum altitude and economical 261 mph (421 km/h) at optimum altitude; certificated ceiling 25,000 ft (7620 m); range 776 miles (1249 km) at standard maximum take-off weight with 50 passengers, or 1,883 miles (3030 km) at optional maximum take-off weight with 50 passengers
Weights: empty 27,886 lb (12650 kg); maximum take-off 41,865 lb (18990 kg) standard or 45,899 lb (20820 kg) optional
Dimensions: span 95 ft 1.75 in (29.00 m); length 82 ft 10 in (25.247 m); height 27 ft 3.5 in (8.317 m); area 753.50 sq ft (70.00 m²)
Payload: between 46 and 58 passengers within the context of a 13,400-lb (6078-kg) maximum payload

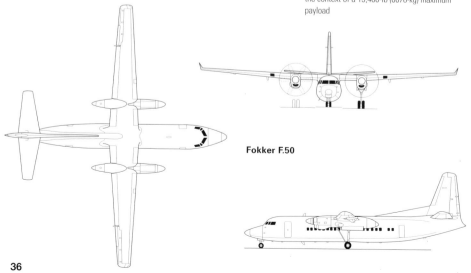

Fokker F.50

First flown on 30 November 1968, the Fokker 100 is a modernized development of the F.28 Fellowship Mk 4000 twin-turbofan airliner. The type was first flown with two Tay Mk 620 turbofans, but an option was later added for the 15,100-lb st (67.17-kN) Tay Mk 650 engine. As well as updated avionics (including an EFIS flight deck) and a general modernization of systems, the F.100 also introduced a large measure of composite materials in its structure, a revised wing of greater span and improved aerofoil section for better cruising performance and high subsonic speeds, and a lengthening of the fuselage to allow the carriage of up to 107 passengers in a five-abreast seating arrangement inside a redesigned cabin.

The type was offered at three maximum take-off weight options with differing fuel quantities, and deliveries began in February 1988. The primary variant was the standard F.100, although other models offered included the F.100QC quick-change model, with a large port-side door in the forward fuselage for a maximum freight payload of 25,353 kg (11500 kg); and the Executive Jet 100 VIP and corporate shuttle. At the time of Fokker's bankruptcy in March 1996, 277 F.100 transports had been completed.

A lower-capacity version of the F.100 was developed as the F.70, with its fuselage reduced in length by 15 ft 2 in (4.62 m) for the carriage of up to 79 passengers on the power of two Tay Mk 620 turbofans. The F.70 recorded its maiden flight on 2 April 1993, received its certification in October 1994 and entered airline service in March 1995. The last of 47 F.70 transports was delivered in April 1997. Variants that had been offered by the time of Fokker's collapse included the standard F.70 and the F.70A for the North American market, with an additional main deck cargo hold, reducing seating capacity to 70.

Specification: Fokker 100
Origin: Netherlands
Type: two-crew regional narrow-body transport
Powerplant: two Rolls-Royce·Tay Mk 620 turbofan engines each rated at 13,850 lb st (61.61 kN) dry
Performance: cruising speed, maximum 532 mph (856 km/h) at 25,500 ft (7770 m) and economical 368 mph (593 km/h) at 25,500 ft (7770 m); certificated ceiling 35,000 ft (10670 m); range between 1,484 and 1,933 miles (2389 and 3111 km) with 50 passengers, depending on maximum take-off weight option
Weights: empty between 54,217 and 54,558 lb (24593 and 24747 kg), depending on weight option; maximum take-off between 95,000 and 101,000 lb (43090 and 45810 kg), depending on weight option
Dimensions: span 92 ft 1.5 in (28.08 m); length 116 ft 6.75 in (35.53 m); height 27 ft 10.5 in (8.51 m); area 1,006.46 sq ft (93.50 m²)
Payload: up to 107 passengers within the context of a maximum payload of between 24,486 and 26,442 lb (11108 and 11993 kg), depending on weight option

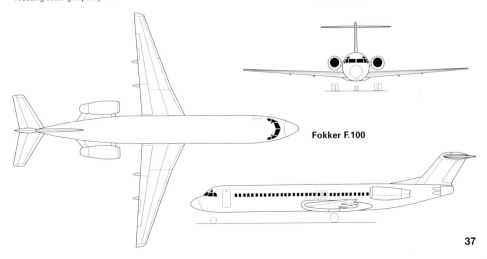

Fokker F.100

ILYUSHIN Il-86 AND Il-96

Designed to provide Soviet-bloc airlines with a medium-range wide-body airliner comparable in terms of operating efficiency with contemporary Western airliners, the Il-86 carries up to 350 passengers on four examples of the 28,660-lb st (127.48-kN) Kuznetsov NK-86 turbofan designed specifically for this application. This powerplant provides for a nominal (but seldom achieved) range of 2,235 miles (3600 km) with an 88,183-lb (40000-kg) payload after take-off at a maximum weight of 458,554 lb (208000 kg). The dimensional data for the Il-86 include a span of 157 ft 8.25 in (48.06 m), length of 195 ft 4 in (59.54 m), height of 51 ft 10.5 in (15.81 m) and area of 3,444.56 sq ft (320.00 m²).

The Il-86 first flew on 22 December 1976, and Aeroflot received its first aeroplane in September 1979 for service from December 1980. The Il-86, which received the NATO reporting designation 'Camber', failed to live up to Soviet hopes in terms of its performance and operating economics, thereby removing all possibility of sales to customers outside the Soviet bloc, and production ended in 1993 after the completion of just 104 aircraft.

Ilyushin felt that there was little wrong with the basic design of the Il-86. It was therefore retained in the Il-96, which was otherwise a new design introducing a measure of more advanced materials. Other major changes were the more advanced engines, the 'glass' flight deck with an HUD and the controls for a triplex fly-by-wire control system, and a wing typified by a supercritical aerofoil section and tip-mounted winglets. The initial version was the Il-96-300, which first flew on 28 September 1988 and entered service early in 1993. Production has been notably slow, and by the later part of 2000 only 11 aircraft had been delivered.

Specification: Ilyushin Il-96-300
Origin: USSR
Type: three/five-crew medium/long-range wide-body transport
Powerplant: four Aviadvigatel (Soloviev) PS-90A turbofan engines each rated at 35,273 lb st (156.90 kN) dry
Performance: cruising speed, maximum and economical 553 mph (889 km/h) at between 33,135 and 39,700 ft (10100 and 12100 m); certificated ceiling 39,700 ft (12100 m); range 6,835 miles (1100 km) with a 33,069-lb (15000-kg) payload and 4,660 miles (7500 km) with an 88,183-lb (40000-kg) maximum payload
Weights: empty operating 257,937 lb (117000 kg); maximum take-off 476,190 lb (216000 kg)
Dimensions: span 197 ft 2.5 in (60.11 m) over the winglets; length 181 ft 7.25 in (55.35 m); height 57 ft 7 in (17.55 m); area 4,215.29 sq ft (391.60 m²)
Payload: between 235 and 300 passengers within the context of an 88,183-lb (40000-kg) maximum payload

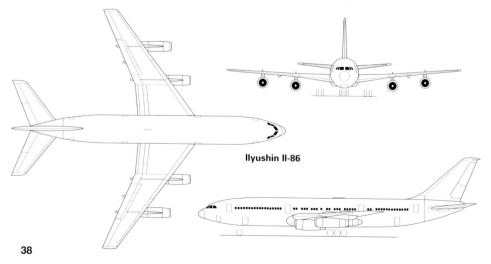

Ilyushin Il-86

ILYUSHIN Il-114

The Il-114 was schemed from the early 1980s as a successor to the Antonov An-24, and first flew on 29 March 1990. Both prototypes were lost during the Il-114's development and certification programmes, which were then delayed as much by the withdrawal of Russian government funding as by difficulties with the airframe and the engine, and production by TAPO at Tashkent in Uzbekistan saw the completion of the first aeroplane to the full production standard only in August 1992. Three of the first five aircraft were used for the completion of the flight certification effort by April 1997, paving the way for a Russian and Uzbek government decision for joint promotion of the type, which entered service in August 1998.

The Il-114 is a conventional low-wing monoplane made largely of light alloy but including, by weight, about 10 per cent of composite materials. The fuselage is of circular section and comprises a two-crew flight deck and a cabin carrying up to 64 passengers. Provision was made at the design stage for the rearrangement of the cabin for a higher-density seating arrangement to permit the carriage of a larger number of passengers, the removal of the seating to allow the aeroplane to operate in a cargo role, and the lengthening of the fuselage for standard accommodation of between 70 and 75 passengers. Power is provided by two TV7-117 turboprop engines driving propellers with six blades of carbon fibre-reinforced plastics construction.

Variants include the Il-114-100 (Il-114PC up to 1997) export model, with Sextant avionics and two 2,750-shp (2051-kW) Pratt & Whitney Canada PW127H turboprops driving Hamilton Standard propellers for increased range and operating economy; the Il-114M, with TV7M-117 turboprop engines and provision for a 15,432-lb (7000-kg) payload at a higher maximum take-off weight; and the Il-114MA variant of the Il-114M, with Pratt & Whitney Canada engines for the carriage of up to 74 passengers over 1,243-mile (2000-km) stage lengths.

Specification: Ilyushin Il-114
Origin: USSR
Type: two-crew regional narrow-body transport
Powerplant: two Klimov TV7-117S turboprop engines each rated at 2,466 shp (1839 kW)
Performance: cruising speed, maximum 311 mph (500 km/h) at optimum altitude and economical 292 mph (470 km/h) at optimum altitude; certificated ceiling 26,500 ft (8075 m); range 621 miles (1000 km) with 54 passengers
Weights: empty operating 33,069 lb (15000 kg); maximum take-off 50,044 lb (22700 kg)
Dimensions: span 98 ft 5.25 in (30.00 m); length 88 ft 2 in (26.88 m); height 30 ft 7 in (9.32 m); area 881.59 sq ft (81.90 m²)
Payload: up to 64 passengers within the context of a 14,330-lb (6500-kg) maximum payload

Ilyushin Il-114-100

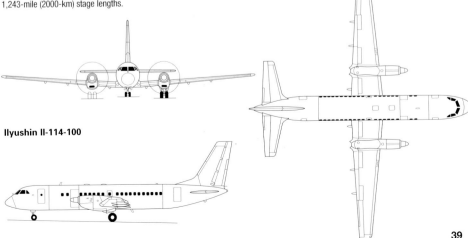

RAYTHEON BEECH MODEL 1900 AIRLINER

The Model 1900 Airliner resulted from Beech's realization that, with the end of Model 99 Airliner production in 1975, it had removed itself from the market for regional and commuter airliners, whose sales were accelerating rapidly in the second half of the 1970s. In 1979, therefore, Beech announced its intention of re-entering the market with one or more new types including, as short-term solutions, a pair of Model 200 Super King Air derivatives: these were the 13-passenger Model 1300 and 19-passenger Model 1900 with a lengthened fuselage. The first Model 1900 flew on 3 September 1982, with two PT6A-65B turboprops flat-rated at 1,100 shp (820 kW) for good performance under 'hot-and-high' conditions and a fuselage whose centre-section part was lengthened by 14 ft 0 in (4.27 m) by comparison with that of the Model 200.

The new type entered service in February 1984. Only three aircraft had been completed before the company switched to the Model 1900C, with an upward-opening cargo door in the port rear side of the cabin, and later to the Model 1900C-1, with integral fuel tanks. After delivering 225 Model 1900C aircraft, Beech switched in 1991 to the Model 1900D, with the height of the cabin increased by 1 ft 2 in (0.36 m) to provide genuine standing headroom and a 28.5 per cent increase in cabin volume, an increased cabin pressurization differential, larger cabin windows and door, winglets at the tips of the wing for superior 'hot-and-high' performance, a pair of ventral strakes under the rear fuselage to improve directional stability, and two more powerful PT6A-67D turboprops.

The Model 1900 is one of the few 19-passenger airliners to remain in production in the early 2000s, when Raytheon Beech's orders for the type had reached 695 aircraft, of which 672 had been delivered.

Specification: Beech Model 1900D Airliner
Origin: USA
Type: one/two-crew regional, commuter and executive narrow-body transport
Powerplant: two Pratt & Whitney PT6A-67D turboprop engines each flat-rated at 1,279 shp (954 kW)
Performance: maximum cruising speed 326 mph (524 km/h) at 16,000 ft (4875 m); certificated ceiling 25,000 ft (7620 m); range 1,726 miles (2778 km) with 10 passengers
Weights: empty operating 10,615 lb (4815 kg); maximum take-off 16,950 lb (7688 kg)
Dimensions: span 57 ft 11.8 in (17.67 m) over winglets; length 57 ft 10 in (17.63 m); height 15 ft 6 in (4.72 m); area 310.00 sq ft (28.80 m²)
Payload: up to 19 passengers within the context of a 4,250-lb (1928-kg) maximum payload

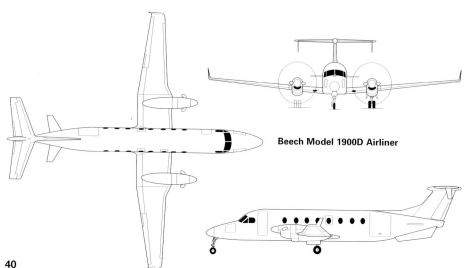

Beech Model 1900D Airliner

The Saab 340 37-seat regional transport was originally developed in partnership with Fairchild and was initially known as the Saab Fairchild SF-340. It first flew on 25 January 1983 with 1,630-shp (1215-kW) General Electric CT7-5A2 turboprops. From November 1985, the 340 was a wholly Swedish programme. The 340 gained certification in March 1984 and the 340A production model was delivered from June 1984. Production lasted to 1999 and amounted to 456 35-passenger aircraft, including the 340B, with 1,750-shp (1305-kW) CT7-9B turboprops for improved 'hot-and-high' performance; and the 340B+, with Saab 2000 features for improved field performance, greater cabin comfort (through better seats for a typical load of 33 passengers and an optional active noise-control system) and lower-cost maintenance. The primary data for the 340B include a cruising speed of 325 mph (522 km/h), range of 1,047 miles (1685 km) with 35 passengers, maximum take-off weight of 29,000 lb (13155 kg), span of 70 ft 4 in (21.44 m), length of 64 ft 8.75 in (19.73 m) and area of 450.00 sq ft (41.81 m²).

First flown on 26 March 1992 for service from September 1994, the Saab 2000 is a development of the 340 with accommodation for between 50 and 58 passengers in a lengthened fuselage and carried by a wing increased in area by some 33 per cent through a 15 per cent increase in span. Other features are a new and more capable powerplant with the engines located farther from the fuselage to reduce the noise perceived in the cabin, slower-turning and therefore quieter propellers with six swept blades, an advanced flight deck, and a slightly more advanced structure making greater use of composite materials. The overall object of the programme was to provide an attractive blend of turboprop economy with the speed and quietness of turbofan-powered aircraft. Sales were sluggish, however, and production ceased in 1999 after the completion of only 60 aircraft.

Specification: Saab 2000
Origin: Sweden
Type: two-crew regional narrow-body transport
Powerplant: two Rolls-Royce North America (Allison) AE2100A turboprop engines each flat-rated at 4,152 shp (3096 kW)
Performance: cruising speed, maximum 423 mph (682 km/h) 25,000 ft (7620 m) and economical 369 mph (594 km/h) at 31,000 ft (9450 m); certificated ceiling 31,000 ft (9450 m); range 1,782 miles (2868 km) with maximum payload
Weights: empty operating 31,966 lb (14500 kg); maximum take-off 50,705 lb (23000 kg)
Dimensions: span 81 ft 2.25 in (24.76 m); length 89 ft 6 in (27.28 m); height 25 ft 4 in (7.73 m); area 600.00 sq ft (55.74 m²)
Payload: up to 58 passengers within the context of a 13,007-lb (5900-kg) maximum payload

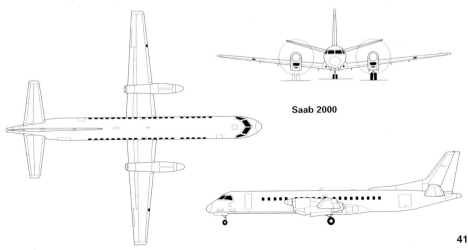

Saab 2000

TUPOLEV Tu-134 'CRUSTY'

In 1957, the USSR issued a requirement for a successor to the piston-engined Ilyushin Il-14 'Crate'. Tupolev responded with its Tu-124, which was essentially a three-quarter-scale version of the Tu-104 'Camel' transport, the civil counterpart of the Tu-16 'Badger' bomber. The Tu-124 first flew in June 1960 and entered service in 1962 as the world's first turbofan-powered short/medium-range transport. Although popular and reliable, the Tu-124 was not fully optimized for airline service, and to meet an Aeroflot demand for a superior type, Tupolev extrapolated the Tu-124A with the engines moved to pod-mounted positions on the rear fuselage under a T-tail, the centre section revised to increase span by 11 ft 3.75 in (3.45 m), and the fuselage lengthened by 5 ft 3 in (1.60 m).

Development proceeded via six prototypes and pre-production aircraft. Production was authorized in 1964, and the type was redesignated the Tu-134 before entering service in September 1967 with a cabin layout for 64 passengers, soon increased to 72 in two cabins. Most of the production aircraft had a revised 'solid' nose with weather radar in place of the Tu-124's glazed nose. In 1970, a new variant entered service as the Tu-134A, with an APU to make the type independent of ground services, strengthened wings and landing gear for operation at higher weights, and the fuselage lengthened by 8 ft 10.25 in (2.70 m) for a maximum of 84 passengers. Production ended in the late 1970s after the delivery of some 700 aircraft, so later models resulted from conversion rather than production programmes.

The baseline version of these later models was the Tu-134B, with a forward-facing crew compartment. Other differences from the basic Tu-134A standard include a power-plant of two 14,991-lb st (66.68-kN) D-30 III turbofans and a maximum take-off weight of 104,938 lb (47600 kg). Subvariants of the Tu-134B are the 90-passenger Tu-134B-1 and the 96-passenger Tu-134B-3.

Specification: Tupolev Tu-134A 'Crusty'
Origin: USSR
Type: three-crew short/medium-range narrow-body transport
Powerplant: two PNPP 'Aviadvigatel' (Soloviev) D-30 II turbofan engines each rated at 14,991 lb st (66.68 kN) dry
Performance: cruising speed, maximum 559 mph (900 km/h) at 27,885 ft (8500 m) and economical 466 mph (750 km/h) at 36,090 ft (11000 m); certificated ceiling 39,040 ft (11900 m); range 2,175 miles (3500 km) with an 8,818-lb (4000-kg) payload or 1,243 miles (2000 km) with an 18,111-lb (8215-kg) payload
Weights: empty operating 63,933 lb (29000 kg); maximum take-off 103,616 lb (47000 kg)
Dimensions: span 95 ft 1.75 in (29.00 m); length 121 ft 8.75 in (37.10 m); height 29 ft 7 in (9.02 m); area 1,370.29 sq ft (127.30 m²)
Payload: up to 76 passengers within the context of an 18,000-lb (8165-kg) maximum payload

Tupolev Tu-134

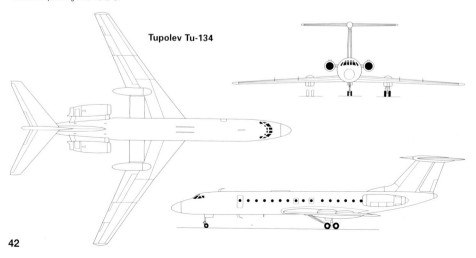

TUPOLEV Tu-154 'CARELESS'

In the first half of the 1960s, Aeroflot issued a requirement for a turbine-powered airliner to replace the obsolescent Antonov An-10 'Cat', Ilyushin Il-18 'Coot' and Tupolev Tu-104 'Camel' transports on stages up to 3,728 miles (6000 km) long. Tupolev's Tu-154 response was in essence an enlarged development of the Tu-134 with a much-revised wing (incorporating wide-span slats, triple-slotted flaps and four-section spoilers) and a powerplant of three turbofans in the tail. The first Tu-154 flew on 3 October 1968, and the type entered service in February 1972 only after a protracted development programme. This basic version is powered by three 20,944-lb st (93.16-kN) KKBM (Kuznetsov) NK-8-2 turbofans, and carries between 128 and 167 passengers.

The improved Tu-154A was introduced in 1973 with three 23,148-lb st (102.97-kN) NK-8-2U turbofans and greater fuel capacity: the additional fuel is not usable in flight, but can be transferred to the standard tanks at an airport where fuel may be scarce or expensive. Introduced in 1977, the Tu-154B features improved high-lift devices and spoilers, as well as more modern avionics for improved landing capability under adverse weather conditions. The Tu-154B was also produced in two subvariants as the Tu-154B-1 and Tu-154B-2, the former intended for domestic flights in the USSR with up to 160 passengers, and the latter built from 1980 as the more prolific member of the family with features including an automatic flight-control and navigation system, a revised cabin for up to 180 passengers, and centre-section tankage integrated into the main tankage. The Tu-154C is a freighter conversion of the Tu-154B.

The Tu-154M was introduced in 1984 and is a modernized version of the Tu-154B with a completely new powerplant for improved range. Other changes are a redesigned tailplane and revisions to the slats and spoilers. Among this model's subvariants are the Tu-154S freighter and the Tu-154M Model 1995 with the Zhasmin (jasmine) automatic flight and navigation system. Production has so far exceeded 1,000 aircraft.

Specification: Tupolev Tu-154M 'Careless'
Origin: USSR
Type: three-crew medium/long-range narrow-body transport
Powerplant: three PNPP 'Aviadvigatel' (Soloviev) D-30KU-154-II turbofan engines each rated at 23,369 lb st (103.95 kN) dry
Performance: cruising speed, maximum 590 mph (950 km/h) at 39,040 ft (11900 m); certificated ceiling 39,040 ft (11900 m); range 4,101 miles (6600 km) with maximum fuel and a 12,015-lb (5450-kg) payload, or 2,324 miles (3740 km) with maximum payload
Weights: empty operating 121,914 lb (55300 kg); maximum take-off 220,459 lb (100000 kg)
Dimensions: span 123 ft 2.5 in (37.55 m); length 157 ft 1.75 in (47.90 m); height 37 ft 4.75 in (11.40 m); area 2,168.46 sq ft (201.45 m²)
Payload: up to 180 passengers within the context of a 39,683-lb (18000-kg) maximum payload

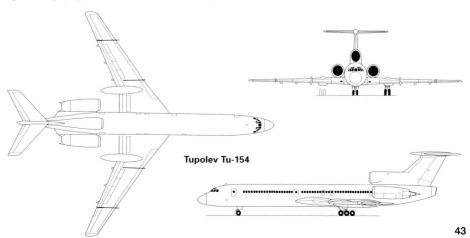

Tupolev Tu-154

TUPOLEV Tu-204 AND Tu-214

The Tu-204 first flew on 2 January 1989 and was certificated in January 1995 for service from April 1995. The Tu-204-100 initial version is powered by PS-90 turbofans. A higher-weight model, also powered by the PS-90 engines, has been developed as the Tu-204-200 but is now known as the Tu-214. It first flew on 21 March 1996, to offer a maximum take-off weight of 242,504 lb (110000 kg). The Tu-204-120 is a westernized model with 43,070-lb st (191.66-kN) Rolls-Royce RB.211-535E4B turbofans, and first flew on 14 August 1992. Sirocco Aerospace International was formed by an Egyptian company to market the type, and in 1996 ordered 30 Tu-204-120 passenger and -120C cargo aircraft. The first Tu-204-120 was delivered in November 1998.

A derivative of the Tu-204-200/Tu-214 is also being developed with Rolls-Royce engines as the Tu-204-220. This is a joint effort by Sirocco and Tupolev, and is essentially a higher-weight version of the Tu-204-120C freighter with a strengthened floor, revised cargo door and no passenger windows.

The Kaman Aircraft Production Organization in Tatarstan is producing a separate long-range version of the Tu-214 operating at higher weights than the baseline variant but still powered by PS-90 engines. Small numbers of this model, which has the official support of the Tatarstan government, have been ordered. The other major derivative is the lower-capacity but longer-range Tu-204-300, which was originally designated the Tu-234 and recorded its maiden flight on 8 July 2000. Offering 160-passenger accommodation, the Tu-204-300 has a fuselage shortened by 19 ft 8.25 in (6.00 m), and with the same fuel as the Tu-204-100 has a range of 5,748 miles (9250 km). There could also be a Tu-234C freighter with Rolls-Royce engines. By a time late in 2000, deliveries of all variants amounted to some 20 aircraft.

Specification: Tupolev Tu-204-100
Origin: USSR
Type: two/four-crew medium-range narrow-body transport
Powerplant: two Aviadvigatel PS-90 turbofan engines each rated at 35,582 lb st (158.34 kN) dry
Performance: cruising speed, maximum 527 mph (849 km/h) at optimum altitude; certificated ceiling 41,010 ft (12500 m); range 3,045 miles (4900 km) with maximum payload
Weights: empty operating 125,485 lb (56920 kg); maximum take-off 227,072 lb (103000 kg)
Dimensions: span 137 ft 10 in (42.00 m); length 150 ft 11 in (46.00 m); height 45 ft 7 in (13.90 m); area 1,980.62 sq ft (184.00 m²)
Payload: between 170 and 214 passengers within the context of a 46,297-lb (21000-kg) maximum payload

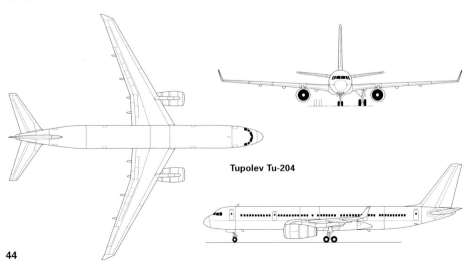

Tupolev Tu-204

YAKOVLEV Yak-42 AND Yak-142

The success of Yakovlev's Yak-40 regional airliner persuaded Aeroflot and the design bureau to press ahead with the creation of a related transport retaining the same basic design although in a form revised to a larger size and fitted with more powerful engines and modestly swept flying surfaces. The result was the Yak-42 (later accorded the NATO reporting designation 'Clobber'), which first flew on 6 March 1975 in the form of an initial prototype with flying surfaces swept at 11°. There followed a second prototype with its flying surfaces swept at 23°, and as this second machine proved generally superior, a third prototype followed with the same basic format but incorporating a number of improvements thought necessary for the production model.

The Yak-42 entered service in 1980 as a partial replacement for the Tu-134, and was characterized by a maximum take-off weight of 119,050 lb (54000 kg) for the carriage of 120 passengers over a range of 951 miles (1530 km). The type's production has been undertaken at an apparently leisurely tempo, and deliveries have reached only about 190 aircraft. There have been a number of variants. The Yak-42D, introduced in 1988, is a Dalnii (range) development of the baseline model with more fuel and a rearranged interior. Certificated in July 1997, the Yak-42D-100 is a development with AlliedSignal avionics but a Russian autopilot. The Yak-42ML is the Mezhdunarodnye Linii (international routes) development of the Yak-42 baseline model that appeared in 1981 with a more comfortable cabin. Originally known as the Yak-42A and first completed in 1998, the Yak-142 is the modernized version of the Yak-42D, with AlliedSignal digital avionics as well as a number of aerodynamic and structural improvements. The type offers a range of 1,733 miles (2790 km) with 120 passengers.

Specification: Yakovlev Yak-42D 'Clobber'
Origin: USSR
Type: two/three-crew short-range and regional narrow-body transport
Powerplant: three ZMDB Progress (Lotarev) D-36 I turbofan engines each rated at 14,330 lb st (63.74 kN) dry
Performance: cruising speed, maximum 503 mph (810 km/h) at 25,000 ft (7620 m) and economical 460 mph (740 km/h) at optimum altitude; certificated ceiling 31,495 ft (9600 m); range 2,485 miles (4000 km) with maximum fuel and 42 passengers, or 1,733 miles (2790 km) with 104 passengers, or 1,336 miles (2150 km) with a 23,148-lb (10500-kg) payload, or 1,218 miles (1960 km) with maximum payload
Weights: empty 72,752 lb (33000 kg); maximum take-off 126,765 lb (57500 kg)
Dimensions: span 114 ft 5.25 in (34.88 m); length 119 ft 4.25 in (36.38 m); height 32 ft 3 in (9.83 m); area 1,614.64 sq ft (150.00 m²)
Payload: up to 120 passengers within the context of a 29,762-lb (13500-kg) maximum payload

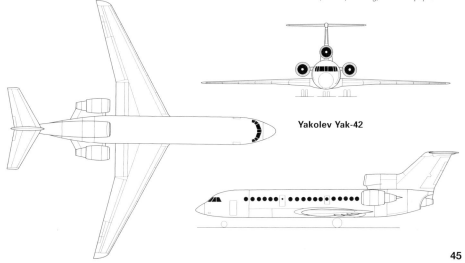

Yakolev Yak-42

ACES COLOMBIA (COLOMBIA)

Main base and hub: Bogotá
Type of operation: International, regional and domestic scheduled and charter passenger and cargo
Personnel: 1,800
Founded in August 1971 and starting operation early in the following year, ACES Colombia began with services to destinations within Colombia but moved into the international market during 1986, initially with charter operations, to which scheduled services were later added. Miami was the first international destination, but others are now included in the 37-destination network operated by ACES Colombia, which is

Fleet (orders):
(4) x Airbus A319-100
4 x Airbus A320-200
6 x ATR 42-300
5 (1) x ATR 42-500
4 x Boeing Advanced
  Model 727-200
9 x De Havilland Canada
  DHC-6 Twin Otter Series 300

currently the country's second largest airline after Avianca, the Colombian national flag carrier.

AER LINGUS (IRELAND)

Main bases and hubs: Dublin, Cork, Shannon and Manchester
Type of operation: International, regional and domestic scheduled and charter passenger and cargo
Personnel: 5,635
The account of the Irish state airline begins on 22 May 1936, when Aer Lingus Teoranta was registered as a private company to operate airline services, and this organization operated its first service on 27 May of the same year with a flight from Dublin to Bristol using a De Havilland D.H.84 Dragon. Aer Rianta, which was created by the Irish government on 5 April 1937 to operate international air routes with the De Havilland D.H.89 Dragon Rapide, also came to constitute a part of the current airline. With the outbreak of World War II (1939–45), all Irish air services were suspended temporarily, although on 28 October 1939 the service between Dublin and Liverpool was reopened for continued operation throughout the war with a pair of D.H.89B aircraft and one Douglas DC-3.

On 9 November 1945, the airline resumed its service from Dublin to Croydon with a DC-3, and this was followed on 17 June of the next year by a service linking Dublin and Paris. On 26 February 1947, Aerlinte Eireann Teoranta was formed as a subsidiary of Aer Rianta to operate transatlantic services, and for this purpose three Lockheed L-749A Constellations were delivered on 17 September 1947, but the service was then postponed indefinitely and the aircraft sold to the British Overseas Airways Corporation.

Aer Lingus later became the third airline in the world to order the radical turboprop-powered Vickers Viscount in November 1951, and on 7 March 1964 the first two Type 707 Viscounts were delivered to Dublin for a service debut on 11 April of the same year. Aer Lingus was the first airline in the world to operate the Fokker F.27 Friendship, its first two aircraft of this type being delivered on 19 November 1958 for a service debut on the routes linking Dublin with Glasgow and Liverpool on 15 December of the same year.

On 28 April 1958, Aerlinte Eireann Teoranta finally started its New York service using a Lockheed L-1049 Super Constellation leased from the American airline Seaboard and

Fleet (orders):
(4) x Airbus A319-100
1 (5) x Airbus A320-200
6 x Airbus A321-200
2 x Airbus A330-200
5 (1) x Airbus A330-300
3 x Boeing Model 737-400
7 x Boeing Model 737-500

Western. Following the success of this service, Aerlinte Eireann Teoranta ordered three examples of the four-turbojet Boeing Model 720-048. The first of these machines was delivered on 25 October 1960 and the airline's first turbojet service was operated on 14 December from Dublin to New York via Shannon. By the end of April 1961, the Boeings had taken over the transatlantic service from the Constellations, and in mid-1964 the Model 720-048 aircraft had been replaced by Boeing Model 707-348C airliners.

On 14 May 1965, Aer Lingus took delivery of its first BAC One-Eleven 208AL twin-jet airliner. This type entered service on the routes to Paris from Dublin and Cork on 6 June of the same year, and the type was then successively introduced on many of the airline's European services. The One-Eleven was then supplemented and finally supplanted by the Boeing Model 737-248 (which is now the mainstay of the airline's fleet) and the first model 737 was delivered to Dublin on 28 March 1969. In January 1967, the airline ordered two examples of the Boeing Model 747-148 'jumbo jet', taking delivery of the first of these long-range, high-capacity transports on 15 December 1970. The Model 747s were at first operated on the airline's own transatlantic routes, but loads were generally insufficient for the viable operation of the two aircraft, which were therefore leased to other airlines for most of their lives. Aer Lingus Teoranta and Aer Rianta were then integrated to fly an extensive international and regional network.

Aer Lingus is currently seeking to reduce capacity and operating costs.

RIGHT: *With its mixed fleet of twin-jet aircraft, Aer Lingus operates to most parts of Europe.*

AÉRO CONTINENTE (PERU)

Main base and hub: Lima
Type of operation: International, regional and domestic scheduled and charter passenger
Personnel: not available

Founded and established in operation during the first half of 1992 to take advantage of tax breaks accorded to airlines created for services outside the Peruvian capital region, Aéro Continente at first concentrated on charter services to support the oil industry. Aéro Continente expanded into scheduled services during July 1993, initially with three Boeing aircraft (one Model 727-100 and two Model 737-200 machines). Aéro Continente is currently Peru's more important airline, operating a network of domestic services as well as one international route to Miami. Late in 1999, the airline collaborated with an investment group to create Aéro

Fleet (orders):
1 x Antonov An-32
3 x Boeing Model 727-100
1 x Boeing Model 737-100
4 x Boeing Model 737-200
1 x Boeing Advanced Model 737-200
1 x Boeing Model 767-200ER
2 x BAE Systems Jetstream 31
1 x Fairchild F-27J

2 x Fairchild F.28 Fellowship Mk 1000

Continente Chile to create a domestic schedule linking Santiago with Peru's other major cities with a fleet comprising eight Model 737-200 aircraft.

Aéro Continente is Peru's major airline.

AEROFLOT – RUSSIAN INTERNATIONAL AIRLINES (ARIA) (RUSSIA)

Main base and hub: Moscow
Type of operation: International, regional and domestic scheduled and charter passenger and cargo
Personnel: not available

The origins of Aeroflot date back to 11 November 1921, when the airline Deruluft was formed by the USSR and Germany to operate services between the two countries. In March 1923, Dobrolet (Soviet Volunteer Air Fleet Company) began operations from Moscow to Odessa and Georgia, with other services to the central area of Asian Russia. Meanwhile, other airlines were formed during April 1925 in the Ukraine as Ukvozduchput and in Georgia as Zakavia. These four airlines were the predecessors of Aeroflot, which finally came into being in 1932.

Fleet (orders):
11 x Airbus A310-300
10 x Boeing 737-400
4 x Boeing Model 767-300ER
2 x Boeing 777-200ER
11 x Ilyushin Il-62M
2 x Ilyushin Il-76M
10 x Ilyushin Il-76T
14 x Ilyushin Il-86
6 (6) x Ilyushin Il-96-300
(17) x Ilyushin Il-96M
1 (2) x Ilyushin Il-96T
1 x McDonnell Douglas DC-10-30F

11 x Tupolev Tu-134A
1 x Tupolev Tu-154B
21 x Tupolev Tu-154M
1 x Tupolev Tu-204-100

Up to the time of the collapse of the USSR in 1989, Aeroflot was the world's largest airline, with a huge network of scheduled domestic and international passenger and cargo services as well as the ability to carry out charter flights on a worldwide basis. In addition to its airline activities, Aeroflot was also responsible for all the USSR's civil airports, navigation services, flying clubs and training as well as every aspect of aerial agriculture, forest fire patrol, aerial survey and air ambulance work.

By the standards of Western airlines, Aeroflot's re-equipment programme after World War II was very slow: the Ilyushin Il-12 did not enter service until 1948 and the Ilyushin Il-14 not until six years later, and both of these aircraft were decidedly inferior to the Western airliners of the period. However, on 15 September 1956, Aeroflot put into service its first turbojet-powered transport, the Tupolev Tu-104, on the Moscow–Irkutsk route, and at the time this was the only jet airliner service in the world.

In the period between 1959 and 1963, Aeroflot operated no fewer than five completely new types of aircraft, namely the Antonov An-10 and An-24, the Ilyushin Il-18, and the Tupolev Tu-114 and Tu-124. From the early 1960s the airline introduced two major types in the forms of the Tupolev Tu-154 and Ilyushin

Il-62, and these two types operated some 73 per cent of Aeroflot's passenger flights until well into the 1980s. The airline took the credit for being the first airline in the world to operate passenger services with a supersonic transport, in the form of the Tupolev Tu-144, on 26 December 1975, when a service was inaugurated between Moscow and Alma Alta.

Up to the time of the USSR's collapse, Aeroflot operated both an extensive domestic network (serving some 3,600 destinations) and an international network covering 86 countries in Africa, the Americas, Asia and Europe. Most of these flights originated from Moscow, and on the shorter domestic routes the aircraft used were mainly the Yakovlev Yak-40, Antonov An-24 and Tupolev Tu-134, while on the shortest of the routes the ageing Antonov An-2 biplane was still used. At that time, the airline's equipment plans included substantial further purchases of types such as the Tupolev Tu-134 and Tu-154, Ilyushin Il-62, Il-76 and Il-86, Yakovlev Yak-42 and Antonov An-26, An-28 and An-32.

In its current form, Aeroflot – Russian International Airlines

RIGHT: *Aeroflot still flies mainly aircraft of Soviet origin, but is adopting Western types.*

(ARIA) is the international division of Aeroflot and as such is the successor to the original Aeroflot, all of whose domestic operations have been transferred to the host of airlines that have sprung up in the Commonwealth of Independent States (CIS) since the demise of the USSR. As such, ARIA remains the only officially designated international airline in Russia and flies scheduled passenger and cargo flights to 135 cities in more than 100 countries, and has also introduced regular services to nine capitals within the CIS and six cities within the Russian Federation. Nothing is more indicative of the airline's new nature and ambitions than the nature of its recent re-equipment, with the Ilyushin Il-96-300 and Boeing Model 767-300 introduced in 1994, and plans well advanced for the lease of further Western airliners pending full delivery of the Tupolev Tu-204.

AEROLÍNEAS ARGENTINAS (ARGENTINA)

Main bases and hubs: Buenos Aires
Type of operation: Scheduled passenger and cargo services
Personnel: 5,830

On 14 May 1949, the Argentine ministry of transport assumed control over the operations of all the country's airlines, with the exception of the air force-operated LADE, to create Aerolíneas Argentinas. The four airlines that were incorporated were Aeroposta Argentina, formed in 1928, Aviación del Literal Fluvial Argentino, formed in 1938, Flota Aérea Mercante Argentina, formed on 8 February 1946, and Zonas Oeste y Norte de Aerolíneas Argentinas, formed on 23 February 1946.

The amalgamation of these airlines into a single entity was formalized on 1 January 1950 as Aerolíneas Argentinas began operations under its own name. At this time, the airline operated a highly mixed fleet of aircraft inherited from its predecessors, namely Short Sandringham flying boats from ALFA, Douglas DC-4 and DC-6 landplanes from FAMA, plus various Avro York, Vickers Viking, Avro Lancastrian and Convair CV-240 landplanes from ZONDA, and the ubiquitous Douglas DC-3 from all of them.

In March 1950, Aerolíneas Argentinas began regular services with Douglas DC-6s to New York, while the CV-240s and DC-3s were used mainly for domestic services, the last of the DC-3s being retired only in 1962. A measure of more modern equipment began to reach the airline in March 1959, when Aerolíneas Argentinas received its first turbojet-powered airliner in the former of the De Havilland Comet 4, and began its first international service with this type on 19 May of the same year with a service linking Buenos Aires and New York.

The airline's domestic and regional networks were upgraded into the jet age when the first of four Sud-Aviation Caravelle VINs was delivered on 15 January 1962, and the operator's CV-240s were replaced by the turboprop-powered Hawker Siddeley HS

Fleet (orders):
4 x Airbus A340-200
(6) x Airbus A340-600
3 x Boeing Model 737-200
25 x Boeing Advanced Model 737-200
1 x Boeing Model 737-200C
7 x Boeing Model 747-200B
1 x Boeing MD-83
5 x Boeing MD-88

748 from 18 January 1962. The British-built airliner began between Buenos Aires and Bahia Blanca in April 1962.

On 23 November 1966, the airline took delivery of its first Boeing Model 707-387, and this and later deliveries soon replaced the Comet, of which the last two were sold in November 1971. For use on its domestic and regional services Aerolíneas Argentinas ordered the Boeing Model 737-287, and before the delivery of the first of these machines on 27 February 1970, the airline leased a Boeing Model 737-204 from Britannia Airways between 24 January and 28 April 1970. The American twin-jet transports were complemented by a leased Hughes Airwest Boeing Model 727-2M7 delivered on 3 December 1977. On 1 December 1978, Aerolíneas Argentina's first Boeing Model 727-287 three-jet transport was delivered, and the airline was able to upgrade its domestic and regional services with the introduction of the Fokker F.28 Fellowship, of which the first was received on 13 January 1975.

On its long-haul routes to North America, Europe, South Africa and the Far East, Aerolíneas Argentinas operates six examples of the Boeing Model 747-287B, the first of these having been delivered in on 16 December 1976, and at one time also flew one Boeing Model 747SP-087.

AEROLITORAL (MEXICO)

Main bases and hubs: Mexico City and Monterrey
Type of operation: International, regional and domestic scheduled passenger
Personnel: not available

Founded and starting operations in the middle of 1989, Aerolitoral concentrates on feeder-line services to Mexico's main airports, and currently flies more than 260 scheduled flights per day between various Mexican and American cities, the latter including El Paso, Houston, Phoenix, San Antonio and

Fleet (orders):
12 x Fairchild Dornier Metro 23
6 x Fairchild Dornier Metro III
13 x Saab 340B

Tucson, all in the south of the country.

AERO LLOYD (GERMANY)

Main base and hub: Frankfurt-am-Main and Munich
Type of operation: International charter passenger services
Personnel: not available

Aero Lloyd Flugreisen is a privately owned operator established on 20 December 1980 to begin operations in March 1981 with three Aérospatiale SE.210 Caravelle 10R aircraft. The operator initially flew charter flights to popular destinations in the Mediterranean, and a tour operator, Air Charter Market, also used Aero Lloyd's aircraft and became a shareholder. From May to July 1982 a DC-9-32 was in service. The operator started to expand from 1986, when the first MD-80 was introduced, and over the years, up to 22 MD-82/83/87 aircraft were flown for scheduled as well as charter services. Aero Lloyd flew its first scheduled services in October 1988; the schedule included services within Germany as well as routes to London, Paris and

Fleet (orders):
7 (1) x Airbus A320-200
7 (5) x Airbus A321-200
4 x Boeing (McDonnell Douglas) MD-83

Zurich. Aero Lloyd pulled out of the scheduled market in 1992 after Lufthansa had taken a holding in the airline. Aero Lloyd disposed of its last DC-9-32 at the end of 1993, and signalled its entry into the larger charter market with its first order for Airbus A320 aircraft, of which the first entered service in January 1996. The switch to an all-Airbus fleet continues, the first A321 being delivered in 1998, and the change should be completed in 2001.

AEROMÉXICO (AEROVÍAS DE MÉXICO) (MEXICO)

Main bases and hubs: Mexico City, Cabo San Lucas, Guadalajara, Monterrey and Tijuana
Type of operation: International, regional and domestic scheduled passenger and cargo services
Personnel: 6,845

One of the two Mexican national airlines, the other being Mexicana Airlines (Compañía Mexicana de Aviación de CV), the airline now known as Aeroméxico was created on 1 September 1934 as Aeronaves de México, and domestic services were launched with the inauguration of a link between Mexico City and Acapulco. Between 1952 and 1962, Aeronaves took over several other Mexican operators, including Líneas Aéreas Mexicanas SA (LAMSA), Aerovías Reforma SA, Aerolíneas Mexicanas SA, and Guest Aerovías México, of which the last had been operating transatlantic services.

Aeronaves was nationalized in July 1959, and a Pan American holding in the airline was acquired by the Mexican government at that time. The airline's first major international route, from Mexico City to New York, was launched in

Fleet (orders):
9 (1) x Boeing Model 757-200
4 x Boeing Model 767-200ER
1 x Boeing 767-300ER
14 x Boeing MD-82
10 x Boeing MD-83
7 x Boeing MD-87
10 x Boeing MD-88
16 x McDonnell Douglas DC-9-30

December 1957 with Bristol Britannia 302 turboprop-powered airliners which were later replaced by Douglas DC-8 turbojet-powered machines. In 1970, as part of a government plan to rationalize Mexico's highly fragmented air transport industry, domestic operators within Mexico were integrated into a system of eight smaller operators under the overall control of Aeronaves de México, which changed its name to Aeroméxico in February 1972.

BELOW: *The core of Aeromexico's short-haul operations is aircraft of the MD-80 series.*

AEROPOSTAL – ALAS DE VENEZUELA (VENEZUELA)

Main base and hub: Caracas
Type of operation: International, regional and domestic scheduled and charter passenger and cargo
Personnel: not available

One of the oldest of the smaller airlines still operating in South America, Aeropostal was created in 1933 as Línea Aérea Venezolana to operate the services that had been operated since 1930 by a French company, the Compagnie Générale Aéropostale, until they were nationalized by the Venezuelan government. The company ceased operations in 1994, but came back into existence during January 1997 after its defunct assets

Fleet (orders):
1 x Boeing Advanced Model 727-100
7 x McDonnell Douglas DC-9-30
9 x McDonnell Douglas DC-9-50

were sold to a private company, Alas de Venezuela. Aeropostal concentrates on domestic services, but operates a small number of international flights to 12 destinations in Central America, the northern part of South America, the Caribbean and the USA.

AIR 2000 (UNITED KINGDOM)

Main bases and hubs: Manchester and London (Gatwick)
Type of operation: International, regional and domestic scheduled and charter passenger and cargo
Personnel: 2,345

Established by First Choice Holidays in 1986 for the start of operations in April 1987 with a fleet that initially comprised two Boeing Model 757 aircraft operating from Manchester, Air 2000 is now the second largest air charter operator in the UK. The company later absorbed Unijet and Leisure International Airways, and now operates charter services from 15 British

Fleet (orders):
4 (5) x Airbus A320-200
5 (1) x Airbus A321-200
13 (8) x Boeing Model 757-200
4 x Boeing Model 767-300ER

and Irish airports to leisure resorts, as well as scheduled services to destinations in Cyprus and Spain.

AIR AFRIQUE (11 WEST AFRICAN COUNTRIES)

Main bases and hubs: not available
Type of operation: International, regional and domestic scheduled and charter passenger and cargo
Personnel: 4,440

Air Afrique was established in March 1961 as a result of the Treaty of Yaoundé, and is the 'national' carrier of the West African states of Benin, Burkina Faso, the Central African Republic, Chad, Congo, Ivory Coast, Mali, Mauritania, Niger, Senegal and Togo. Air Afrique started operations in August 1961, and now serves destinations in a large number of African states as well as southern Europe; the company also flies to New York. The airline has suffered severe financial problems, and in July 1998 was

Fleet (orders):
4 x Airbus A300-600R
2 x Airbus A300B4-200
1 x Airbus A310-300
2 x Airbus A330-200
1 x Antonov An-12 'Cub'
2 x Boeing Model 737-300

forced to suspend some of its longer-haul services after creditors demanded the return of four leased Airbus A310-300 aircraft.

BELOW: *Strong French connections have resulted in Air Afrique buying numerous Airbus machines.*

AIR ALGÉRIE (ALGERIA)

Main base and hub: Algiers
Type of operation: International, regional and domestic scheduled and charter passenger and cargo
Personnel: not available
Air Algérie came into practical existence in May 1953, when the country was still part of French North Africa, as a result of the merger of the Compagnie Générale de Transports Aériens and the Compagnie Air Transport. After Algeria's independence, the government took a majority shareholding in 1963 and full control in 1972. Air Algérie now operates a domestic, regional and international network linking Algerian airports with destinations in Africa, Europe and the Middle East, and is the national flag carrier of Algeria.

Fleet (orders):
2 x Airbus A310-200
2 x Boeing Model 727-200
8 x Boeing Advanced Model 727-200
13 x Boeing Advanced Model 737-200
2 x Boeing Model 737-200C
3 x Boeing Model 737-300
(5) x Boeing Model 737-600
(3) x Boeing Model 737-800
3 x Boeing Model 767-300
1 x Boeing Model 767-300ER
2 x De Havilland Canada DHC-6 Twin Otter Series 300

7 x Fokker F.27 Friendship Mk 400
2 x Lockheed Martin L-100-30 Hercules
4 x Raytheon Beech Model 1900D Airliner

AIR ATLANTA ICELANDIC (ICELAND)

Main base and hub: Keflavik
Type of operation: International scheduled and charter passenger and freight services
Personnel: 1,180
Air Atlanta Icelandic came into being in January 1986, founded by Captain Arngrimur Johannsson and his wife Thora Gudmundsdottir as a specialized wet-lease operator supplying other airlines with aircraft complete with crews and other services. The new company's first contract was for the use of a Boeing Model 707 by Caribbean Airways on the service linking Barbados and London. In August 1988, the company brought a second Model 707 into service, this time for Air Afrique on a service that flew Muslim pilgrims between West Africa and Saudi Arabia for the Hajj. In May 1991, the Icelandic company bought its first wide-body aeroplane, a Lockheed L-1011 TriStar, and two years later there came the three Boeing Model 747 aircraft to feature on the Icelandic register. These Model 747 aircraft were wet-leased for several years to Saudia, now Saudi Arabian Airlines. Air Atlanta also started operating its own charter series from

Fleet (orders):
1 x Boeing Model 747-100
3 x Boeing Model 747-200B
1 x Boeing Model 747-300
1 x Lockheed Martin L-1011-100 TriStar

1993, and the fleet continued to expand: Boeing Model 737-200F machines were used for freighting, and a Model 737-300 was used in June 1995 to inaugurate a scheduled service between Iceland and Berlin. The British and African markets proved to be the most successful for Air Atlanta Icelandic, and the operator's aircraft flew in the markings of companies including Air-India, Tunis Air, Caledonian and Monarch. During 1999, several of the TriStar and all of the Model 737 aircraft were replaced by additional Model 747-100, -200 and -300 aircraft.

BELOW: *Air Atlanta flies examples of three earlier variants of the Model 747 transport.*

AIR CANADA (CANADA)

Main bases and hubs: Calgary, Halifax, Montreal, Toronto and Vancouver
Type of operation: International, regional and domestic scheduled and charter passenger services
Personnel: not available

Air Canada began life as Trans-Canada Air Lines Ltd (TCA), the flag carrier for the Dominion of Canada. At this time the operator's main shareholder was Canadian National Railways, an organization wholly owned by the government of Canada. The airline flew its first scheduled service on 1 September 1937 using a Lockheed Model 10-A Electra on the route between Vancouver and Seattle. In the following March, the operator added its first mail service, in this instance between Vancouver and Winnipeg. One year later, on 1 April 1939, Trans-Canada flew its first coast-to-coast service between Seattle and Montreal with intermediate halts at Vancouver, Toronto and Ottawa.

TCA began a transatlantic service on 22 July 1943 between Montreal and London with modified Avro Lancaster bombers, an altogether superior capability being offered by the Canadair DC-4M which flew its first service between Montreal and London on 15 April 1947. The availability of this new type helped the airline to enlarge its route network, and this soon extended south to points such as Florida, in the USA, and destinations in Mexico.

The airline's next milestone was the introduction of the Lockheed L-1049G Super Constellation, which operated its first service across the Atlantic on 14 May 1954. On 1 April 1955, TCA became the first airline in the Americas to operate the turboprop-powered Vickers Viscount 724, which entered service on the route linking Montreal and Winnipeg. The first pure-jet airliner used by TCA was the Douglas DC-8-43, of which the first was delivered on 7 February 1960 for a service debut on 1 April of the same year on the route linking Montreal

Fleet (orders):
35 (13) x Airbus A319-100
34 (3) x Airbus A320-200
(12) x Airbus A321-200
4 (4) x Airbus A330-300
12 (1) x Airbus A340-300
(5) x Airbus A340-500
3 x Boeing Model 747-400 Combi
9 x Boeing Model 767-200
14 x Boeing Model 767-200ER   25 x Bombardier CRJ-100ER
7 (4) x Boeing Model 767-300ER   17 x McDonnell Douglas DC-9-30

and Vancouver. Exactly two months later the route between Montreal and London being added.

In 1964, Trans-Canada Air Lines adopted its current title of Air Canada, together with a new livery, modified in 1977 to the current scheme. On 11 February 1971, Air Canada took delivery of its first wide-body airliner in the form of a Boeing Model 747-133 and, together with the Lockheed L-1011 TriStars that were delivered from 14 January 1973 and the Douglas DC-8-63, this 'jumbo jet' type operated the airline's long-haul routes into the mid-1980s, when the first of Air Canada's Airbus wide-body airliners was delivered.

Under the terms of the Air Canada Act of 1977, the airline became a direct wholly owned subsidiary of the government of Canada, but has been completely privatized since July 1989. Through its domestic service Connector Partners, another 54 communities and destinations in Canada and the USA are linked to the Air Canada network. Together with its regional airlines, Air Canada now offers services to over 120 destinations, including over 90 cities in North America, eight cities in Europe, 11 points in the Caribbean, and a number of destinations in Asia. In 2000, Air Canada secured a majority shareholding in Canadian Airlines, which is being integrated into Air Canada.

AIR CHINA (CHINA)

Main base and hub: Beijing Capital Airport
Type of operation: International, regional and domestic scheduled passenger and cargo services
Personnel: 12,900

The airline now known as Air China was created in 1988 by renaming of the Beijing-based international division of the Civil Aviation Administration of China (CAAC), which was the Chinese equivalent of the Soviet Aeroflot organization and therefore responsible for all civil aviation matters in China. In 1988, the various operating divisions of the CAAC were formed into separate airlines each with its own name. Air China is the largest of the airlines currently operating in China, and has two subsidiary operations, located in Inner Mongolia and Tianjin.

The first direct link with CAAC can be located in 1939, when in the north-west of China the governments of China and the USSR established the Sino-Soviet Aviation Corporation to provide services between China and the USSR. The company

Fleet (orders):
(8) x Airbus A318
4 x BAE Systems 146-100
19 x Boeing Model 737-300
7 (3) x Boeing Model 737-800
4 x Boeing Model 747-200F
6 x Boeing Model 747-400
8 x Boeing Model 747-400 Combi
6 x Boeing Model 767-200ER   5 x Boeing Model 777-200
3 x Boeing Model 767-300   2 (3) x Boeing Model 777-200ER
1 x Boeing Model 767-300ER

became known as Hamiata as its main terminals were Hami in China and Alma Ata in the USSR. The immediate predecessor of the current airline was the People's Aviation Corporation of China (SKOGA), which was established in 1952 by the USSR and China to take over and expand the transport services that had been undertaken by the CATC and CNAC, themselves created in March 1943 and July 1930, whose operations and aircraft had been transferred to Formosa in 1949 by the Kuomintang nationalist party as it was being defeated by the communists in the final stages of the Chinese Civil War. On its creation, SKOGA took over Hamiata, and Aeroflot helped to place the new Chinese organization on a firmer technical footing by providing it with aircraft in the form of several examples of the Lisunov Li-2, which was the Soviet-made version of the Douglas DC-3.

SKOGA's first service connected Beijing (then Peking) with Hankow, Kunming and Canton, as well as Chia, Irkutsk and Alma Ata so that the growing Chinese air network was linked with that of the USSR. In 1954, the Chinese government assumed full control of the airline and renamed it the Civil Aviation Administration of China (CAAC) or Minhaiduy. For the first four years of its operations the CAAC relied on the Li-2, some of which may still be in service in remoter areas, but gradually more modern equipment was introduced, namely the Ilyushin Il-14 with a powerplant of two piston engines and, in 1960, the Ilyushin Il-18, with its powerplant of four turboprops.

In December 1961, the CAAC broke with its practice of operating only Soviet-built aircraft when it placed an order for the six examples of the Vickers Viscount 843 four-turboprop airliner. The first was delivered on 6 July 1963 for a service debut in March 1964 on the route linking Peking and Shanghai.

In 1962, the airline revised its title to the Department of International Affairs of the General Administration of Civil Aviation of China, but the airline retained its abbreviated title of CAAC. To replace some of its ageing Soviet types, the CAAC bought four Hawker Siddeley HS 121 Trident 1E turbofan-powered airliners from Pakistan International Airlines in 1970, to be followed from 19 November 1971 by the first of four new Trident 2E airliners. The next type introduced on CAAC services was the Ilyushin Il-62, the first two aircraft of an order for five being delivered in late 1972 and operating the airline's first long-haul services from early in 1973. On 23 August 1973, the CAAC received its first Boeing Model 707-3JB, and with this type the airline started a service from Peking to Tokyo in August 1974. The CAAC then introduced the Boeing Model 747, initially in the form of the Model 747SP-J6, of which the first of three was delivered on 29 February 1980. Since that time, the airline has been equipped mainly with Boeing airliners, although in the early 1990s Air China ordered three Airbus transports.

Currently Air China operates passenger and cargo services to many countries in the Asian, African, European and American continents as well as a modest network of domestic and regional services derived largely from the total of 171 domestic services that CAAC operated to link 29 provinces of the country.

BELOW: *Like many other long-haul operators, Air China flies several Model 747 variants.*

AIR EUROPA (SPAIN)

Main base and hub: Balearic and Canary Islands
Type of operation: International, regional and domestic scheduled and charter passenger
Personnel: 1,840

Created in February 1984 but starting services only in November 1993, Air Europa was originally a member of the Airlines of Europe Group. The operator now specializes in package tour services linking nations in northern and western Europe with holiday locations in the Balearic and Canary Islands, although it also operates scheduled Spanish and

Fleet (orders):
3 x Boeing Model 737-300
5 x Boeing Model 737-500
10 x Boeing Model 737-800
1 x Boeing Model 757-200
2 x Boeing Model 767-200ER
1 (2) x Boeing Model 767-300ER

transatlantic services to a few destinations in the Caribbean and North America.

AIR FRANCE (FRANCE)

Main base and hub: Paris Charles de Gaulle
Type of operation: International, regional and domestic scheduled passenger and cargo services
Personnel: 59,000

France was an early entrant into the field of commercial airline operations as several pioneering companies were formed in 1919 after the end of World War I. The most significant of these was the Lignes Aériennes Farman (later the Compagnie Générale de Transports Aériens, or CGTA), which flew the nation's first international service on 8 February 1919 from Paris to London. Between 1919 and 1926, the CGTA expanded its route network to Belgium, Germany, the Netherlands and Scandinavia. During the same period, the Compagnie Franco-Roumaine de Navigation Aérienne led the way to the south-east with a network of routes to the Balkans, Czechoslovakia and Poland, while the Lignes Aériennes Latecoere (LAT) explored the route into western Africa as far south as Dakar, and within South America pending the development of a viable commercial air service across the South Atlantic: this last was finally achieved in 1930. Other air routes pioneered during this period of great French civil air transport expansion stretched across the Sahara, central Africa and as far east as Tananarive in Madagascar.

By 1923, the powerhouse of French airline operations was Air-Union, which came into existence by the amalgamation of the Compagnie des Messageries Aériennes and the Compagnie des Grands Express Aériens. Other major operators of the time were the Compagnie Internationale de Navigation Aérienne (CIDNA) which went east to Czechoslovakia and Turkey, and Air-Orient, which was an Air-Union subsidiary that extended farther into the Middle East and Far East to reach Hong Kong and Saigon during 1938 after Air-Union had become Air France.

The key date for French civil aviation is 1933, when the CGTA, CIDNA, Air-Orient and Air-Union merged to form the Société Centrale pour l'Exploration de Lignes Aeriennes. The consolidated company operated as Air France and bought

Fleet (orders):
6 x Airbus A310-200
4 x Airbus A310-300
(15) x Airbus A318
26 (12) x Airbus A319-100
13 x Airbus A320-100
45 (1) x Airbus A320-200
5 (3) x Airbus A321-100
9 x Airbus A321-200
(11) x Airbus A330-200
(8) x Airbus A330-300
21 (1) x Airbus A340-300
(10) x Airbus A380-800
6 x Boeing Advanced Model 737-200
9 x Boeing Model 737-200
25 x Boeing Model 737-500
2 x Boeing Model 747-200B
8 x Boeing Model 747-200B Combi
11 x Boeing Model 747-200F

2 x Boeing Model 747-300 Combi
7 x Boeing Model 747-400
6 x Boeing Model 747-400 Combi
5 x Boeing Model 767-300ER
14 (10) x Boeing Model 777-200ER
(10) x Boeing Model 777-300ER
5 x EADS/BAE Systems Concorde (4 in operation)

the assets of the Compagnie General Aéropostale (successor to LAT) on 30 August. At this time, Air France possessed 259 aircraft and had inherited a very substantial route network, and immediately laid and implemented plans for the disposal of all its single-engined types, elimination of duplicated routes, and increased service frequencies. Domestic services within France were allocated to an affiliate, Air Bleu, and this was completely revised in 1937 to improve France's internal mail service.

Just before the outbreak of World War II, exploratory flights were made for the proposed transatlantic service to North America via the Azores and Bermuda, and at the time of France's defeat in June 1940, Air France's surviving aircraft

BELOW: *Air France flies Model 747 variants for freight as well as passenger services.*

were evacuated from France to North Africa, whence they joined the Allied cause.

Limited services were resumed in 1945, and in 1946 Air France's first transatlantic service was inaugurated by Douglas DC-4 airliners of Air France Transatlantique. Air France was nationalized on 1 January 1946 as the Société Nationale Air France, and on 16 June 1948 the modern Air France was formed by the merger of the parent company with Air Bleu and Air France Transatlantique. A period of consolidation and expansion followed, including the introduction of turbine power in 1953. Since that time, Air France's network has expanded into one of the largest in the world, with an intricate series of European routes complemented by long-haul services to most other parts of the world excluding Australasia.

AIR-INDIA (INDIA)

Main bases and hubs: Bombay and Delhi
Type of operation: International, regional and domestic scheduled passenger and cargo
Personnel: not available
Established in October 1932, Tata Airlines became a publicly quoted company in 1946 and was renamed Air-India, then Air-India International in 1948. By this time, India had become independent of the UK, and Air-India was the new nation's national airline, soon operating international flights to destinations as far distant as London. The airline was nationalized in 1953, soon after this transferring the operation of all domestic services to Indian Airlines so that it could concentrate on its international route network. In 1962, the airline became Air-India once again. It later added a domestic route network again, and in the late 1990s was revealed by the Indian government as a candidate for partial privatization. The airline's domestic route network currently covers much of India, while its regional and international services extend to many parts of the world.

Fleet (orders):
3 x Airbus A300B4-200
9 x Airbus A310-300
4 x Boeing Model 747-200B
2 x Boeing Model 747-300
   Combi
6 x Boeing Model 747-400

AIR JAMAICA (JAMAICA)

Main bases and hubs: Kingston and Montego Bay
Type of operation: International, regional and domestic scheduled passenger and cargo
Personnel: not available
The national airline of Jamaica, Air Jamaica was created in October 1968 and began operations in April of the following year. The airline's first overseas destinations were Miami and New York in the USA, with destinations in Europe added from 1974. The airline currently operates services to more than 15 destinations in the Caribbean, Europe and North America, and its subsidiary for intra-island and Caribbean regional services is Air Jamaica Express, formerly known as Trans-Jamaican Airlines. This links five Jamaican and several Caribbean destinations using two Fairchild Dornier Do 228-200 and two Shorts 360-300 aircraft.

Fleet (orders):
4 x Airbus A310-300
7 (1) x Airbus A320-200
2 (1) x Airbus A321-200
1 x Airbus A340-300
2 x Boeing MD-83

ABOVE: *Airbus machines are the mainstay of Air Jamaica's medium- and long-haul flights.*

AIR KAZAKHSTAN (KAZAKHSTAN)

Main base and hub: Almaty
Type of operation: International, regional and domestic scheduled and charter passenger and cargo
Personnel: not available
The national airline of Kazakhstan, Air Kazakhstan was created in October 1996 out of Aeroflot's Kazakhstan Division after the dissolution of the USSR. The original name was Kazakhstan Airways, but this was declared bankrupt in 1996 and re-emerged under its present designation. The airline currently flies to a number of domestic and regional destinations inside and outside the Commonwealth of Independent States, and also to cities in the Asia, Europe and the Middle East. Air Kazakhstan is based in Almaty, and is 50 per cent state-owned, with the other 50 per cent being in the hands of a commercial bank.

Fleet (orders):
2 x Airbus A310-300
1 x Antonov An-24
10 x Antonov An-24B
12 x Antonov An-24RV
1 x Antonov An-72
3 x Boeing Advanced Model 737-200
1 x Ilyushin Il-76T
2 x Ilyushin Il-86
5 x Tupolev Tu-134A
10 x Tupolev Tu-154B
4 x Tupolev Tu-154M
2 x Yakovlev Yak-40
1 x Yakovlev Yak-42D

AIR LIBERTÉ (FRANCE)

Main base and hub: Paris (Orly)
Type of operation: International, regional and domestic scheduled and charter passenger and cargo
Personnel: 2,800
Currently flying a route network linking some 35 destinations, Air Liberté is an independent operator that was created in July 1987 and began services in the following year. The company was rescued from bankruptcy in September 1996 by British Airways' purchase of a majority holding, and later merged its operations with those of another British Airways subsidiary, TAT European Airlines. In May 2000, the airline was bought by Taitbout Antibes, which plans to merge AOM French Airlines into it.

Fleet (orders):
2 x ATR 42-300
2 x ATR 72-200
4 x Boeing MD-82
10 x Boeing MD-83
3 x Fokker F.28 Fellowship Mk 2000
3 x McDonnell Douglas DC-10-30

AIR LITTORAL (FRANCE)

Main bases and hubs: Montpellier and Nice
Type of operation: International, regional and domestic scheduled and charter passenger and cargo
Personnel: not available
Operating an important network of domestic services in central and southern France since its creation in 1972, Air Littoral has also flown services to a number of neighbouring countries since 1981. It is currently planned that Air Littoral will be merged with Air Liberté and AOM French Airlines to create a major grouping second only to Air France in the French air transport business.

Fleet (orders):
10 x ATR 42-500
17 x Bombardier CRJ-100ER
5 x Fokker 70
1 x Fokker 100

BELOW: *The CRJ-100 provides Air Littoral with an excellent regional transport capability.*

AIR MALTA

Main base and hub: Luqa International Airport
Type of operation: International, regional and domestic
scheduled and charter passenger and cargo services
Personnel: 1,880
Created on 30 March 1973 and starting operations in April of
the following year, Air Malta is the national airline of Malta. Air
Malta has flown only jet-powered aircraft, its initial equipment
being Hawker Siddeley Trident machines leased from British
Airways. The airline's route network was gradually expanded
with charter as well as scheduled services to European
destinations such as Amsterdam, London, Munich, Paris and
Zurich as well as North African destinations including Cairo and
Tripoli. The airline's next equipment was the Boeing Model
720, supplemented from 1978 by the Boeing Model 737-200
which then replaced the Model 720. In the spring of 1990, Air
Malta received its first two Airbus A320 aircraft, and from

Fleet (orders):
2 x Airbus A320-200
2 x Boeing Advanced Model
   737-200
6 x Boeing Model 737-300

September 1994 added the BAe RJ-70, but these latter aircraft
were sold to Azzurra Air, an Italian company in which Air Malta
has a 48 per cent stake, in 1998. Air Malta also has
shareholdings in Mediterranean Aviation (Med Avia), which
operates CASA C-212 Aviocar aircraft, and in Malta Air Charter,
which links Malta with the small island of Gozo, using Mil
Mi-8 helicopters. Model 737-300 aircraft have been added to
the operator's fleet steadily since 1993.

AIR MAURITIUS (MAURITIUS)

Main base and hub: Port Louis
Type of operation: International, regional and domestic
scheduled and charter passenger and cargo
Personnel: 2,000
Established in June 1967 and starting operations two months
later as an air handling company with flight operations starting
only in 1972, Air Mauritius is the national airline of the island
republic of Mauritius. International operations began in 1977,
and Air Mauritius currently flies a network of services linking
the island with 29 destinations in Africa, Asia, Europe and the

Fleet (orders):
(2) x Airbus A319-100
5 x Airbus A340-300
1 x ATR 42-300
2 x ATR 42-500
2 x Boeing Model 767-200ER

Middle East. Air Mauritius is based at Port Louis, the capital of
this Indian Ocean republic.

AIR NEW ZEALAND (NEW ZEALAND)

Main bases and hubs: Auckland, Los Angeles, Honolulu,
Brisbane and Sydney
Type of operation: International, regional and domestic
scheduled passenger and cargo services
Personnel: 9,175
Formed in April 1940, Tasman Empire Airways Ltd (TEAL) was
originally owned by the governments of New Zealand (50 per
cent), Australia (30 per cent) and UK (20 per cent). The airline
operated its first service with a Short S.30 flying boat on 10 April
of the same year, this inaugural flight linking Waite Harbour,
Auckland, and Rose Bay, Sydney, across the Tasman Sea. By the
end of World War II, the airline was flying the service to Sydney
four times a week with two S.30 'boats' that were replaced on 29
October 1947 by Short Sandringham flying boats. As a result of
engine problems, the Sandringham 'boats' were non-operational
from 23 February to 17 June 1948. In this gap, the service was
operated by Douglas DC-4 four-engined airliners leased from
Australian National Airways and Trans Australian Airways.
   To replace the problem-ridden Sandringhams, TEAL bought
four examples of the Short Solent 4 flying boat late in 1949, and

Fleet (orders):
2 x Boeing Advanced Model
   737-200
1 x Boeing Model 737-200QC
13 x Boeing Model 737-300
8 x Boeing Model 747-400
4 x Boeing Model 767-200ER
10 x Boeing Model 767-300ER

the first of these was delivered on 29 September for a service
debut on 14 November of the same year. Further expansion of the
airline's capabilities occurred on 2 October 1950 with the
operation of the first service from Wellington to Sydney, followed
in June 1951 by the start of services from Christchurch to
Melbourne and on 27 December by the 'Coral Route' from
Auckland to Papeete in Tahiti via Suva and Aitutaki.
   In May 1954, the UK government relinquished its interest in
TEAL to the Australian government, and in the same year the
airline's first landplane, a Douglas DC-6, operated its first service
between Auckland and Fiji on 14 May. Three more DC-6 aircraft
were handed over to TEAL in May 1954 by the New Zealand

government, which had assumed ownership of the aircraft from British Commonwealth Pacific Air Lines after its sale to QANTAS.

After a lengthy evaluation by TEAL and QANTAS, it was announced in May 1958 that the Lockheed L-188 Electra four-turboprop airliner would replace the DC-6, and the first of three such aircraft was delivered on 15 October 1959 for its first operational service over the Tasman route on 1 December. By the end of the year, all three Electra airliners were in service.

It had long been the ambition of the New Zealand government to complete its ownership of TEAL, and on 1 April 1961 this became a reality when it bought Australia's 50 per cent interest.

With the expansion of services in the Far East and to the USA imminent at a time of burgeoning business and tourist traffic, the title Tasman Empire Airways Ltd seemed a little incongruous, and on 1 April 1965 the airline's name was changed to Air New Zealand. To cope with the expansion programme that was now necessary, the airline ordered three examples of the Douglas DC-8-52 four-turbojet airliner, the first of these being delivered on 19 July 1965 and the other two following at short intervals. The DC-8 inaugurated the airline's first jet service on 3 October 1965 on the route linking Christchurch and Sydney, while on 14 December the airline started one of its most prestigious routes, namely Auckland to Los Angeles via Nandi and Honolulu. On 13 March 1966, the DC-8 operated the airline's first service to Hong Kong via Sydney, soon adding a service from Auckland to Singapore.

Following this considerable enlargement of its route network,

Air New Zealand (ANZ) looked carefully to the future and appreciated that larger numbers of more capacious aircraft would be needed, and the type it selected was the Douglas (soon to be McDonnell Douglas) DC-10-30, a triple-turbofan transport of which three examples were ordered on 15 September 1970. The first of these wide-body airliners reached the airline on 27 January 1973, and the DC-10-30 flew its inaugural service between Auckland and Sydney on 7 February of the same year.

During 1976–77, the government of New Zealand discussed the feasibility and commercial advantage of merging the domestic airline, New Zealand National Airways Corporation (NZNAC), with Air New Zealand, and after agreement had been reached, the two operators merged under the name Air New Zealand. The fleet at that time was eight DC-10, three DC-8, eight Boeing Model 737 and 18 Fokker F.27 Friendship aircraft, the first two and last two types being contributed by ANZ and NZNAC respectively. From September 1975 until October 1980, an aircrew interchange agreement with British Airways meant that Air New Zealand operated the route Auckland to London (Heathrow) via Los Angeles, where the New Zealand crew was replaced by a British crew.

In April 1980, the government of New Zealand granted permission for the airline to place an order for five Boeing Model 747-219B four-turbofan airliners.

BELOW: *ANZ has eight Model 747-400 aircraft.*

AIR NIPPON (JAPAN)

Main base and hub: Tokyo (Haneda)
Type of operation: International, regional and domestic scheduled passenger services
Personnel: not available

Originally called Nihon Kinkyori Airways (NKK), the operator now known as Air Nippon was established on 13 March 1974 by Japan Air Lines, All Nippon Airways, TOA Domestic and other interests, and began operations on 10 October of the same year. The operator's remit at that time was the provision of government-subsidized feeder services between Japan's larger airports and smaller towns and island communities within the Japanese home islands group. The airline began its life with De Havilland Canada DHC-6 Twin Otter and NAMC YS-11 airliners,

Fleet (orders):
4 x Airbus A320-200
1 x Boeing Model 737-400
19 x Boeing Model 737-500
1 (2) x Bombardier Dash 8-300
2 x Bombardier DHC-6 Twin
   Otter Series 300
3 x NAMC YS-11A-200
2 x NAMC YS-11A-500

each powered by two turboprop engines, and while these types are still operated, the airline now also flies twin-turbofan types such as the Airbus A320 and Boeing Model 737, as its route network and passengers numbers have grown considerably.

AIR PHILIPPINES (PHILIPPINES)

Main base and hub: Subic Bay and Manila
Type of operation: Domestic scheduled and charter passenger and cargo
Personnel: 840
Air Philippines was established in February 1995 and began services in February of the following year. The operator currently flies a network linking 13 destinations within the Philippines, and plans at some time in the future to expand into international services.

Air Philippines is based in Luzon, at Ninoy Aquino

Fleet (orders):
9 x Boeing Model 737-200
3 x Boeing Advanced Model
 737-200
1 x Boeing Model 737-400
1 x NAMC YS-11-100
1 x NAMC YS-11A-200

International Airport, and operates to a number of major Filipino cities.

AIR TRANSAT (CANADA)

Main bases and hubs: Quebec, Halifax, Montreal, Toronto and Vancouver
Type of operation: International and domestic scheduled and charter passenger
Personnel: 2,135
Starting services in November 1987 after being established in December 1986, Air Transat concentrates its efforts on domestic services within Canada and international services mainly to destinations in Europe during the summer. In the winter, however, the operator switches its major effort to flights to destinations in the USA and the Caribbean.

Air Transat is based at Montreal International Airport,

Fleet (orders):
2 x Airbus A310-300
2 x Airbus A330-200
1 x Airbus A330-300
5 x Boeing Model 757-200
1 x Lockheed
 L-1011 TriStar
3 x Lockheed
 L-1011-100 TriStar
4 x Lockheed
 L-1011-150 TriStar

6 x Lockheed
 L-1011-500 TriStar

located at Mirabel.

AIR UKRAINE (UKRAINE)

Main base and hub: Kiev
Type of operation: International, regional and domestic scheduled and charter passenger and cargo
Personnel: not available
Since its creation out of the Ukrainian Division of Aeroflot after the dissolution of the USSR, Air Ukraine has been the national airline of the Ukraine. It flies a major network of services inside the Ukraine and to a number of destinations in the CIS and also in China, the Middle East, North Africa and southern Europe.

Fleet (orders):
8 x Antonov An-24B
6 x Antonov An-24RV
1 x Antonov An-26
7 x Antonov An-30
(4) x Antonov An-140
1 x Ilyushin Il-62M
1 x Ilyushin Il-76M
1 x Let L-410UVP-E
1 x Let L-410UVP
6 x Tupolev Tu-134A

8 x Tupolev Tu-154B
2 x Tupolev Tu-154M

AIR WISCONSIN
(UNITED STATES OF AMERICA)

Main bases and hubs: Chicago (O'Hare), Denver and Outagamie
Type of operation: Domestic scheduled passenger and cargo
Personnel: 2,500
Air Wisconsin began operations in August 1965, and in 1985, 1990 and 1998 absorbed Mississippi Valley Airlines, Aspen Airways and Mountain Air Express respectively. During 1991, United Airlines bought Air Wisconsin but then sold it in 1993. The airline currently operates scheduled feeder-line services

Fleet (orders):
8 (1) x Bombardier CRJ-200LR
1 x BAE Systems 146-100
11 x BAE Systems 146-200
5 x BAE Systems 146-300
23 x Fairchild Dornier 328-100

under the United Express logo to move passengers into and out of United Airlines' hubs at Chicago and Denver.

AIRBORNE EXPRESS
(UNITED STATES OF AMERICA)

Main base and hub: Wilmington
Type of operation: International and domestic charter cargo
Personnel: 22,995
Airbourne Express was created in 1979 after the Airborne Freight Corporation had bought Midwest Air Charter, and started operations in April 1980. The airline operates specialized overnight small-package delivery services to a considerable number of destinations, both large and small, within the USA. It also operates services to Canada and, to a

Fleet (orders):
14 x Boeing Model 767-200
4 x Boeing model 767-200ER
30 x McDonnell Douglas DC-8-60
2 x McDonnell Douglas DC-9-10
43 x McDonnell Douglas DC-9-30
29 x McDonnell Douglas DC-9-40

lesser extent, Mexico and to a number of destinations in the Caribbean.

AIRTOURS INTERNATIONAL
(UNITED KINGDOM)

Main base and hub: Manchester
Type of operation: International charter passenger
Personnel: not available
Established in October 1990 and flying services from March 1991, Airtours International is the second-largest British tour operator, flying services largely on behalf of the companies of the Airtours Group. These services originate from a number of British airports, and have as their destination holiday resorts in Africa, the Caribbean, Europe and North America. In November 1993, the operator bought the Cardiff-based European Airways, which was integrated within Airtours International, and in February 1996, the

Fleet (orders):
13 x Airbus A320-200
4 x Airbus A321-200
3 x Airbus A330-200
1 x Airbus A330-300
6 x Boeing Model 757-200
3 x Boeing Model 767-300ER
4 x McDonnell Douglas DC-10-10
1 x McDonnell Douglas DC-10-30

Airtours Group bought Spies, the largest Scandinavian tour company, thereafter integrating the operational aspects of the two groupings' airlines, Airtours International and Premiair.

AIRTRAN AIRWAYS
(UNITED STATES OF AMERICA)

Main bases and hubs: Orlando and Atlanta
Type of operation: Regional and domestic scheduled passenger
Personnel: 3,900
This airline was created in June 1993 and began services in October of the same year with the original designation Conquest Sun Airlines. The operator changed its name to AirTran Airways during August 1994. It was the first airline to take delivery of the new Boeing Model 717, which took place in 1999. AirTran Airways currently flies more than 275 services

Fleet (orders):
17 (33) x Boeing Model 717-200
4 x Boeing Advanced Model 737-200
31 x McDonnell Douglas DC-9-30

per day over a route network that embraces the eastern and central parts of the USA.

ALASKA AIRLINES
(UNITED STATES OF AMERICA)

Main bases and hubs: Anchorage, Portland and Seattle
Type of operation: International, regional and domestic scheduled and charter passenger and cargo services
Personnel: not available
Established in 1932, McGee Airways flew its first service, between Anchorage and Bristol Bay, using a Stinson three-passenger transport, in the same year. McGee later merged with Star Airways, and the combined operator later changed its name to Alaska Star Airlines and then in 1944, following further

Fleet (orders):
4 x Boeing Model 737-200C
4 x Boeing Model 737-200QC
40 x Boeing Model 737-400
13 (5) x Boeing Model 737-700
(11) x Boeing Model 737-900
6 x Boeing MD-82
27 x Boeing MD-83

RIGHT: *Air Alaska flies an all-Boeing fleet including the Model 737 in several variants.*

consolidation and further mergers with several smaller companies, to Alaska Airlines.

In 1951, Alaska Airlines started a service between Seattle and Fairbanks via Anchorage using the Douglas DC-4 four-engined airliner, and moved into the jet age in 1961 when it introduced the ill-starred Convair CV-990. Further re-equipment and expansion followed, the latter including the 1968 absorptions of two other regional carriers in the forms of Cordova Airlines and Alaska Coastal Airlines. By the early 1980s, Alaska Airlines had standardized on the Boeing Model 727 three-turbofan airliner as its basic equipment, but then

added the smaller Boeing Model 737 transport with its powerplant of two turbofans. More mergers have since occurred, the most recent being with Jet America in 1987, and Alaska Airlines is now Alaska's 'national' airline.

Now operating a fleet of twin-turbofan aircraft in the forms of the Model 737 and the MD-80 series of updated and stretched derivatives of the McDonnell Douglas DC-9 family, Alaska Airlines currently operates services in conjunction with Horizon Air Industries, which is its regional sister airline in the Alaska Air Group holding company.

Alaska Airlines is based at Seattle.

ALFA AIRLINES (TURKEY)

Main base and hub: Istanbul
Type of operation: International and regional charter passenger services
Personnel: 500

Air Alfa Hava Yollari was founded in 1992 but is now known as Alfa Airlines, and began charter operations in the spring of 1994 with Boeing Model 727-200 aircraft to destinations located mainly in Belgium, France and Germany, where large populations of expatriate Turks provided a good but very competitive market for Turkish operators. During 1994, the airline received its first Airbus A300, and this marked a switch towards the more lucrative package holiday market. By 1996, the airline's fleet had grown to five A300 aircraft, and in the same year the operator

Fleet (orders):
2 x Airbus A300B4-100
2 x Airbus A300-600R
3 x Airbus A321-100

was taken over by Kombassan Holdings, a multi-faceted company located in the Anatolian town of Konya. A leased Boeing Model 757 replaced one of the Model 727 aircraft, but this lease was not long-lasting, and the operator's small fleet began to grow with newer aircraft, including Airbus A321 machines.

ALITALIA (ITALY)

Main bases and hubs: Milan and Rome
Type of operation: International, regional and domestic scheduled passenger and cargo services
Personnel: 20,770

Aerolinee Italiane Internationale was established on 16 September 1946 by the Italian government (47.5 per cent), British European Airways (40 per cent) and a number of private investors (12.5 per cent) and, following its merger with Linee Aeree Italiane (LAI; created in 1946 by the Italian government and TWA), on 1 September 1957, was renamed Alitalia. The combined airlines operated as a single entity from 6 October 1957, and at this time BEA's interest was reduced to 9 per cent before being completely sold in 1961.

Alitalia began domestic operations on 5 May 1947 from Turin to Catania via Rome using Fiat G.12 transport aircraft leased from the Italian Air Force and, like LAI, soon expanded into a major domestic, regional and intercontinental force. The first international flights were in 1947 to Cairo, Tripoli and Lisbon, with the G.12 transports supplemented and then supplanted by Savoia-Marchetti SM.95 and Avro Lancastrian aircraft. In the early 1950s, these original aircraft, which can be most charitably described as obsolescent, were gradually replaced by Douglas DC-4 and later by Douglas DC-6 four-engined transports of altogether superior capability.

Fleet (orders):
(12) x Airbus A319-100
6 (5) x Airbus A320-200
23 x Airbus A321-100
7 x Boeing Model 747-200B
3 x Boeing Model 747-200F
1 x Boeing Model 747-400F
9 x Boeing Model 767-300ER
(6) x Boeing Model 777-200ER
3 x Boeing MD-11

5 x Boeing MD-11 Combi
89 x Boeing MD-82

Alitalia had to abandon the service linking Rome and London for lack of competitive equipment, but upon the delivery of its first Convair CV-340 on 24 April 1953 was able to resume the route. Alitalia took delivery of its first Douglas DC-8-42 four-turbojet airliner on 28 April 1960, and on the following day confirmed its full entry into the turbine-powered era with the first of its Sud-Aviation Caravelle VIN twin-turbojet airliners. The smaller type entered operational service on the service between Rome and London on 23 May 1960, while the DC-8's first service took place on 1 June 1960 with a flight from Rome to New York.

The next landmark for Alitalia was its entry into the operation of wide-body airliners with the receipt of its first

ABOVE: *The MD-82 is numerically the most important of Alitalia's short-haul aircraft.*

Boeing Model 747-143 on 13 May 1970, followed by that of its first McDonnell Douglas DC-10-30 on 6 February 1973. Alitalia has since developed into a considerably more capable and far-ranging airline operating a mixed fleet of Airbus, Boeing and McDonnell Douglas aircraft.

Based in Rome, Alitalia has a number of regional and domestic subsidiaries and affiliates, providing an effective service of feeder services linking into and out of the operator's primary routes.

ALL NIPPON AIRWAYS (JAPAN)

Main bases and hubs: Fukuoka, Osaka Kansai International Airport and Tokyo
Type of operation: International, regional and domestic scheduled and charter passenger and cargo services
Personnel: 14,640
The operator now known as All Nippon Airways was established in December 1952 as the Japan Helicopter and Airplane Transport Company (JHATC) and started operations almost exactly one year later in December 1953 with a service between Tokyo and Osaka using De Havilland Dove twin-engined light transports. Since that time, the company has grown to become Japan's largest civil air operator, with some 55 per cent of the domestic market.

JHATC changed its name to All Nippon Airways in December 1957, and in March of the following year merged with Kyokuto Airlines, a domestic operator that had started operations in March 1953 with a network of routes linking Osaka with points in southern Japan. In spite of strong competition from Japan Air Lines and the country's very significant railway network, All Nippon Airways grew rapidly and vigorously as the requirement for domestic travel flowered, and in November 1963, All Nippon Airways absorbed Fujita Airlines, following in 1965 with Central Japan Airlines in 1965 and Nagasaki Airways during 1967.

Meanwhile, All Nippon Airways had moved into the jet age with the lease of a Boeing Model 727 three-turbofan transport

Fleet (orders):
21 x Airbus A320-200
8 x Airbus A321-100
(5) x Airbus A340-300
11 x Boeing Model 747-100B
3 x Boeing Model 747-200B
14 x Boeing Model 747-400
9 x Boeing Model 747-400
   Domestic
11 x Boeing Model 767-200
32 x Boeing Model 767-300
10 x Boeing Model 767-300ER
12 (1) x Boeing Model 777-200

4 (3) x Boeing Model 777-200ER
5 (4) x Boeing Model 777-300
(6) x Boeing model 777-300ER

from the manufacturer during 1964, and this machine entered service linking Tokyo and Sapporo in May of that year. A number of routes were later transferred to Nihon Kinkyori Airways (now Air Nippon), a third-level operator formed in March 1974 by Japan Air Lines, ANA, Toa Domestic and other Japanese airlines to operate government-subsidized feeder services to isolated island communities and remote mainland destinations.

All Nippon Airways inaugurated its first international scheduled operations with services to Los Angeles and Washington, DC.

All Nippon Airways is based at Hameda Airport, situated outside Tokyo.

65

ALOHA AIRLINES
(UNITED STATES OF AMERICA)

Main base and hub: Honolulu
Type of operation: International, regional and domestic scheduled and charter passenger and cargo
Personnel: not available

The airline now known as Aloha Airlines was established in July 1946 as Trans-Pacific Airlines for charter services in the Hawaiian Islands, later extended to the US trust territories in the Pacific Ocean. In June 1949, the operator received certification for scheduled services, and in 1958 changed its name to Aloha Airlines. The airline currently operates services

Fleet (orders):
13 x Boeing Advanced Model 737-200
3 x Boeing Model 737-200C
3 x Boeing Model 737-300C
2 (3) x Boeing Model 737-700

in Hawaii and to the American trust territories as well as two destinations in the west of the continental USA.

AMERICA WEST AIRLINES
(UNITED STATES OF AMERICA)

Main bases and hubs: Phoenix, Des Moines and Las Vegas
Type of operation: Domestic and regional scheduled passenger services
Personnel: 13,370

America West Airlines was created in September 1981 specifically to provide low-fare regional air services from its base at Phoenix, Arizona, and started scheduled operations on 1 August 1983 with three Boeing Model 737 twin-turbofan aircraft and 280 employees. The airline's network initially extended between Colorado Springs, Kansas City (since discontinued), Los Angeles, Phoenix and Wichita, but has since become considerably larger in size and scope. America West Airlines currently operates an extensive hub-and-spoke system centred on the increasingly popular Phoenix Sky Harbor International Airport. It serves numerous cities in the

Fleet (orders):
(15) x Airbus A318
20 (9) x Airbus A319-100
45 (11) x Airbus A320 200
14 x Boeing Advanced Model 737-200
44 x Boeing Model 737-300
2 x Boeing Model 737-300QC
13 x Boeing Model 757-200

USA as well as several destinations in Canada and Mexico.

In order to expand its operations in Arizona, the airline acquired De Havilland Canada Dash 8 aircraft to provide feeder services to Yuma and Flagstaff from a time in the spring of 1987. Las Vegas and Des Moines were then developed as other important centres for operations, with 'Nite Flite' services connecting the city with numerous other destinations.

AMERICAN AIRLINES
(UNITED STATES OF AMERICA)

Main bases and hubs: Chicago O'Hare, Miami, Dallas/Fort Worth and San Juan
Type of operation: International, regional and domestic scheduled passenger services
Personnel: 93,000

American Airlines, currently ranked second in the USA in terms of the numbers of passengers carried and first in the world in terms of sales, was formed on 11 April 1934, taking over the interests of American Airways.

American Airlines received its first mail contracts in 1934, covering the route between Fort Worth and Los Angeles. On 9 September 1934, the airline introduced the all-metal cantilever monoplane Vultee V1-A on its Great Lakes to Texas services, supplementing its transcontinental Curtiss Condor sleeping service.

RIGHT: *American Airlines flies an enormous fleet of Airbus, Boeing and Fokker aircraft.*

Fleet (orders):
35 x Airbus A300-600R
60 x Boeing Advanced Model 727-200
55 (63) x Boeing Model 737-800
102 (23) x Boeing Model 757-200
8 x Boeing Model 767-200
22 x Boeing Model 767-200ER
49 x Boeing Model 767-300ER
28 (19) x Boeing Model 777-200ER
7 x Boeing MD-11
229 x Boeing MD-82

43 x Boeing MD-83
4 x Boeing MD-87
75 x Fokker 100
5 x McDonnell Douglas DC-9-30

American Airlines was one of the sponsors of the most successful US airliner of the period leading up to World War II, namely the Douglas DC-3, which was developed from the DC-2. The operator had received its first DC-2 on 4 November 1934. Services with this type on the route between New York and Chicago were initiated in December of the same year.

American Airlines took delivery of its first DST (Douglas Sleeper Transport), a development of the DC-2 with a widened and lengthened fuselage, on 7 June 1936 and placed this type in service on the route between New York and Chicago on 25 June of the same year, and then received its first DC-3 on 18 August.

By 1942, during World War II, American Airlines was operating 74 Douglas DC-3s and the airline, like many other US carriers, began the movement of troops and essential equipment. On 20 June 1942, American Airlines began regular services across the North Atlantic, following early in 1943 with flights to India. Towards the end of World War II, modified Consolidated Liberators were drafted into service for the first all-freight service from Los Angeles to New York, which started on 1 August 1944 and was supplemented by a DC-3 service from 15 October 1944.

On 1 June 1945, American Export Airlines and American Airlines amalgamated, thereby creating a very large operator. On 24 October, American Export operated its first commercial transatlantic flight from New York to Hurn Airport, near Bournemouth, England. In 10 November 1945, American Export became American Overseas, and the full merger of the two airlines took effect on 5 December.

With the end of World War II, the Douglas four-engined transport was developed to meet a US Army requirement, and many C-54 Skymasters were released for civil service with the designation DC-4. American Airlines received 50 for service first on the route linking New York and Chicago (February 1946) and then on the transcontinental route between New York and Los Angeles (7 March 1946). The airliner remained in passenger service until December 1948, with the last DC-4 freight service taking place at the end of 1958. The DC-4 was replaced in passenger service by the Douglas DC-6, of which American Airlines received its first machine on 24 November 1946. American Airlines was the first operator to place the DC-6 in service, initially on its route between New York and Chicago. American Airlines took delivery of its first Convair CV-240 on 1 June 1948.

In December 1951, American Airlines ordered 25 examples of the Douglas DC-7, and took delivery of the first of these machines on 10 October 1953. American Airlines placed the DC-7 in service in direct competition with TWA on the non-stop service between New York and Los Angeles on 29 November 1953. During 1958, American Airlines operated only piston-engined aircraft, in the form of 85 DC-6, 58 DC-7 and 58 CV-240 transports.

American Airlines then became the second operator, after National Airlines, to place an order for the Lockheed L-188 Electra, with its radical powerplant of four turboprop engines, on 15 December 1955. The first of these aircraft was accepted on 27 November 1958, and entered service on 23 January 1959 for the New York to Chicago service. The Electra was the mainstay of American Airline's short- and medium-haul fleet until the arrival of the Boeing Model 727, and the last L-188 remained in service until 1971.

On 25 January 1959, American Airlines began the first jet domestic service using its own aircraft, a Boeing Model 707-123, on the route between New York and Los Angeles. The first Model 707 was initially handed over on 25 October 1958, and after trials was redelivered on 16 March 1959. One other four-engine jet type to enter service with the airline was the Convair CV-990, which began serving the New York to Chicago route on 18 March 1962.

The airline decided that it should replace the turboprop-powered Electra with a faster and more economical turbofan-powered type, and ordered 25 examples of the Boeing Model 727-238, of which the first was delivered on 25 January 1964. Like many other American Airlines aircraft, the Model 727 first entered service on the New York to Chicago route on 12 April 1964. To complement the Model 727s on shorter-range routes, American Airlines in July 1963 ordered the first 15 of an eventual 30 examples of a British twin-turbofan airliner, the BAC One-Eleven 401, and the first of these aircraft was accepted on 23 December 1965 for service from 6 March of the following year. By the end of 1969, American Airlines had an all-jet fleet comprising 27 One-Eleven, 100 Boeing Model 707, 22 Model 720, and 98 Model 727 airliners.

American Airline's first wide-body transport was a Boeing Model 747 leased from Pan American, and this made its debut on 2 March 1970 between Los Angeles and New York. American Airlines started to operate its own Model 747 'jumbo jet' aircraft in June 1970. On 29 July 1971, the airline received its first Douglas (soon McDonnell Douglas) DC-10-10, and it was this machine that flew the airline's first flight between Los Angeles and Chicago on 5 August 1971.

On 30 November 1970, American Airlines bought Trans Caribbean Airways, whose routes it started to operate with its own aircraft on 2 March 1971. In August of the same year, American Airlines started using the Model 707 on a new service across the Pacific from the US west coast to Sydney in Australia, but this service ended in 1974.

During the rest of the 1970s and into the mid-1980s, American Airlines concentrated on consolidation of its position as a pre-eminent American airline, and it was not until 4 November 1982 that it took delivery of a new type of airliner, a Boeing Model 767-223, of which 10 had entered service by December 1984 in the first stage of an expansion and re-equipment programme, giving American Airlines a force of 86 such aircraft complemented by 71 examples of the Boeing Model 767. At the lower end of the range/payload spectrum, American Airlines on 12 May 1983 received the first of its initial order for 20 McDonnell Douglas MD-82 twin-turbofan airliners. This aeroplane entered revenue-earning service two days later, and while the order for 20 aircraft was quite large by the standards of the day, in 1984 American Airlines contracted for a further 86 such aircraft (19 and 67 for delivery in 1984–85 and 1986–87 respectively), together with an option for a further 100 aircraft of the same type.

In common with other major airlines, American Airlines took measures from September 2001 to reduce capacity and boost operating efficiency in the face of an airline slump.

AMERICAN EAGLE AIRLINES (UNITED STATES OF AMERICA)

Main bases and hubs: Dallas/Fort Worth, Chicago (O'Hare), Los Angeles, Miami and New York (John F. Kennedy)

Type of operation: International, regional and domestic scheduled passenger and cargo

Personnel: 10,765

Fleet (orders):
30 x ATR 42-300
29 x ATR 72-210
12 x ATR 72-500
(25) x Bombardier CRJ-700
1 x EMBRAER RJ-135ER
37 (12) x EMBRAER RJ-135LR
50 x EMBRAER RJ-145LR
106 x Saab 340B

Created in 1984 and starting operations in November of the same year, American Eagle Airlines was established by the amalgamation of the services of Executive Airlines, Flagship Airlines, Simmons Airlines and Wings West Airlines under the overall designation American Eagle. All of these small airlines were later bought by AMR Eagle, part of the AMR Corporation which also owns American Airlines. Further growth came from the 1992 purchase of Metroflight Airlines by Simmons Airlines, and in 1998 Simmons Airlines, Flagship Airlines and Wings West Airlines merged to create American Eagle Airlines, which absorbed Business Express in December 2000. American Eagle Airlines is in effect the regional airline supporting the long-range services of American Airlines, flying more than 1,700 services per day to link some 135 American, Bahamian, Canadian and Caribbean destinations.

ANSETT AUSTRALIA (AUSTRALIA)

Main base and hub: Melbourne

Type of operation: International, regional and domestic scheduled passenger and cargo services

Personnel: 14,875

Fleet (orders):
20 x Airbus A320-200
23 x Boeing Model 737-300
2 x Boeing Model 747-400
8 x Boeing Model 767-200
1 x Boeing Model 767-200ER
1 x Boeing Model 767-300ER
7 x BAE Systems 146-200
2 x BAE Systems 146-200QT   3 x BAE Systems 146-300

Reginald M. Ansett formed Ansett Airways in February 1936 with a Fokker Universal as its equipment, and the new airline began services between Melbourne and Hamilton on 17 February of the same year. By 1939, the airline's route network had swelled to include those between Melbourne and Adelaide, Broken Hill and Sydney. Ansett operated no services in the course of World War II, but resumed operations on 5 February 1946 with three war-surplus Douglas C-47s acquired late in the preceding year. The revived Ansett started with routes linking Melbourne with Adelaide, Canberra and Hamilton, soon extended to Brisbane and Hobart.

Early in 1952, Ansett started on a programme of expansion by the purchase of Barrier Reef Airways which operated a small network of seaplane services from Brisbane to Hayman Island, Sydney and Townsville, and by the acquisition in 1953 of the bankrupt Trans-Oceanic Airways' routes. In 1954, the three operations were consolidated into a single network, and with the delivery of its first Convair CV-240 on 23 April of the same year the airline was able to offer low-fare services between state capitals in competition with Trans-Australia Airlines and Australian National Airways. In March 1957, Ansett revealed a further expansion plan requiring the purchase of additional CV-240 and 340 aircraft as well as more advanced turboprop-powered airliners in the form of four Vickers Viscount 832 and three Lockheed L-188 Electra aircraft.

On 4 October of the same year, Ansett Transport Industries, the parent group of which Ansett Airways was a member, bought Australian National Airways to form Ansett-ANA, a title retained until late 1968, when the name Ansett Airlines was adopted. Further consolidation of this growing operator followed with the purchase on 5 February 1958 of Butler Air Transport, which was renamed Airlines of New South Wales on 15 December of the following year, and then of Guinea Airways, which was renamed Airlines of South Australia.

The first of the Electra and Viscount aircraft were received on 27 February and 12 March 1959 respectively. The Electras remained operational as passenger but later freight transports up to 1984, when they were sold to Turbo Power International of the USA. Further turboprop equipment was also secured in 1959 in the form of the first of a rapidly growing fleet of Fokker F.27 Friendships, of which the first was accepted on 5 October. The type remains in service in both its basic and its updated F.50 forms with the parent company and its four principal subsidiaries right up to the present.

The airline received its first pure jet aircraft on 9 September 1964, when it took delivery of its initial Boeing Model 727-77 three-turbofan airliner, and this type entered revenue-earning service on 2 November of the same year. From 13 April 1967, the Model 727 aircraft were complemented on shorter routes by the Douglas DC-9-31.

In January 1969, Ansett acquired MacRobertson Miller Airlines, which was renamed Airlines of Western Australia in July 1981. During the 1970s, additional Model 727 aircraft, in the form of Model 727-277 machines, were taken on strength, and

69

throughout most of the 1980s 13 of these aircraft constituted the single largest element in Ansett's fleet. Ansett also decided to standardize on the Boeing Model 737 twin-turbofan type in place of the DC-9, and first of 12 Model 737-277 airliners was delivered on 15 June 1981.

In 1979, Ansett Transport Industries, itself created in 1946 and the parent organization for R. M. Ansett's transport interests, was taken over by the New Corporation and TNT Ltd. Further growth and consolidation followed, and in July 1981 Ansett created another subsidiary as Airlines of North Australia. Two

years later, on 8 June 1983, the airline moved into the wide-body arena with the receipt of the first of its six Boeing Model 767-277 airliners. Further advanced equipment followed in the form of the Airbus A320-200, BAe 146 and Fokker F.28 Fellowship.

Since 1987, Ansett has been involved in a joint venture to set up Ansett New Zealand, bought Eastwest Airlines and Kendell Airlines and, before its recent disposal of these assets, owned part of America West and Ladeco. During 1994, Ansett absorbed its subsidiary airlines (Ansett West Australia, Ansett Express and Eastwest) to become Ansett Australia.

ARKIA ISRAELI AIRLINES (ISRAEL)

Main bases and hubs: Tel Aviv, Yafo and Sde Dov
Type of operation: International, regional and domestic scheduled and charter passenger and cargo
Personnel: 1,350

Created in 1949 by El Al and the Israeli labour federation, Arkia Inland Airlines undertook its first services within Israel from the following year. In 1972, Arkia bought a half share in Kanaf Airlines and Aviation Services, resulting in the creation of Kanaf Arkia Airline and Aviation Services, and during 1980 Kanaf Arkia bought Arkia to consolidate the two operators' service under the designation Arkia Israeli Airlines. The operator is Israel's second-

Fleet (orders):
3 (1) x ATR 72-500
2 x Boeing Model 737-200
1 x Boeing Model 757-200
2 x Boeing Model 757-300
8 x Bombardier Dash 7

largest airline, and with the exception of a service to Amman in neighbouring Jordan, its scheduled services are flown in Israel. Arkia also flies charter services to Europe.

ASIANA AIRLINES (SOUTH KOREA)

Main base and hub: Seoul
Type of operation: Regional and domestic scheduled and charter passenger services
Personnel: 5,835

Created as recently as December 1988 and beginning operations in the same month, Seoul Air International was established by the Kumho Group within the context of the policy enunciated by the South Korean government for the creation of a second national flag carrier airline to complement Korean Air Lines.

Asiana Airlines is based at Seoul airport, and in the summer of 2001 this operator's route network included 13 destinations in South Korea and 44 destinations in 12 other countries characterized by strong economic links with South Korea.

Fleet (orders):
(8) Airbus A321-100
5 (1) x Airbus A321-200
(3) x Airbus A330-200
(3) x Airbus A330-300
22 x Boeing Model 737-400
3 x Boeing Model 737-500
3 x Boeing Model 747-400
5 x Boeing Model 747-400 Combi
4 (3) x Boeing Model 747-400F
9 x Boeing Model 767-300

1 x Boeing Model 767-300 Freighter
1 (1) x Boeing Model 767-300ER
(9) x Boeing Model 777-200ER

BELOW: *Asiana flies a large fleet of modern Airbus and Boeing aircraft, the latter including the Model 747.*

ATLANTIC SOUTHEAST AIRLINES (UNITED STATES OF AMERICA)

Main base and hub: Dallas/Fort Worth and Atlanta
Type of operation: Regional and domestic scheduled passenger
Personnel: not available

Atlantic Southeast Airlines was established in March 1979 and began operations in June of the same year, and as what is now a subsidiary of Delta Air Lines provides feeder-line services for its owner. Atlantic Southwest Airlines flies to 80 destinations in the eastern part of the USA from its two hubs.

Fleet (orders):
19 x ATR 72-210
42 (37) x Bombardier CRJ-200ER
(30) x Bombardier CRJ-700
47 x EMBRAER EMB-120 Brasilia
2 x EMBRAER EMB-120 Brasilia Advanced

Atlantic Southeast also flies to three international destinations, two in Canada and one in Mexico.

ATLAS AIR (UNITED STATES OF AMERICA)

Main base and hub: Miami
Type of operation: International and regional scheduled and charter cargo
Personnel: not available

Atlas Air is a dedicated air freight operator, and was established in April 1992 for the start of operations in 1993 over a network that currently comprises more than 100 destinations in 46 countries around the world.

Atlas Air is based at Miami International Airport. The airline specializes in the provision, on a long-term basis, of

Fleet (orders):
14 x Boeing Model 747-200F
3 x Boeing Model 747-300 Combi
7 (4) x Boeing Model 747-400F
1 x Boeing Business Jet

Boeing Model 747 freighter aircraft to boost the capacity of other operators.

AUSTRIAN AIRLINES (AUSTRIA)

Main bases and hubs: Vienna, Graz, Klagenfurt, Linz and Salzburg
Type of operation: International, regional and domestic scheduled passenger and cargo services
Personnel: 5,370

Otherwise known as Oesterreichische Luftverkehrs AG, Austrian Airlines was created on 30 September 1957 by the merger of Air Austria and Austrian Airways, neither of which had started operations at that time, and assumed the name of its predecessor of the period between the two world wars, itself absorbed into Deutsche Lufthansa on 1 January 1939 after the German annexation of Austria.

Austrian Airlines received its first airliner, a Vickers Viscount, on 23 February 1960, but up to this time ran its services with four Viscount 779 machines leased from Fred Olsen Air Transport. The new airline's first service was flown on 31 March 1958 on the route linking Vienna and London via Zurich, and in order to cope with the demands of its route network, which was growing rapidly during the early 1960s, the airline placed an order for the Sud-Aviation Caravelle VIR on 29 October 1962 and received the first of these machines on 18 February 1963.

On 30 April 1966, Austrian Airlines received the first of its two Hawker Siddeley HS 748 twin-turboprop airliners ordered for the operation of domestic services as well as routes into neighbouring countries. These aircraft were particularly useful

Fleet (orders):
6 (7) x Airbus A320-200
3 x Airbus A321-100
2 (2) x Airbus A321-200
4 x Airbus A330-200
2 x Airbus A340-200
3 x Boeing MD-82
2 x Boeing MD-83
5 x Boeing MD-87
6 x Fokker 70

for their STOL capability, allowing successful operation into airports in mountainous regions, and remained in service up to 6 September 1970.

In the later 1960s, Austrian Airlines expanded its horizons to include long-range routes, and the operation of such services was initially made possible by the lease of a Boeing Model 707-329 from the Belgian operator Sabena on 1 April 1969. This aeroplane was used on the route linking Vienna and New York up to 1971, when it was returned to Sabena. In that year, the airline received a considerable boost to its short-range operations with the acceptance on 10 June 1971 of its first Douglas DC-9-32 twin-turbofan transport, and the receipt of further aircraft of the same type permitted Austrian Airlines to withdraw its fleet of Caravelles, the last of which made its ultimate revenue-earning flight on 26 July 1972.

On 24 September 1973, Austrian Airlines leased a

71

McDonnell Douglas DC-8-73CF for use on cargo flights from Vienna to Hong Kong, a service that was flown between 29 September 1973 and 5 December 1974, when the aeroplane was returned to Overseas National Airways.

On 25 August 1975, the airline received its first McDonnell Douglas DC-9-51, which entered service early the following month, and on 30 October 1977 it became one of the launch customers for the MD-80, the lengthened and up-engined derivative of the DC-9, receiving its first such MD-81 on 3 October 1980. The advent of the DC-9-51 and MD-81 allowed Austrian Airlines to dispose of its DC-9-32 fleet to Texas International.

The MD-81 has since been complemented by the MD-82, MD-83 and two subvariants of the MD-87 as the mainstay of Austrian Airlines' medium-range operations, with responsibility for short-range services entrusted to the Fokker 50, 70 and 100. The airline has also increased its capacity on high-density routes by the introduction of the Airbus A310 with other Airbus wide-body airliners in service or on order for further augmentation of capacity.

In 1964, Austrian Airlines established Austrian Airtransport as a subsidiary for the operation of charter and inclusive tour services using aircraft drawn from the parent company. Another subsidiary is Austrian Air Services, which flies local services with Swearingen SA 226 Metros, of which the first was delivered on 25 January 1980 for a service debut on 1 April of the same year. Austrian Airlines now flies scheduled passenger and cargo services from Graz, Klagenfurt, Linz and Salzburg as well as Vienna to a growing number of destinations in Eastern Europe, Western Europe and the Middle East plus a limited number of destinations in Africa, Asia and North America.

AVIANCA (COLOMBIA)

Main base and hub: Bogotá
Type of operation: International, regional and domestic scheduled and charter passenger and cargo
Personnel: 3,215
Avianca is the national airline of Colombia, and was established in June 1940 through the merger of SCADTA, dating from 1919, and Servicio Aéreo Colombiano, dating from 1933. Avianca currently flies a network of scheduled and charter services linking 12 Colombian destinations as well as an international network extending to 19 destinations in South

Fleet (orders):
3 x Boeing Model 757-200
4 x Boeing Model 767-200ER
2 x Boeing Model 767-300ER
12 x Boeing MD-83
10 x Fokker 50

America, the Caribbean, Europe and the USA, the latter pair each represented by two destinations.

BIMAN BANGLADESH AIRLINES (BANGLADESH)

Main base and hub: Dhaka
Type of operation: International, regional and domestic scheduled and charter passenger and cargo services
Personnel: not available
Biman Bangladesh Airlines was created on 4 January 1972 as the national flag carrier of the new state of Bangladesh, previously known as East Pakistan. One month later, the airline began to operate its first services, with a Douglas DC-3 on routes from Dhaka to Chittagong, Sylhet and Jessore. The DC-3 was obsolete even as it entered service, and was soon replaced by a pair of Fokker F.27 Friendship Series 200 airliners that were delivered on 3 and 7 March 1972. During September 1972, the airline added two new F.27 Friendship Series 600 aircraft to its fleet, one of them donated by the Dutch government. For a short time in 1972, the airline also flew leased Douglas DC-6 aircraft.

Biman Bangladesh flew its first international service on 28 April 1972 on the route between Dhaka and Calcutta using an F.27 Friendship Series 200, and on 1 January 1973 started a weekly service from Dhaka to London (Heathrow) with a Boeing Model 707-321 four-turbofan airliner leased from

Fleet (orders):
4 x Airbus A310-300
2 x BAE Systems ATP
3 x Fokker F.28 Fellowship Mk 4000
6 x McDonnell Douglas DC-10-30

Donaldson International. On 30 December of the same year, Biman Bangladesh took delivery of its first Model 707-351, and over the following eight years received additional Model 707 and F.27 aircraft to permit the expansion of the airline's route network to a number of other Asian destinations.

Domestic services were limited by the capacity of the F.27s which were the only suitable aircraft in service for this task, and to improve capability in the regional as well as domestic markets, Biman Bangladesh bought two examples of the Fokker F.28 Fellowship, these aircraft being accepted in September and November 1981. By this time, the airline was planning a considerable improvement in its long-range capacity, and moved into the market for wide-body aircraft

with the purchase of two McDonnell Douglas DC-10-30 three-turbofan airliners. These aircraft were delivered in August 1983, and this type started a high-capacity service to London on 22 October of the same year.

Further expansion has been limited by the poverty of Bangladesh and thus of its airline, but the F.27 aircraft have

ABOVE: *The A310-300 gives Biman Bangladesh a modern medium-haul capability.*

been replaced by BAE Systems ATP twin-turboprop transports and the DC-10 fleet has expanded to six, with further capability offered by the introduction of the Airbus A310-300.

bmi BRITISH MIDLAND
(UNITED KINGDOM)

Main bases and hubs: Birmingham, London (Heathrow) and East Midlands
Type of operation: International and regional scheduled passenger services
Personnel: 6,320

The origins of British Midland can be found in the establishment by Air Schools, during October 1938, of a reserve flying school at Burnaston near Derby. During World War II, this trained pilots and navigators for the Royal Air Force, and expanded with the establishment of another training school near Wolverhampton. On 21 August 1947, the company started a small-scale charter service with a combination of British Taylorcraft Auster, Miles Gemini and Miles Messenger aircraft, and the success of this commercial transport effort persuaded Air Schools early in 1949 to expand its commercial air transport capability. On 16 February of that year, Derby Aviation was registered as an airline. The new operator started scheduled passenger services on 18 July 1953 with a single De Havilland D.H.89A Rapide on the route between Derby and Jersey via Wolverhampton.

In April 1955, Derby Aviation bought its first Douglas DC-3 for greater capacity and speed on the service to and from the Channel Islands, and this machine flew its first such service on 1 May of the same year. The success of this service is attested by the fact that Derby Airlines was by the summer of 1958 operating

Fleet (orders):
5 (8) x Airbus A320-200
10 (1) x Airbus A321-200
(4) x Airbus A330-200
7 x Boeing Model 737-300
2 x Boeing Model 737-400
9 x Boeing Model 737-500
3 x Fokker 70
6 x Fokker 100

three DC-3 airliners, mainly for tour charters from Derby to Austria, France, Italy, Spain and Switzerland. The airline was also operating scheduled services from Derby to British destinations such as Glasgow, the Isle of Man and Jersey as well as international destinations such as Antwerp and Ostend.

On 12 March 1959, the operator changed its name to Derby Airways as a reflection of its growing involvement in scheduled and charter operations. By 1960, the operator had a fleet of eight Douglas DC-3 transports and was carrying over 20,000 passengers a year on its scheduled services, together with a considerably larger number on its charter flights.

On 30 July 1964, Derby Airways announced that it was changing its name to British Midland Airways, a change that took place on 1 October 1964, and the growing capability of this company meant that on 1 February 1965 the airline was able to introduce its first turboprop-powered type in the form of the

Handley Page Dart Herald Mk 211. In April of the same year, BMA moved to its current base, the newly opened East Midlands Airport at Castle Donington, and in the same month it added new services to Palma and Gerona, adding Newquay during 1966.

In January 1967, British Midland Airways took delivery of its first four-turboprop airliner, the Vickers Viscount 736, which entered service to complement the Canadair Argonaut aircraft which had been operating on its scheduled flights since 1961. Autair International pulled out of scheduled operations in 1969, and British Midland Airways gained several of its routes, including the London–Teesside link: this service was originally flown by the Viscount but was later taken over by the airline's new BAC One-Eleven 523, of which the first was accepted on 17 February 1970.

On 15 April 1970, British Midland Airways moved into the long-range market with the purchase of a Boeing Model 707 which was placed in service on charter flights across the Atlantic, and to Africa and the Far East. In 1974, the airline dropped out of the inclusive charter market, however, and after that, the airliner operated a total of 11 Model 707 transports in other roles, including the lease of several aircraft to other operators.

On 29 February 1972, Channel Airways ceased operations, and British Midland Airways secured this operator's scheduled routes to the Channel Islands from Bournemouth and Southend. This required additional capacity, and British Midland Airways therefore bought 11 Viscounts in 1972. Up to 26 August 1976, when the first McDonnell Douglas DC-9 was accepted, the

Viscount constituted the core of British Midland Airways' fleet. To complement the medium-range DC-9, British Midland Airways also operated the short-range Fokker F.27 Friendship twin-turboprop airliner, including three leased from Air UK and one from NLM, on its low-density routes in the UK and the international routes to Amsterdam, Brussels and Paris. Later equipment has included the ubiquitous Boeing Model 737 twin-turbofan type in three variants as well as the Fokker 70 updated and lengthened development of the F.27 and also the Fokker 100.

In 1968, it should be noted, British Midland Airways was bought by Minster Assets, an investment and banking group, but in 1978 the directors of the airline succeeded in a management buy-out. In 1982, British Midland formed Manx Airlines to operate scheduled services from the Isle of Man. British Midland Airways, which had traded as British Midland since 1964, formally became British Midland in 1985, and two years later, in March 1987, the Airlines of Britain Holdings (ABH) group was established as a holding company for British Midland and its subsidiaries. Scandinavian Airlines System (SAS) took a 24.9 per cent stake in ABH in 1988, then increased this to 35 per cent in March 1992, and to 40 per cent in 1994. In May 1999 the airline applied for approval to operate its first transatlantic services, and in the same year adopted its current designation.

RIGHT: *bmi has fixed on Airbus aircraft as the core of its medium- and long-haul services.*

BRAATHENS (NORWAY)

Main base and hub: Oslo
Type of operation: International, regional and domestic scheduled and charter passenger and cargo
Personnel: 5,170
Braathens SAFE (Braathens from March 1998) was established in 1946 as a subsidiary of the Braathens shipping company, its initial operations being charter flights to destinations in the Far East and South America. In September 1996, the airline began domestic services in Sweden after its purchase of Transwede, these services being expanded after August 1998 by the purchase of Malmö Aviation Schedule.

Fleet (orders):
5 x Boeing Model 737-400
17 x Boeing Model 737-500
9 (4) x Boeing Model 737-700

Braathens is the largest Norwegian airline, and currently operates a network linking 15 Norwegian, four Swedish and 10 other European destinations.

BRITANNIA AIRWAYS (UNITED KINGDOM)

Main bases and hubs: Birmingham and London (Gatwick)
Type of operation: International and regional charter passenger and cargo
Personnel: not available
Now the UK's largest charter operator, with flights from some 20 airports to holiday destinations in the Mediterranean region and also in Brazil, the Caribbean, Thailand and the southern USA, Britannia Airways was created in December 1961 as Euravia. This flew services with Lockheed Constellation airliners on behalf of Universal Sky Tours. Euravia switched to the Bristol Britannia in 1964, and at the same time changed

Fleet (orders):
2 (2) x Boeing Model 737-800
19 x Boeing Model 757-200
6 x Boeing Model 767-200ER
6 (1) x Boeing Model 767-300ER

its name to Britannia Airways. In 1965 Britannia was bought by the International Thomson Organisation which later bought Horizon Travel and its charter air arm, Orion Airways,

which was merged into Britannia. In 1998, Thomson bought a Scandinavian tour operator, the Fritidsresor Group, whose air charter arm, Blue Scandinavia, then became Britannia A.B. In 2000, the German holiday operator Preussag bought the whole of the Thomson group within the consolidation of the package tour industry in the European Union.

BRITISH AIRWAYS (UNITED KINGDOM)

Main bases and hubs: Birmingham, Glasgow, London (Heathrow), London (Gatwick) and Manchester
Type of operation: International, regional and domestic scheduled and charter passenger and cargo services
Personnel: 65,640

British Airways can be traced back to an origin on 31 March 1924, when four pioneering British airlines (British Marine, Daimler Airways, Handley Page Air Transport and Instone Air Lines, the earliest of them coming into existence on 25 August 1919 and flying its first service on the same date) merged to create Imperial Airways for the development of air routes to the dominions and British possessions/mandates in the Middle East, India, the Far East, Australasia and Africa. It also operated a few European routes, the most important of them being that between London and Paris.

In 1935, British Airways was established by the amalgamation of three small independent airlines, and concentrated its commercial effort on the operation of air services within the continent of Europe. Then an act of Parliament on 24 November 1939 served to merge Imperial Airways and British Airways, this creating the British Overseas Airways Corporation (BOAC), although it was not until 1 April 1940 that the two previous operators' combined fleet of 82 aircraft was formally taken over as the equipment of the new airline.

BOAC operated only limited services in World War II, but after the revival of more extensive services following the end of hostilities in Europe during May 1945, a separate division of BOAC was created during August 1946 to operate a growing

Fleet (orders):
(12) x Airbus A318
19 (20) x Airbus A319-100
5 x Airbus A320-100
5 (21) x Airbus A320-200
4 x Boeing Advanced Model 737-200
7 x Boeing Model 737-300
34 x Boeing Model 737-400
8 x Boeing Model 737-500
12 x Boeing Model 747-200B
3 x Boeing Model 747-200B Combi
56 x Boeing Model 747-400
2 x Boeing Model 747-400F
47 x Boeing Model 757-200
21 x Boeing Model 767-300ER
5 x Boeing Model 777-200
35 (5) x Boeing Model 777-200ER
7 x EADS/BAE Systems Concorde

network of routes throughout the UK and Europe, and this was designated British European Airways (BEA). In July and August 1950, BEA experimentally used a new turboprop airliner, the Vickers Viscount 630, on the routes linking London with Edinburgh and Paris, thus pioneering turbine propulsion for civil purposes, and in April 1953 the world's first true turboprop service was inaugurated on the route between London and Nicosia with the Viscount 701. Meanwhile, BOAC had started the first true jet service in May 1952 with the De Havilland Comet 1, which was powered by four turbojets, on the route linking London and Johannesburg, and on 4 October

BELOW: *Despite its use of Airbus machines, BA is still primarily a 'Boeing airline'.*

1958, BOAC operated the first jet service across the Atlantic to New York with the Comet 4, an enlarged and much improved development of the Comet 1.

In March 1964, BEA began scheduled services with the De Havilland Trident 1C three-turbofan airliner, which was the first civil type with the ability to land in zero-visibility conditions. Through the 1960s, BEA and BOAC continued to enlarge their route networks and fleets, and the development of the mass air transport market during this period, as tourism started to boom, .resulted in the establishment of BEA Airtours (later British Airtours) as BEA's separate charter and inclusive tour subsidiary. Starting with a fleet of Comet 4B airliners which were later replaced by altogether more capable Boeing Model 707-436 machines transferred from BOAC, the operator was finally equipped with Boeing Model 737-236 and Lockheed L-1011-200 TriStar 200 two- and three-turbofan airliners for the short- and long-haul routes respectively.

On 31 October 1970, BEA took over Cambrian Airways and BKS/Northeast Airlines for incorporation in its Regional Division.

On 22 April 1970, BOAC took delivery of its first Boeing Model 747-136 four-turbofan airliner, and flew its first North Atlantic services with this pioneering wide-body airliner almost exactly one year later. By the provisions of the Civil Aviation Act of 1971, the British Airways Board was created on 1 September 1972 to rejoin the two divisions and British Air Services within a single organization, but the BEA and BOAC names were retained until 1 April 1974.

One of the most important events in aviation history took place on 21 January 1976, when the first supersonic airliner developed in the Western world was introduced to revenue-earning service: this airliner was the Aerospatiale/BAC Concorde, and it first entered service on the route linking London and Bahrain.

British Airways was privatized in 1987, and in 1988 took over British Caledonian Airways. Throughout the 1980s, the airline introduced large numbers of American narrow- as well as wide-body aircraft, most of them Boeing types, for its very large network of domestic, regional and intercontinental services. In the 1990s, it started to add Airbus aircraft.

British Airways has shed many jobs and severely trimmed capacity in light of the airline slump following the September 2001 terrorist attacks on the USA.

BRITISH EUROPEAN (UNITED KINGDOM)

Main bases and hubs: Birmingham, Exeter, Jersey and London (Gatwick and City)
Type of operation: International, regional and domestic scheduled passenger and cargo
Personnel: 1,300
The operator now known as British European was created in November 1979 on the basis of the Jersey-based Intra Airways, and in 1983 became part of the Walkersteel Group, owner of the Blackpool-based Spacegrand Aviation, the two airlines were merged fully in 1985 as Jersey European Airways, whose name was changed to British European in 2000. Operating in its own right as an Air France franchisee, British European now flies domestic services linking 17 British destinations and also operates services to six European

Fleet (orders):
4 x Bombardier CRJ-200ER
3 x Bombardier Dash 8-200
6 x Bombardier Dash 8-300
(4) x Bombardier Dash 8Q-400
3 x BAE Systems 146-100
7 x BAE Systems 146-200
6 x BAE Systems 146-300
(12) x BAE Systems RJ-100
1 x Shorts 360 Advanced

destinations. British European flies most of its scheduled services from Birmingham and London (Gatwick and Stansted), and also operates a staff movement service between Toulouse and Bristol for Airbus personnel.

BRITISH REGIONAL AIRLINES (UNITED KINGDOM)

Main bases and hubs: Manchester, Belfast, Cardiff, Edinburgh, Glasgow, Inverness, Leeds, Bradford and Southampton
Type of operation: International, regional and domestic scheduled and charter passenger and cargo
Personnel: 1,410
It was in 1991 that Manx Airlines (Europe) was established, and in 1995 this became a franchisee of British Airways operating under the British Airways Express logo. In September 1996, the operator became British Regional Airlines, which currently flies services linking 19 British destinations, and also operates flights to 17 destinations on the European mainland.

Fleet (orders):
1 x ATR 72-200
10 x BAE Systems ATP
1 x BAE Systems 146-100
1 x BAE Systems 146-300
12 x BAE Systems Jetstream 41
18 (5) x EMBRAER RJ-145ER

In August 1997, British Regional Airways became the first British operator of the EMBRAER RJ-145 regional transport, which has since become the numerical mainstay of this airline. The airline's parent group was floated on the stock market in June 1998.

BWIA WEST INDIES AIRWAYS (TRINIDAD AND TOBAGO)

Main base and hub: Port of Spain (Piarco International Airport)

Type of operation: International and regional scheduled passenger and cargo services

Personnel: 2,700

Fleet (orders):
6 x Boeing Model 737-500
5 x Boeing MD-83
(1) x Bombardier Dash 8-300
4 x Lockheed L-1011-500 TriStar

On 27 November 1939, Lowell Yerex, a New Zealander who had earlier established the Honduran airline Transportes Aéreos Centro-Americanos, formed British West Indian Airways. The new airline flew its first service, with a Lockheed L-18 Lodestar from Port of Spain in Trinidad via Tobago to Barbados on 26 November 1940. On 11 May 1943, the airline became a limited company and, on behalf of the British government, the British Overseas Airways Corporation took an interest in the airline. This took place within the context of World War II, and during this period, British West Indian Airways purchased additional Lockheed twin-engined aircraft for an expansion of its route network to the Leeward and Windward Islands in 1943, between Kingston and both St Kitts and Port of Spain in 1944, and between Port of Spain and Georgetown on 6 September of the same year.

Early in 1947, the government of Trinidad bought Yerex's 28 per cent interest in the airline, and at the same time British South American Airways acquired a 47 per cent shareholding, on 1 October purchasing the balance of the shares via its subsidiary British International Airlines, by which name British West Indian Airways was known up to 24 June 1948. On 30 July 1949, British South American Airways was amalgamated with the British Overseas Airways Corporation, which now assumed control of the West Indian operator. During this period, the airline's equipment comprised three types of twin-engined transport, namely the Lockheed Lodestar, Douglas DC-3 and Vickers Viking Mk IA; the first of an eventual eight of this last type was received on 20 July 1948, and the type remained in service up to 1950.

In October 1949, British West Indian Airways took over British Caribbean Airways, which brought with it services between Nassau in the Bahamas and two cities in Florida, namely Miami and Palm Beach. Further expansion followed late in 1952 when British South American Airways transferred to British West Indian Airways the international services of Bahamas Airways, which it had bought in August 1948, leaving Bahamas Airways as a domestic operator. In June 1953, British West Indian Airways contracted for four examples of the world's first turbine-engined airliner, the Vickers Viscount, in the form of the Viscount 702 variant, and took delivery of the first of these machines on 28 July 1955 for a service debut on the route between Trinidad and San Juan in Puerto Rico on 2 December 1955.

British West Indian Airways was the first Caribbean operator of a turboprop-powered type – the Viscount. On 29 April 1960, it started a transatlantic service, between Trinidad and London via Barbados and New York, with another turboprop-powered type, a Bristol Britannia 312 leased from the British Overseas Airways Corporation. In November 1961, the government of Trinidad and Tobago secured a 90 per cent holding in the company, and bought the remaining 10 per cent in 1967.

The airline sold its last Viscounts in 1965, when the operator launched its first service with a pure jet type, namely the Boeing

ABOVE: *Four L-1011-500 turbofan aircraft provide BWIA with its long-haul strength.*

Model 727-78, of which the first was received on 21 December 1964. On 15 December of the following year, British West Indian Airways started to operate another jet type in the form of a leased Boeing Model 720-048, and this was followed by Boeing Model 707 airliners during December 1968. British West Indian Airways eventually flew 13 examples of the Model 707, of which one made the operator's inaugural jet service to London in April 1974.

From 1976, the Model 727 was replaced by the McDonnell Douglas DC-9-51, the first of which was leased from Finnair and received on 24 July 1976. The Model 707 was finally replaced by the Lockheed L-1011-500 TriStar, the first of which was received on 28 January 1980 and still flies the airline's long-haul flights.

On 1 January 1980, Trinidad and Tobago (BWIA International) Airways was formed by the merger of BWIA with the other government-owned airline, Trinidad and Tobago Air Services. This merger allowed the combined airlines to fly scheduled passenger and cargo services from Piarco Airport (Port of Spain) to 11 points in the Caribbean as well as other services to Miami, New York, Toronto and London. The name was later changed to the current designation.

CANADA 3000 AIRLINES (CANADA)

Main base and hub: Toronto
Type of operation: International, regional and domestic scheduled and charter passenger and cargo
Personnel: 2,150
Created in April 1988 and starting services in December of the same year, Canada 3000 Airlines flies domestic services linking 13 destinations and also international services to 40 destinations in Australia, Europe and the USA.

In November 2001, Canada 3000 was Canada's second largest airline when it went out of business, a casualty of the

Fleet (orders):
(8) x Airbus A319-100
8 x Airbus A320-200
4 x Airbus A330-200
5 x Boeing Model 757-200

downturn in the world airline business since the September 2001 terrorist attacks on the USA.

CARGOLUX (LUXEMBOURG)

Main base and hub: Luxembourg
Type of operation: International scheduled and charter cargo
Personnel: 1,235
Cargolux was created in March 1970 and began operations in May of the same year, then rising to become the most important all-freight operator in Europe. The operator currently flies scheduled freight services to 45 destinations in nearly every part of the world.

Cargolux was the first operator of the Boeing Model 747-400F freighter, and in September 1997 Lufthansa, the second

Fleet (orders):
10 (2) x Boeing Model 747-400F

largest single shareholder, sold its 33.7 per cent holding to SAir Logistics of South Africa.

CATHAY PACIFIC AIRWAYS (CHINA)

Main base and hub: Hong Kong
Type of operation: International scheduled and charter cargo
Personnel: 13,160
Cathay Pacific Airways was established on 24 September 1946 to implement a freight service between Shanghai and Sydney. The airline received its first equipment, one Douglas DC-3 two-engined transport, late in the same month, and this machine was followed on 3 October by two more of the same type. In 1948, the John Swire organization took a majority shareholding in the operator, and since that time various Swire groups have held an interest in Cathay Pacific.

On 7 September 1949, the company took delivery of its first Douglas C-54 Skymaster four-engined transport, allowing it to

Fleet (orders):
14 (6) x Airbus A330-300
15 x Airbus A340-300
4 x Boeing Model 747-200F
19 x Boeing Model 747-400
3 (2) x Boeing Model 747-400F
5 x Boeing Model 777-200
7 x Boeing Model 777-300

expand its route network during the following five years to Calcutta, Saigon and Borneo. Cathay Pacific received its first pressurized aeroplane, a Douglas DC-6, on 1 December 1954, and on 9 June 1958 followed with its first new aeroplane, in the form of one DC-6B. Further commercial success and

79

expansion followed, and within 12 months, Cathay Pacific was able to take delivery of its first turbine-powered aircraft, one Lockheed L-188 Electra four-turboprop transport, on 1 April 195. Exactly a fortnight later, Cathay Pacific became the first airline in Asia to put this type into service. In 1959, Cathay Pacific merged with Hong Kong Airways, an associate of the British Overseas Airways Corporation flying Vickers Viscount airliners between Far Eastern destinations.

Technical competitiveness has always been important to Cathay Pacific, so in 1961 the airline ordered a single example of the Convair CV-880 four-jet transport, and this machine arrived on 20 February 1962 for a debut in revenue-earning service on the route linking Hong Kong and Tokyo via Manila on 8 April of the same year. During the 1960s, Cathay Pacific bought another eight examples of the CV-880, the last of them reaching the operator on 26 June 1970. Late in 1970, however, it was clear that Cathay Pacific's swelling level of success required greater payload capability, and the airline opted for the Boeing Model 707. Two such aircraft were bought from Northwest Orient Airlines, the first being received and entering service on 1 July and 3 August 1971 respectively. Cathay Pacific eventually acquired 12 Model 707 transports from Northwest Orient, the last arriving in August 1974, and the availability of this type allowed the retirement of the CV-880, which flew its last Cathay Pacific service on 15 September 1972.

Between 1971 and 1974, Cathay Pacific's rate of expansion continued, and this persuaded the airline to investigate the advantage of operating wide-body aircraft. During March 1974, therefore, Cathay Pacific placed an order for two examples of the Lockheed L-1011-1 TriStar three-turbofan; the airline took delivery of the first of these machines on 8 August 1975 and placed this machine in service on 16 September of the same year.

By the second half of the 1980s, Cathay Pacific was planning a westward expansion of its route network to points as far distant as London, and accordingly placed an order in October 1978 for the Boeing Model 747-267B with a powerplant of four Rolls-Royce RB.211 turbofans. The airline took delivery of the first of these machines on 20 July 1979, and operated its first service to London with this type on 17 July 1980. Eventually the airline operated a large fleet of such 'jumbo jets' on passenger and freight operations to a growing number of long-haul destinations. Further capability has been provided by the adoption of the Boeing Model 777 airliner and the A330 and A340 airliners produced in Europe by Airbus.

Cathay Pacific flies to 47 international destinations from its base at Hong Kong International Airport.

BELOW: *For its medium/long-haul services, Cathay Pacific has Airbus and Boeing aircraft.*

CHINA AIRLINES (TAIWAN)

Main base and hub: Taipei
Type of operation: International, regional and domestic scheduled passenger and cargo services
Personnel: 9,000

China Airlines is the national flag carrier of the Republic of China (Taiwan), and was established on 16 December 1959 by a number of retired Taiwanese air force personnel. The airline's first equipment was a pair of Consolidated PBY-5A Catalina amphibian flying boats, and these were initially operated on domestic charter services. The airline moved forward to scheduled domestic services during October 1962 with a

Fleet (orders):
12 x Airbus A300-600R
(7) x Airbus A340-300
9 (12) x Boeing Model 737-800
9 x Boeing Model 747-200F
12 x Boeing Model 747-400
5 (10) x Boeing Model 747-400F
2 x Boeing MD-11

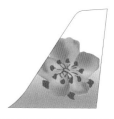

mixed fleet of Douglas DC-3 and DC-4 aircraft as well as a number of Curtiss C-46 Commando transports. In 1965, China Airlines became the national flag carrier of Taiwan.

ABOVE: *China Airlines is Western-oriented, and flies Airbus and Boeing aircraft.*

Late in 1969, China Airlines moved into the world of turbine-powered aircraft with the receipt of the first of two NAMC YS-11 twin-turboprop airliners, but before this, the airline had launched its first international service on 2 December 1966 with a Lockheed L-1049H Super Constellation on the route linking Taipei and Saigon. The L-1049H operated this service up to March 1976, when it was replaced by the airline's first Boeing Model 727-109 three-turbofan airliner. The L-1049H remained in service up to 1970, being used only for charter work within South-East Asia.

To allow expansion of its route network and payload capability, China Airlines placed an order for two examples of the Boeing Model 707-309C four-turbofan transport, and the first of these was received on 7 November 1969. In February 1970, the availability of this long-haul type allowed the inauguration of a new route to San Francisco via Tokyo, and intermediate halts at Los Angeles and Honolulu were later added.

From 1971 to 1977, China Airlines operated four examples of the Sud-Aviation Caravelle for domestic and charter work, but in 1976 these were replaced by three examples of the Boeing Model 737-281 twin-turbofan airliner, of which the first was received on 9 April 1976. At much the same time,

China Airlines was also improving its long-haul capability with the acceptance of the first Boeing Model 747 four-turbofan wide-body aircraft in the form of the Model 747-132 and Model 747SP, of which the first examples were delivered on 16 May 1975 and 6 April 1977 respectively.

In order to expand its position in the regional market, China Airlines has operated the Airbus A300 since 22 June 1982, while for the long-haul routes that do not require the capacity of the Model 747, two Boeing Model 767-209 twin-turbofan airliners were ordered; the first of these entered service between Taipei and Hong Kong on 30 December 1982. On this date, China Airlines became the first airline in Asia to operate the type and the first airline in the world to operate both the A300 and Model 767.

China Airlines currently operates a fleet of Airbus and Boeing aircraft. The most important change in recent years has been the adoption of the Model 737-800 version of the Model 737 twin-turbofan series in moderately large numbers for an improvement of the airline's short-haul capabilities.

CHINA EASTERN AIRLINES (CHINA)

Main bases and hubs: Shanghai (Hingqiao and Pudong)
Type of operation: International, regional and domestic scheduled and charter passenger and cargo
Personnel: 9,000
Established in June 1985, China Eastern Airlines had its origins in the Huadong Administration of the Civil Aviation Administration of China, and later took over China General Aviation. The airline is currently the second largest in China, and flies scheduled services linking 31 domestic destinations, as well as services to 21 international destinations.

China Eastern was the first Chinese airline to offer its shares on the international market, and in 1998 it joined forces

Fleet (orders):
10 x Airbus A300-600R
4 x Airbus A319-100
17 (2) x Airbus A320-200
5 x Airbus A340-300
(5) x Airbus
  A340-500/600
3 x Boeing MD-11
3 x Boeing MD-11F
3 x Boeing MD-82

9 x Boeing MD-90-30

with China Ocean Shipping to create China Cargo Airlines, the country's first all-freight airline.

CHINA NORTHERN AIRLINES (CHINA)

Main bases and hubs: Shenyang, Changchun, Dalian, Harbin and Sanya
Type of operation: International, regional and domestic scheduled and charter passenger
Personnel: 8,000

China Northern Airlines was established in 1990 as the successor to Swan Airlines, and currently flies scheduled services between 37 domestic destinations and also to six international destinations.

China Northern Airlines also operates charter services to

Fleet (orders):
4 x Airbus A300-600R
(10) x Airbus A321-200
17 x Boeing MD-82
10 x Boeing MD-90-30
10 x XAC Y7-100

destinations in Japan and Korea as well as several South-East Asian countries.

CHINA SOUTHERN AIRLINES (CHINA)

Main bases and hubs: Guangzhou (Baiyum), Zhengzhou, Changsha, Haikou, Guiyang, Guilin, Shenzen, Wuhan, Xiamen and Zhuhai
Type of operation: Regional and domestic scheduled and charter passenger
Personnel: not available

China Southern Airlines was established in 1991 and is currently the largest aviation undertaking in China. The operator flies scheduled services between 64 Chinese destinations, and also to 19 international destinations.

Fleet (orders)
20 x Airbus A320-200
19 x Boeing Model 737-300
9 x Boeing Model 737-500
18 x Boeing Model 757-200
4 x Boeing Model 777-200
5 x Boeing Model 777-200ER

In terms of numbers, China Southern Airlines carries 25 per cent of all Chinese passengers.

COMAIR (SOUTH AFRICA)

Main base and hub: Johannesburg
Type of operation: International, regional and domestic scheduled passenger and cargo
Personnel: 360

Created in July 1946 by a quartet of ex-South African Air Force officers, Commercial Air Services Pty Ltd began domestic services in 1948. Thereafter the operator grew slowly, but in 1996 it became a franchisee of British Airways.

Comair currently operates a schedule of approximately 420 flights per week linking four destinations within South Africa,

Fleet (orders):
6 x Boeing Advanced Model
  727-200
3 x Boeing Model 737-200
7 x Boeing Advanced Model
  737-200

as well as six international destinations in the southern half of Africa.

CONDOR (GERMANY)

Main bases and hubs: Frankfurt, Düsseldorf, Munich and Stuttgart
Type of operation: International scheduled and charter passenger and cargo
Personnel: 2,700

Founded in December 1955 for a start to operations in March of the following gear, Deutsche Flugdienst was created to provide charter air services for the rapidly developing German market for holidays in the Mediterranean region. This market underwent a downturn in the later part of the decade, and Deutsche Flugdienst was taken over by Lufthansa during 1960. The operator's name was changed to Condor in October 1961,

Fleet (orders):
14 x Boeing Model 757-200
13 x Boeing Model 757-300
9 x Boeing Model 767-300ER

and in October 1992 the company, now the largest tour operator in Germany, absorbed Sudflug. Condor now flies services to Asia, Africa and the Americas as well as to the Mediterranean.

CONTINENTAL AIRLINES
(UNITED STATES OF AMERICA)

Main bases and hubs: Cleveland, Denver, Guam, Honolulu, Houston and Newark
Type of operation: International, regional and domestic scheduled passenger services
Personnel: not available

Continental Airlines can trace its history back to 6 April 1926, when Varney Speed Lines (South West Division) started life with contracts to carry air mail for the US Post Office. Varney Air Lines was taken over by United Air Lines on 30 June 1930, but in 1934 this operation again became a separate entity as Varney Air Transport, which on 15 July of that year began passenger and air mail services on the route linking El Paso with Albuquerque and Pueblo using three examples of the Lockheed Vega high-wing transport. In 1936, Varney Air Transport bought the route between Pueblo and Denver from Wyoming Air Service, and with this expansion of its route network moved base from El Paso to Denver, where it changed its name to Continental Airlines on 1 July 1937.

During World War II, Continental Airlines was one of the many operators that carried out military transport and training duties for the US Army Air Forces, but it reverted to civil operations in 1945 and in 1948 was sufficiently well re-established to buy the latest short-haul equipment in the form of the Convair CV-240. At the end of 1954, Continental Airlines bought Pioneer Airlines and its extensive route network in Texas and New Mexico. On 1 May 1957, Continental Airlines started a service on the route linking Chicago and Los Angeles via Kansas City and Denver; flown with Douglas DC-7B four-engined airliners, this operation marked Continental Airlines' emergence as a main-line trunk carrier within the USA. Continental Airlines started to use the Vickers Viscount 812 four-turboprop airliner on the Chicago

Fleet (orders):
65 x Boeing Model 737-300
66 x Boeing Model 737-500
36 x Boeing Model 737-700
53 (24) x Boeing Model 737-800
(15) x Boeing Model 737-900
41 x Boeing Model 757-200
(15) x Boeing 757-300
5 (5) x Boeing Model 767-200ER
4 x Boeing Model 767-300ER
(10) x Boeing 767-400ER
16 (2) x Boeing Model 777-200ER

4 x Boeing MD-81
52 x McDonnell Douglas MD-82
6 x McDonnell Douglas MD-83
17 x McDonnell Douglas DC-10-30

to Los Angeles service on 26 May 1958, thereby moving into the field of turbine-powered civil aircraft, and went one step further on 8 June 1959 when it started to operate the Boeing Model 707-124 turbojet-powered airliner.

In 1963, Continental Airlines again moved its main base, this time to Los Angeles, and by 1969 had further enlarged its route network to the west by the inclusion of destinations such as the Hawaiian Islands, which was served from Chicago in an operation inaugurated on 9 September 1969. On 18 May 1970, Continental Airlines received its first Boeing Model 747 wide-body transport with a powerplant of four turbofans, and the availability of this high-capacity type did much to speed the growth of the airline even though the Model 747 was later supplemented and then put partially in the shade by the introduction of a larger number of a three-turbofan type, the McDonnell Douglas DC-10 series. Continental Airlines started an expansion to the east in the course of 1974 with services

BELOW: *Continental Airlines operates a very large fleet of what are now all Boeing aircraft.*

83

to destinations such as Miami, followed later by Newark and Washington, DC.

During October 1981, the Texas Air Corporation, parent of Texas International Airlines, bought a controlling interest in Continental Airlines; Texas International Airlines, known until 1969 as Trans-Texas Airways and originally created in 1940 as Aviation Enterprises, had begun scheduled services in October 1947. The operations of Continental Airlines and Texas International Airlines were consolidated and combined from 31 October 1982 to create a single carrier under the name Continental. This was not a good time for airlines, however, as the price of fuel was increasing rapidly and passenger demand was declining as operators were forced to raise their fares, and as a result, Continental was compelled to file for Chapter 11 protection against its creditors in the course of September 1983. Continental's domestic network was reduced from 78 to 25 destinations and its personnel strength declined from 12,000 to 4,200. Following approval by the US bankruptcy court of its plan for reorganization, submitted in September 1985, Continental emerged from Chapter 11 protection during 1986 to operate a network serving 57 domestic destinations from primary hubs at Denver and Houston, and 28 international

destinations in Australasia, Canada, Europe, the Far East and Mexico. In the same year, Continental was integrating the services of New York Air and the People Express Group into its own operation after the purchases of these airlines during February.

Frank Lorenzo, Continental's owner, sold his share in the airline to SAS in August 1990, and Continental once again filed for Chapter 11 protection during December 1990. The airline emerged from a 29-month Chapter 11 reorganization in May 1993 after Air Canada and Texas-based Air Partners had received the approval of the bankruptcy court to invest $450 million. Shortly before this, in March 1993, Continental was a major operator of the Boeing Models 727, 737 and 757 as well as the McDonnell Douglas MD-80 series, but had cancelled firm orders for 20 Airbus A330 and A340 aircraft together with options for 18 more machines of the same types. Shortly after emerging from Chapter 11 protection, however, the airline placed orders for large numbers of modern aircraft.

Like most North American and European operators, Continental Airlines has been badly affected by the airline slump following the September 2001 terrorist attacks on the USA, and is seeking to trim costs.

CONTINENTAL EXPRESS (UNITED STATES OF AMERICA)

Main bases and hubs: Cleveland, Houston and Newark
Type of operation: International, regional and domestic scheduled passenger
Personnel: 4,700
Vercoa Air Service was founded in 1956 and was later renamed Britt Airways before becoming Continental Express in January 1989. This operator later became a wholly owned subsidiary of Continental Airlines, for which it flies feeder-line services. Continental Express currently flies more than 1,000 services per day to more than 100 American destinations from its three hubs. Continental Express also flies scheduled

Fleet (orders):
31 x ATR 42-300
19 x EMBRAER EMB-120 Brasilia
15 (27) x EMBRAER RJ-135ER
8 x EMBRAER RJ-135LR
23 x EMBRAER RJ-145ER
95 (6) x EMBRAER RJ-145LR
75 x EMBRAER RJ-145XR
9 x Raytheon Beech Model
   1900D Airliner

services to five Canadian destinations as well as 11 other destinations in Central America.

CROSSAIR (SWITZERLAND)

Main bases and hubs: Basle, Berne, Geneva, Lugano and Zurich
Type of operation: International, regional and domestic scheduled and charter passenger and cargo
Personnel: 2,945
Established in 1975 and beginning operations in February of the same year, Business Flyers Basel was originally concerned only with charter air operations for business customers. The operator changed its name to Crossair in November 1978 and began to fly scheduled air services in July of the following year. In November 1995, Crossair began to undertake charter services on behalf of Swissair, which is Crossair's majority shareholder. Crossair is currently the second largest regional

Fleet (orders):
(8) x Airbus A320-200
4 x BAE Systems Avro RJ-85
16 x BAE Systems Avro RJ-100
11 x Boeing MD-83
11 (14) x EMBRAER RJ-145LR
(30) x EMBRAER RJ-170
(30) x EMBRAER RJ-190-200
34 Saab 2000
6 x Saab 340B

airline in Europe, and serves more than 30 destinations in Europe, the Middle East and North Africa with charter and scheduled services.

CSA CZECH AIRLINES (CZECH REPUBLIC)

Main base and hub: Prague
Type of operation: International, regional and domestic scheduled passenger
Personnel: 3,875

Fleet (orders):
2 x Airbus A310-300
3 x ATR 42-300
2 x ATR 42-400
4 x ATR 72-200
9 x Boeing Model 737-400
10 Boeing Model 737-500

The operator now known as CSA Czech Airlines came into its current existence on 26 March 1995 as a redesignation of Ceskoslovenské Státní Aerolinie (CSA), which had been established as the Czechoslovak national flag carrier on 28 July 1923. CSA flew its first service on 28 October between Prague and Uzhorod using initially the Aero A.14, but later equipment included the De Havilland D.H.50 and Farman Goliath, purchased from the UK and France respectively. In 1930, CSA started its first international service, in this instance to Zagreb in Yugoslavia, and the international route network was slowly expanded to destinations in Austria, Romania and the USSR. During the 1930s, CSA purchased the Savoia-Marchetti SM.73 from Italy, and four Airspeed Envoy and one Saro Cloud from the UK.

From 15 March 1939, the operations of the CSA and Ceskoslovenská Letecká Spolecnost (CLS) nationalized and private airlines were integrated into those of Deutsche Lufthansa after Germany's annexation of Czechoslovakia, and after the end of World War II CSA reverted to state-owned status, resuming operations on 1 March 1946 with Douglas C-47 and Junkers Ju 52/3m services to a number of European capitals. By the end of 1947, CSA was flying to most European capitals, and was planning larger-scale operations including transatlantic services with the Douglas DC-4. These plans were completely revised after the communist assumption of power in Czechoslovakia during 1948, which led to the adoption of Soviet operating practice.

This meant the effective end of purchases from Western sources in those early days of the Cold War, and CSA had therefore to turn to Soviet sources of supply. Early in 1949, CSA bought the first two of an eventual eight Ilyushin Il-12 twin-engined transports which proved to be very limited in capability. It was only in the mid-1950s that the airline was able to begin any real expansion by the purchase of the Ilyushin Il-14 twin-engined airliner, which was built under licence in Czechoslovakia. A major milestone in the airline's development took place in 1957, when CSA became the first foreign company to operate the twin-jet Tupolev Tu-104A, which entered service at first on CSA's services to Brussels, Moscow and Paris, and on 1 April 1960 succeeded the Il-14 on the service linking Prague and London.

Early in the same year, CSA was finally able to begin the process of retiring its wholly obsolete Il-12 piston-engined aircraft in favour of the larger and more capable Ilyushin Il-18 four-turboprop type. Services to Bombay, Dakar and Djakarta were inaugurated, and discussion was started with the Canadian authorities about the possibility of a service to Montreal via Amsterdam. Thus by 1960, CSA was approaching the stage of becoming the communist world's first airline with a world-wide network.

On 3 February 1962, CSA launched a service to Havana, Cuba, with a leased Bristol Britannia 318. In May 1968, it acquired additional capability by leasing an Ilyushin Il-62 four-turbofan airliner from Aeroflot, a type which CSA later bought. On 4 May 1970, CSA started its first service between Prague and New York via Amsterdam and Montreal, with the Il-62.

BELOW: *CSA has turned its back on Soviet equipment and now flies Western aircraft.*

By the late 1970s, CSA was operating an extensive network of routes between Prague and most European capitals as well as destinations in the Middle and Far East, West Africa, and North and Central America, using the Il-62 for longer-haul services and the Il-18 and Tupolev Tu-134 for shorter-haul services. The airline also flew a domestic network with types such as the Let L-410 Turbolet and Yakovlev transports, including the Yakovlev Yak-40.

With the collapse of the Soviet bloc in the late 1980s, CSA was finally able to start the process of discarding its Soviet-supplied aircraft, which were unreliable and costly to operate, and acquiring more modern aircraft of Western origin.

CUBANA (CUBA)

Main base and hub: Havana
Type of operation: International, regional and domestic scheduled and charter passenger and cargo
Personnel: not available
The national airline of Cuba, Cubana was established in October 1929 as the Compañía Cubana de Aviación Curtiss, becoming the Compañía Nacional de Aviación Cubana after its take-over by Pam-American in 1932. In 1944, the organization became the Compañía Cubana de Aviación, and in 1946 Cubana recorded its first international service to the USA. The

BELOW: *Lack of resources means that Cubana still flies obsolescent Soviet airliners.*

Fleet (orders):
7 x Antonov An-24RV
1 x Antonov An-26
1 x Antonov An-26B
1 x Boeing Model 737-400
5 x Fokker F.27 Friendship Mk 600
7 x Ilyushin Il-62M
2 x Ilyushin Il-76M
2 x Tupolev Tu-154B
3 x Yakovlev Yak-40   2 x Yakovlev Yak-42

airline was nationalized in 1959 after the Cuban rRevolution, and now flies a wide range of services inside Cuba and to a large number of international destinations.

CYPRUS AIRWAYS (CYPRUS)

Main bases and hubs: Larnaca and Paphos
Type of operation: International, regional and domestic scheduled and charter passenger and cargo
Personnel: 1,770
Cyprus Airways was established at Nicosia in 1947 as a joint venture between the government of Cyprus, British European Airways and a number of private individuals. Much of the airline's aircraft and infrastructure was lost in the de facto partition of the island in July 1974, but the company re-established itself at Larnaca and resumed operations in February 1975. The airline

Fleet (orders):
4 x Airbus A310-200
(2) x Airbus A319-100
5 x Airbus A320-200
(2) x airbus A330-200

has a domestic network based on only two destinations, but a larger regional and international network.

DELTA AIR LINES
(UNITED STATES OF AMERICA)

Main bases and hubs: Atlanta, Cincinnati, Dallas/Fort Worth, Frankfurt, Los Angeles, New York, Orlando and Salt Lake City
Type of operation: International, regional and domestic scheduled passenger
Personnel: 72,000

In 1925, C. E. Woolman created Delta Air Services as the world's first commercial crop-dusting company. On 16 June 1929, the company began passenger operations between Atlanta and Birmingham in the American states of Georgia and Alabama respectively, and shortly after this extended the service to Salas in Texas via Jackson, Mississippi. However, passenger services were suspended on 16 September 1930 when Delta did not obtain any of the new airmail contracts that would have provided a measure of the subsidization that was required during the Depression. The successful applicant for the air mail contract was American Airlines, which added some of Delta's routes into its own network.

The airline introduced its current name, Delta Air Lines, during 1934, and in the same year received its first airmail contract for the route linking Charleston and Fort Worth, in South Carolina and Texas respectively, using Travel Air aircraft. In November 1940, Delta Air Lines received its first Douglas DC-3, and by 1942 was flying five DC-3 and four Lockheed L-10A Electra aircraft for services on a network that included Cincinnati, Savannah and New Orleans.

In December 1941, Delta Air Lines had transferred two-thirds of its fleet to aid in the American war effort after the USA entered the war during that month. During February 1942, Delta Air Lines created a modification centre at its Atlanta base, and here 1,000 aircraft were processed. Emergency work on 45 Boeing B-29 Superfortress bombers was also undertaken in 1945.

Returning largely to civil operations as the end of World War II approached, Delta Air Lines was granted the prime service

Fleet (orders):
76 x Boeing Advanced Model 727-200
54 x Boeing Advanced Model 737-200
26 x Boeing Model 737-300
43 (89) x Boeing Model 737-800
118 x Boeing Model 757-200
15 (3) x Boeing Model 767-200
28 x Boeing Model 767-300
57 (1) x Boeing Model 767-300ER
15 (6) x Boeing Model 767-400ER
7 (6) x Boeing Model 777-200ER
15 x Boeing MD-11

120 x Boeing MD-88
16 x Boeing MD-90-30
5 x Lockheed L-1011 TriStar
5 x Lockheed L-1011-250 TriStar
5 x Lockheed L-1011-500 TriStar

between Chicago and Miami during July 1945, and operated this service on a four-times-per-day basis from 1 December 1945 with DC-3 aircraft that flew a route with many intermediate stops for the loading and offloading of passengers. The airline inaugurated a non-stop service during November 1946 using Douglas DC-4 four-engined aircraft, the first of which the airline received on 14 December 1945. Just under three years later, on 5 November 1948, Delta Air Lines accepted the first of an initial three Douglas DC-6 aircraft, and the DC-6 replaced the DC-4 on the Miami route during December of the same year. The DC-6 was replaced by the much superior and fully pressurized Douglas DC-7 on 1 April 1954.

On its shorter-haul services, Delta Air Lines used 20 Convair CV-340, of which the first was delivered on 18 December 1952. Chicago and Southern Air Lines merged with Delta Air Lines on 1 May 1953, and this amalgamation brought many new routes (including international services) and aircraft, the latter including eight undelivered CV-40 and six Lockheed L-649A

BELOW: *Delta Air Lines' substantial fleet comprises Boeing aircraft almost exclusively.*

Constellation aircraft ordered by Chicago and Southern Air Lines. Eventually Delta Air Lines operated 38 of the Convair aircraft, all of which were later upgraded to CV-440 standard. On 1 February 1956, the airline started services to New York and Washington, DC using four Lockheed L-049 Constellations bought from Pan American World Airways.

By the autumn of 1958, the airline's fleet numbered 77 aircraft including 28, 21 and 12 examples of the CV-440, DC-7 and DC-3 respectively. A year later, on 18 September 1959, Delta Air Lines operated its first jet service, from New York to Atlanta, with a Douglas DC-8-11, having received the first of these on 21 July 1959. On 15 May 1960, it flew its first service with another four-engined jet airliner, the Convair CV-880.

Soon after this, it became clear that a modern replacement was needed for the CV-440, and in April 1963, Delta Air Lines contracted for the delivery of an initial 14 examples of the Douglas DC-9-14 twin-jet type. The first of these was delivered on 9 June 1966, and Delta Air Lines was the first airline to operate the DC-9 on a revenue-earning basis when the type entered service on 8 December of the same year.

By 1969, the airline had become an all-jet operator, its fleet comprising 129 aircraft in the form of 68 Douglas DC-9, 45 DC-8 and 16 CV-880 aircraft. Further development of the airline's route network and equipment followed, a notable landmark being the arrival of Delta Air Lines' first wide-body airliner, a Boeing Model 747-132, on 26 September 1970; this flew its first commercial flight on 25 October 1970. On 10 October 1972, Delta Air Lines leased its first McDonnell Douglas DC-10-10 three-turbofan airliner from United Airlines.

On 1 August 1972, Northeast Airlines and Delta Air Lines merged, the former contributing a number of Fairchild FH-227 twin-turboprop and Boeing Model 727 three-turbofan transports to the combined airlines' aircraft fleet, together with many east coast destinations and services to the Bahamas and Bermuda. Delta Air Lines now provided services to 99 cities.

The DC-10 did not last long in service with Delta Air Lines, for the type was replaced by the Lockheed L-1011 TriStar, of which the airline received an initial example on 3 October 1973 for service from 16 November of the same year. Thus in a period of only three years, Delta Air Lines operated all three of the USA's first wide-body airliners.

On 1 May 1978, Delta Air Lines launched a new service to London from New Orleans and Atlanta with two examples of the L-1011-200 TriStar leased from TWA. Through the 1980s, further expansion and re-equipment followed as Delta Air Lines took over Western Airlines in April 1987 and standardized on a combination of the Boeing Model 737 and McDonnell Douglas MD-80/90 series for its short-haul and/or low-density routes, the Boeing Model 727 for medium-haul routes, and a combination of the Boeing Models 757 and 767, the L-1011 TriStar and the McDonnell Douglas (now Boeing) MD-11 for long-haul routes, depending on density.

DHL AIRWAYS
(UNITED STATES OF AMERICA)

Main bases and hubs: five hubs and seven gateways
Type of operation: International, regional and domestic scheduled and charter passenger and cargo
Personnel: not available

DHL Airways came into existence in California during 1969 and started operating in the same year, initially on a small-scale basis for the charter delivery of high-priority documents and packages. The operator grew steadily, and now uses its own aircraft as well as the services of other airlines to undertake services to about 225 countries.

Fleet (orders):
1 x Airbus A300B4-100
5 x Airbus A300F4-200
10 x Boeing Model 727-100F
11 x Boeing Model 727-200F
7 x McDonnell Douglas DC-8-70

BELOW: *As a package delivery specialist, DHL flies freighter versions of several standard types of jet-powered airliner.*

DRAGONAIR (CHINA)

Main base and hub: Hong Kong
Type of operation: International and regional scheduled and charter passenger and cargo
Personnel: 1,175
Coming into existence during 1985, with establishment in May and the start of operations in the following month, Dragonair expanded rapidly in the East Asian market and currently operates passenger services to 27 destinations in Asia and the Pacific, and freight services between Europe, the Middle East and Asia.
 Dragonair is now owned mainly by Chinese interests, of which the largest is China National Aviation Co.

Fleet (orders):
6 (6) x Airbus A320-200
3 (1) x Airbus A321-200
5 (3) x Airbus A330-300
1 x Boeing Model 747-400F

BELOW: *During the 1990s, Dragonair modernized its fleet through the addition of several Airbus types. It is a major force in Far East civil aviation.*

EASYJET (UNITED KINGDOM)

Main bases and hubs: London (Luton) and Liverpool
Type of operation: International, regional and domestic scheduled passenger
Personnel: not available
Created by the Haji-Ioannou family in October 1995 to start operations in November of the same year, easyJet is a pioneer of the low-cost and therefore no-frills type of air service in Europe. The airline currently operates services between seven British and nine European destinations. In common with other low-cost airlines, easyJet has not been badly affected by the

Fleet (orders):
14 x Boeing Model 737-300
3 (29) x Boeing Model 737-700

overall airline slump that followed the September 2001 terrorist attacks on the USA.

EGYPTAIR (EGYPT)

Main base and hub: Cairo International Airport
Type of operation: International, regional and domestic scheduled and charter passenger and cargo services
Personnel: 18,000
It is possible to trace the history of Egyptair back to May 1932, when Misr Airwork was established as a joint undertaking by the Misr Bank of Egypt and Airwork Ltd of the UK. The airline flew its first services in July of the same year, the first route operating between Cairo and Mersa Matruh via Alexandria with De Havilland D.H.84 Dragon aircraft, and by the end of the

Fleet (orders):
7 x Airbus A300-600R
2 x Airbus A300F4-200
(5) x Airbus A318
7 x Airbus A320-200
4 x Airbus A321-200
4 x Airbus A340-200
(2) x Airbus A340-600
1 x Boeing Model 707-320C
1 x Boeing Advanced Model 737-200
4 x Boeing Model 737-500

2 x Boeing Model 747-300 Combi
1 x Boeing Model 767-300ER
3 x Boeing Model 777-200ER

year, further destinations had been added in the forms of Aswan, Asyut and Luxor. The airline started international services, to Lydda and Haifa in Palestine, during 1934 and added Baghdad in 1936. On charter services, the airline initially flew the De Havilland D.H.83 Fox Moth. By 1937, traffic had expanded and Misr Airwork was now operating five examples of the De Havilland D.H.89 Rapide and two examples of the De Havilland D.H.86 Express as well as two examples of the D.H.84 Dragon, and by 1939 the operator's international network from Cairo connected Baghdad, Cyprus, Haifa, Istanbul, Jeddah, Khartoum and Tehran.

During World War II, Misr Airwork was taken over by the Egyptian government, which retained the civil operator's basic route network and increased capacity on some routes by a considerable degree. A new service to Beirut via Palestine was inaugurated during this period.

After the end of World War II, passenger traffic increased steadily and, lacking the aircraft to cope with this increased demand, Misr Airwork suspended operations from 6 April 1946 until a resumption was made possible by the arrival of more modern equipment in the forms of Beech Model 18 twin-engined light transports and Vickers Viking twin-engined medium transport; the first two Vikings were delivered on 1 November 1948. In 1949, Airwork sold its interest in the airline and the company was renamed Misrair.

During the 1950s, the airline introduced the Douglas DC-3 as its standard type, but in March 1954 decided to advance into the turbine-powered age with an order for three examples of the Vickers Viscount 739. The first of these arrived on 23 November 1955 and Misr flew its first Viscount service on 16 March 1956.

Five years later, Misr moved into the era of pure jet propulsion with the receipt of its first de Havilland Comet 4C on 10 June 1960 for a service debut on 16 July of the same year.

On 23 December 1960 Misrair amalgamated with Syrian Airways to form United Arab Airlines. It was planned that other Arab airlines of the Middle East should subsequently become part of this alliance, but the instability of regional politics prevented this from happening. The Syrian element withdrew

from United Arab Airlines in the course of 1961, so the operator became wholly Egyptian once more. Another aircraft type received in this year was the Douglas DC-6B, of which three were delivered.

During 1964, United Arab Airlines expanded, with the re-establishment of Misrair as its domestic and regional element. By this time, Egypt had become closely connected with the USSR, and this fact was reflected in the adoption of a Soviet type, the Antonov An-24 twin-turboprop airliner, of which seven were received, to complement seven DC-6B heavier transports. During the 1960s and early 1970s, the airline had several Soviet types in its fleet, namely the Ilyushin Il-18D between 1968 and 1975, the Ilyushin Il-62, leased in 1971, and the Tupolev Tu-154 between 2 December 1973 and 1975. United Arab Airlines received its first Boeing Model 707-366C on 18 September 1968, and on 10 October 1971 changed its name to EgyptAir, and then to Egyptair on 10 October 1974.

With the bitter end to the Egyptian and Soviet relationship in the mid-1970s, followed by the return of Egyptair's Soviet aircraft, the airline had to acquire new aircraft and opted for the Boeing Model 737 to meet its short-haul requirements and the Airbus A300 for its medium-haul routes. Egyptair had to wait for the delivery of its own aircraft, and in the interim operated Model 737 aircraft leased from Aer Lingus and Transavia from October 1975, and A300 aircraft leased from TEA of Belgium from April 1977.

Egyptair currently operates Airbus and Boeing aircraft to the exclusion of all other types, and has considerably expanded its domestic, regional and international capabilities.

Egyptair flies to international destinations, including major Muslim centres, as well as Amsterdam, Athens, Bangkok, Barcelona, Berlin, Brussels, Budapest, Cape Town, Copenhagen, Düsseldorf, Frankfurt, Geneva, Hamburg, Istanbul, Johannesburg, Larnaca, Los Angeles, Lisbon, London, Lagos, Madrid, Manchester, Manila, Marseille, Milan, Moscow, Munich, Nairobi, Montreal, New York, Osaka, Paris, Rome, Singapore, Stockholm, Sydney, Tokyo, Vienna and Zurich.

EL AL (ISRAEL)

Main base and hub: Tel Aviv
Type of operation: International, regional scheduled and charter passenger and cargo services
Personnel: not available

El Al was created on 11 November 1948 with equipment comprising one Douglas DC-4 and two Curtiss C-46 Commando transports transferred from this Israeli airline's predecessor, the Israeli Air Transport Command (LATA). Israel's national flag carrier, El Al was formed initially to replace the domestic carrier Aviron and also to operate flights that were difficult for the Israeli Air Force to carry out. The new operator's first service, undertaken on 31 July 1949, was a flight linking Tel Aviv and Paris.

Fleet (orders):
2 x Boeing Model 737-700
3 x Boeing Model 737-800
3 x Boeing Model 747-200B
1 x Boeing Model 747-200C
2 x Boeing Model 747-200F
4 x Boeing Model 747-400
7 x Boeing Model 757-200
2 x Boeing Model 767-200
4 x Boeing Model 767-200ER   2 (1) x Boeing Model 777-200ER

El Al bought three examples of the Lockheed L-049 Constellation four-engined airliner in June 1950. These machines reached Israel during May 1951 and entered service between Israel and New York, via Athens or Rome and London, on 16 May of the same year. In addition to its services to European destinations and New York, El Al established a route to South Africa on 1 October 1953, and for a short time in 1955–56, this service to Johannesburg was operated by leased Douglas DC-6B aircraft.

The only turboprop airliner flown by El Al was the Bristol Britannia 313, of which the operator received just two examples from 12 September 1957 for service on the route to New York from 22 December 1957 of the same year. Further modernization to the airline's fleet took place in December 1960, when El Al leased one Boeing Model 707-441 from the Brazilian operator VARIG for its transatlantic service, which was soon entrusted to the Israeli operator's own Model 707 aircraft, of which the first was received on 22 April 1961. By the end of 1961, El Al had retired all its Constellation aircraft, leaving it with Britannia and Model 707 aircraft. El Al kept the Britannia in service up to the mid-1960s, since when the operator has flown only Boeing aircraft, initially in the forms of the Model 707 and Model 720.

On 26 May 1971, El Al took delivery of its first wide-body transport in the form of an initial Boeing Model 747-258B, and since this time, the Model 747 has been the mainstay of El Al's commercial operation for high-density passenger, freight and combined passenger/freight services. These 'jumbo jets' have been complemented more recently by the Boeing Model 757 and Model 767, of which the first example was delivered on 12 July 1983, for additional capability on medium-density routes. On its European and Middle Eastern routes, El Al flies the Boeing Model 737; the airline initially leased two Model 737-2M8 aircraft from Trans European Airlines from 1 November 1980, but then received the first of its own two Model 737-258 aircraft in 1982.

El Al's scheduled international destinations include numerous African, Asian, Chinese, European, Far Eastern, Middle Eastern and North American cities, as well as a surprisingly large number of cities in the republics of the former USSR. The airline also links three Israeli destinations with scheduled services.

BELOW: *After considering Airbus machines, El Al has remained faithful to Boeing.*

EMERY WORLDWIDE
(UNITED STATES OF AMERICA)

Main bases and hubs: Daytona Beach, Atlantic City, Brussels, Charlotte, Dallas/Forth Worth, Los Angeles, Nashville, Orlando, Poughkeepsie and Sacramento
Type of operation: International, regional and domestic scheduled and charter cargo
Personnel: 1,185
Created in 1946 as Emery Air Freight, it initially handled air freight and did not embark on its own air services until 1980, and then rose to become one of the most important air freight operators in the USA. In April 1989, Consolidated Freightways bought the company, and in the following month amalgamated

Fleet (orders):
3 x Boeing Model 727-200F
1 x Boeing Model MD-11 Freighter
5 x McDonnell Douglas DC-10-10F
3 x McDonnell Douglas DC-10-30F
7 x McDonnell Douglas DC-8-60
26 x McDonnell Douglas DC-8-70

it with CF Airfreight to create the current Emery Worldwide. The company operates to a very large number of destinations in some 230 countries across the world, and also flies a major network covering the continental USA.

91

EMIRATES AIRLINE
(UNITED ARAB EMIRATES)

Main base and hub: Dubai
Type of operation: International, regional and domestic scheduled passenger services
Personnel: 6,525

Emirates Airline was established in 1985 as the national flag carrier of the United Arab Emirates, and started services with two Boeing Model 727-200 three-turbofan aircraft (sold to Qatar Airways early in 1995) for its domestic and regional services, and Airbus aircraft for its longer-haul routes, which are being substantially enlarged in capacity and extended by the delivery of

Fleet (orders):
2 x Airbus A300-600R
5 x Airbus A310-300
15 (6) x Airbus A330-200
(6) x Airbus A340-500
(5) x Airbus A380-800
(2) x Airbus A380-800F
1 x Boeing Model 747-400F
3 x Boeing Model 777-200
6 x Boeing Model 777-200ER

3 (1) x Boeing Model 777-300

further Airbus transports as well as Boeing Model 777s.

ETHIOPIAN AIRLINES (ETHIOPIA)

Main base and hub: Addis Ababa
Type of operation: International, regional and domestic scheduled and charter passenger and cargo
Personnel: 3,650

Ethiopian Airlines is the national airline of Ethiopia, and one of the oldest airlines in Africa. This operator was established in 1945 and began operations in April of the following year. Ethiopian Airlines has been much hindered in its developments by the conflicts that have raged over much of this region of Africa during recent decades, and now operates services to 31 domestic destinations as well as to 45 international destinations in Africa, Europe, the Middle East, the Far East and the USA.

Fleet (orders):
2 x Boeing Advanced Model 737-200
4 x Boeing Model 757-200
1 x Boeing Model 757-200PF
2 x Boeing Model 767-200ER
2 x Boeing Model 767-300ER
5 x Fokker 50HP
2 x Lockheed Martin L-100-30 Hercules
4 x De Havilland Canada DHC-6 Twin Otter Series 300

BELOW: *Ethiopian uses mainly Boeing aircraft.*

EVA AIR (TAIWAN)

Main base and hub: Taipei
Type of operation: International, regional and domestic scheduled and charter passenger and cargo services
Personnel: not available

EVA Air was established in March 1989 as Taiwan's first privately owned international air operator, and began operations in 1991. Since that time, the airline has grown both rapidly and extensively, and now has a route network reaching key points in Asia, Australasia, Europe and the USA, with further expansion planned as the international market for air freight continues to grow.

Fleet (orders):
5 x Boeing Model 747-400
10 x Boeing Model 747-400 Combi
1 (2) x Boeing Model 747-400F
4 x Boeing Model 767-200
4 x Boeing Model 767-300ER
4 x (3) x Boeing Model 777-200LR
(4) x Boeing Model 777-300ER
3 x Boeing MD-11

9 x Boeing MD-11 Freighter

RIGHT: *The Model 747 is EVA Air's main type.*

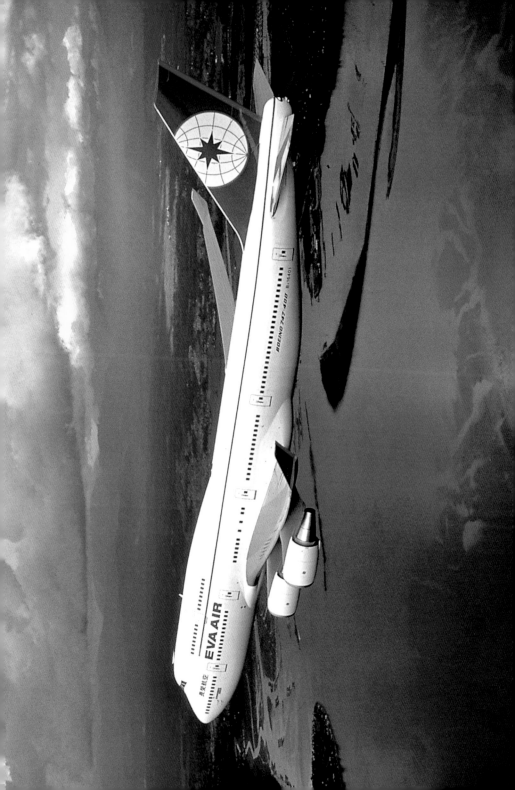

EVERGREEN INTERNATIONAL AIRLINES (UNITED STATES OF AMERICA)

Main bases and hubs: New York (John F. Kennedy), Columbus and Hong Kong
Type of operation: International, regional and domestic scheduled and charter cargo
Personnel: 550

The operator now known as Evergreen International Airlines came into existence in 1960 when Evergreen Helicopters Inc. bought the operating certificate of Johnson Flying Service. Evergreen now undertakes all types of air freight work, including operations on behalf of the US armed forces and also the US Postal Service, and ranges over much of the USA as well as the financially and industrially more important cities of the countries round the Pacific Rim.

Fleet (orders):
6 x Boeing Model 747-100F
2 x Boeing Model 747-200C
2 x Boeing Model 747-200F
2 x McDonnell Douglas DC-9-10
5 x McDonnell Douglas DC-9-30

EXPRESS AIRLINES I (UNITED STATES OF AMERICA)

Main base and hub: Memphis
Type of operation: International, regional and domestic scheduled passenger
Personnel: not available

Created and starting operations in 1985, during February and June respectively, Express Airlines I was established in Memphis to operate feeder-line services largely for Republic Airlines, a regional operator whose aircraft could not operate into and out of the smallest airports. In 1986, Northwest Airlines bought Republic Airlines, and Express therefore started to operate to and from Minneapolis/St Paul as well as Memphis. During 1997, the airline became a wholly owned subsidiary of Northwest Airlines, for which it operates regional and feeder-line services to a large number of American destinations as well as Monterrey in Mexico.

Fleet (orders):
13 (30) x Bombardier CRJ-200LR
19 x Saab 340A
11 x Saab 340B

FEDEX (UNITED STATES OF AMERICA)

Main bases and hubs: Memphis, Brussels, Hong Kong, Miami and Paris (Charles de Gaulle)
Type of operation: International, regional and domestic scheduled and charter cargo
Personnel: not available

Federal Express was created in June 1971 to undertake the delivery of documents and small packages, and has since risen to become the world's largest operator of its type, with a total workforce of 156,385 and the daily delivery of some 2.7 million items to destinations in more than 211 countries.

Fleet (orders):
36 x Airbus A300-600F
42 x Airbus A310-200F
1 x Airbus A310-300F
(10) x Airbus A380-800F
(75) x Ayres Loadmaster
52 x Boeing Model 727-100F
91 x Boeing Model 727-200F
31 x Boeing MD-11 Freighter
1 x Lockheed Martin L-100-30 Hercules
36 x McDonnell Douglas DC-10-10F
22 x McDonnell Douglas DC-10-30F

FINNAIR (FINLAND)

Main bases and hubs: Helsinki, London (Gatwick) and Stockholm
Type of operation: International, regional and domestic scheduled and charter passenger and cargo services
Personnel: 9,215

Finnair is one of the longest-established airlines in the world, for its origins can be traced back to 1 November 1923, when Bruno Lucander created Aero O/Y with financial

Fleet (orders):
4 (2) x Airbus A319-100
1 (7) x Airbus A320-200
4 x Airbus A321-200
9 x ATR 72-200
5 x Boeing Model 757-200
4 x Boeing MD-11
9 x Boeing MD-82
12 x Boeing MD-83
10 x McDonnell Douglas DC-9-50

help from local interests. The new airline flew its first service between Helsinki across the Gulf of Finland to Reval in Estonia using a Junkers F13 floatplane, and its most significant international link was established on the route linking Helsinki with Stockholm on 2 June 1924 in conjunction with the Swedish airline ABA. In 1925, the route on the eastern side of the Baltic Sea was extended southward to Königsberg in East Prussia, and on 29 June 1932, Aero O/Y took delivery of its first Junkers 52/3m three-motor transport, which supplanted the Junkers G 24W floatplane on the Königsberg service.

A major change became evident on 15 June 1937 when Aero O/Y accepted its first landplane in the form of a De Havilland D.H.89 Dragon Rapide, and this soon entered service between Riga and Liepaja. By the time of the Russo-Finnish 'Winter War' of 1939–40, Aero O/Y's fleet comprised two Ju 52/3m and two D.H.89 aircraft. The 'Winter War' resulted in the cancellation of only eight of Aero O/Y's scheduled 389 flights, six of these being attributable to weather conditions rather than Soviet action, but during the 'Continuation War' of 1941–44, when Finland was allied with Germany, all services were cancelled.

Aero O/Y resumed services in August 1945 with domestic services from Hyvinkää to Vaasa, Kerni and Jyväskylä, and in 1946 the government of Finland acquired a 70 per cent shareholding in the airline. Aero O/Y accepted the first of six Douglas DC-3 twin-engined transports on 6 June 1947, and resumed services to Stockholm on 1 November of the same year: Aero O/Y had earlier operated two examples of the Douglas DC-2 from 28 April 1941. The availability of the DC-3 fleet permitted an expansion of the airline's international network, and on 15 April 1951 Düsseldorf and Hamburg were added to the destinations served by the airline, which was now operating under the name Finnair, although this change was not formally adopted until July 1968.

Finnair acquired its first truly modern aircraft on 27 January 1953, when it took delivery of its initial Convair CV-240, and with this type Finnair was able to start a service linking Helsinki with London, via Hamburg and Amsterdam, on 1 September 1954. Finnair also became the first non-Soviet bloc airline to serve Moscow, which it did with the start of a CV-240 service on 18 February 1956.

Finnair missed out the intermediate step of turboprop-powered airliners, and instead proceeded straight to the pure jet type with a January 1958 order for three examples of the Sud-Aviation Caravelle IA; the first of the aircraft was accepted on 18 February 1960 and the type operated its first revenue-earning services on 1 April 1960 on the routes from Helsinki to Stockholm and Frankfurt. Finnair received the first of its larger turbofan-powered Super Caravelle 10B aircraft on 22 July 1964, and this type remained in service up to 30 April 1983, when a final service was flown from Helsinki to Monastir in Yugoslavia.

With the Super Caravelle established as the workhorse of Finnair's international network, the CV-240 replaced the DC-3 on the airline's domestic network. In general, however, Finnair was notably cautious in its expansion after World War II, and it was not until November 1966 that the airline placed its first order for long-haul aircraft in the form of two Douglas DC-8-62CF four-turbofan transports with which to expand its international network to North America. Finnair accepted delivery of its first DC-8 on 27 January 1969, and this soon entered service between Helsinki and New York via two intermediate stops. Finnair was well pleased with the DC-8, and accordingly ordered the Douglas DC-9-10 for its short-haul routes, accepting the first of these aircraft on 24 January 1971. Since that time, Finnair has operated two other variants of the basic DC-9 series, as well as three variants of the lengthened and modernized MD-80 series; the Finnish operator received its first examples of the DC-9-40, DC-9-50 and MD-82 in March 1981, January 1976 and March 1983 respectively.

Finnair received its first wide-body airliner, a McDonnell

BELOW: *Finnair flies a major route network primarily with Airbus and Boeing transports.*

Douglas DC-10-30, on 27 January 1975, and in its original DC-10 and somewhat later updated MD-11 forms, this three-turbofan transport replaced the DC-8-62CF on the North American and most intercontinental routes. In April 1980, Finnair bought the first two of an eventual three Fokker F.27 Friendship twin-turboprop transports from Icelandair for the operation of low-density services to destinations such as Umeå, Vaasa and Turku in the remoter parts of the region.

The F.27 aircraft did not remain in service long and, while it still operates mainly McDonnell Douglas (now Boeing) aircraft, Finnair is now also an operator of Airbus transports for its short- and medium-range services.

FRONTIER AIRLINES (UNITED STATES OF AMERICA)

Main base and hub: Denver
Type of operation: Regional and domestic scheduled passenger
Personnel: not available

Frontier Airlines began life in 1994 as successor to an airline of the same name, flying its first services in July of that year, and has since developed as a low-cost regional airline with services to 24 destinations in the USA. The airline is the second largest user of Denver International Airport.

Fleet (orders):
(6) x Airbus A318
(22) x Airbus A319-100
7 x Boeing Advanced Model 737-200
17 x Boeing Model 737-300

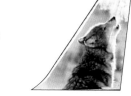

BELOW: *Frontier Airlines flies Airbus and Boeing twin-jets on regional services.*

GARUDA INDONESIA (INDONESIA)

Main bases and hubs: Denpasar and Jakarta
Type of operation: International, regional and domestic scheduled passenger and cargo services
Personnel: 9,765

In 1928, KLM (Royal Dutch Airlines) established the Koninklijke Nederlandsch Indische Luchtvaart Maatschappij (KNILM) for the operation of air services to and in the Netherlands East Indies from 1 November of the same year. During the 1930s, various types of Fokker aircraft were used, and KLM also supplied KNILM with more advanced Douglas DC-2 and Lockheed Model 14 twin-engined aircraft. By 1934, KNILM was operating a network covering seven towns in the Netherlands East Indies and also flying a service to Singapore, and four years later the airline was serving a domestic network of 12 destinations, as well as three international destinations once the cities of Saigon and Darwin had been added to Singapore.

Fleet (orders):
6 (3) x Airbus A330-300
7 x Boeing Model 737-300
12 x Boeing Model 737-400
5 x Boeing Model 737-500
5 x Boeing Model 747-200B
1 x Boeing Model 747-200B Combi
3 x Boeing Model 747-400
5 x Boeing Model 767-300ER
(6) x Boeing Model 777-200ER
2 x Boeing MD-11CF
1 x Boeing MD-11ER
3 x Fokker F.28 Friendship Mk 3000
2 x Fokker F.28 Fellowship Mk 4000
5 x McDonnell Douglas DC-9-30

When the Japanese invaded the Netherlands East Indies in the first months of 1942, all KNILM's services were halted and all possible aircraft were evacuated to Australia and thence, if feasible, to the USA, where the airline re-established itself in New York. Services in the Netherlands East Indies were resumed after the end of World War II in 1945, and on 1 August 1947 KLM absorbed KNILM, which became the KLM Island Division with a fleet of 20 Douglas DC-3 landplanes and eight Consolidated PBY-5A Catalina amphibious flying boats.

Since the end of World War II, a nationalist effort had been fighting to make the Netherlands East Indies into the independent republic of Indonesia, and in August 1950 the republic was proclaimed after the Netherlands had granted full sovereignty in November 1949. On 21 December 1949, Garuda Indonesian Airways came into being as a joint venture between the governments of Indonesia and the Netherlands, and on 31 March 1950 the new operator was officially registered as the successor to KNILM.

Garuda received its first new transport on 28 September 1950, when it took delivery of the first of an eventual 19 Convair CV-240 aircraft for use on major routes, for which feeder operations were undertaken by an eventual 14 examples of the De Havilland D.H.114 Heron, of which the first was delivered in October 1953.

A major change occurred on 12 July 1954, when the Indonesian government nationalized Garuda, and in September 1956, KLM's technical support agreement was terminated. Fleet modernization was now vital, and on 15 March 1957, Garuda ordered three examples of the Lockheed L-188 Electra four-turboprop airliner; the first of these arrived on 14 January 1961, with the other pair following a mere 10 days later. Garuda also wanted to expand its route network as well as provide additional capacity, and as a result it ordered three examples of the jet-powered Convair CV-990. The airline took delivery of the first of these fast jetliners on 3 September 1963, and the type was placed in service on Far Eastern routes to destinations such as Manila and Tokyo, with a link to Amsterdam following in March 1965. During 1968, Garuda replaced the CV-990 aircraft on the Amsterdam service with the Douglas DC-8-55, of which the first was received on 19 July 1966. Garuda also leased a number of extra DC-8 aircraft from KLM.

BELOW: *Garuda flies mainly Boeing aircraft, but has recently become an Airbus customer.*

Further re-equipment followed from 1969, when the airline's regional capability was transmogrified by the introduction of Fokker F.27 Friendship Mk 600 twin-turboprop and Douglas DC-9-32 twin-jet aircraft to complement and then supplant the Convair CV-340 and CV-440 aircraft that had been the mainstays of these services up to that time. Garuda received its first F.27 and DC-9 aircraft on 14 August and 15 October 1969 respectively. The F.27 did not long remain in service with Garuda as it was soon replaced by the Fokker F.28 Fellowship twin-turbofan type. The first of these aircraft was delivered on 19 August 1971, and Garuda became the world's largest operator of this type, with 45 received in Series 1000, 3000 and 4000 forms.

As its longer-haul services were growing rapidly, the advent of the wide-body airliner was very important for Garuda, which entered the market for this type in the early 1970s with an order for the McDonnell Douglas DC-10-30 three-turbofan type as successor to the DC-8. Before receiving its own aircraft, Garuda leased one similar machine from KLM from October 1973 to March 1975.

On 1 January 1963, Garuda had absorbed the domestic operation of De Kroonduif in West New Guinea, but one year later transferred this network to PN Merpati Nusantara. Then, in October 1978, Garuda took over PN Merpati Nusantara, which operated domestic services with a fleet of F.27 Friendships, De Havilland Canada DHC-6 Twin Otter, CASA-Nurtanio NC-212 Aviocar and Vickers Viscount aircraft. Although wholly owned by Garuda, this airline continued to operate semi-independently as Merpati Nusantara Airlines up to September 1989, when it was absorbed fully into Garuda. Many of the older aircraft were still operated, although more modern equipment included seven BAe 748 and Jetstream ATP, three Boeing Model 737-200, up to 40 CASA-IPTN CN-235, 20 F.28 and six Fokker 100 aircraft.

Further consolidation of Garuda's international capability followed the adoption of the Boeing Model 747, of which the airline received its first example on 2 July 1980. Given the growth of tourism and local wealth, Garuda found that its DC-9 fleet lacked adequate capacity and therefore ordered another wide-body type, the Airbus A300B4-220, the first of an eventual nine being accepted on 11 January 1982. The DC-9 was later supplanted by the Model 737, and further capability was added by the introduction of other Airbus types.

GO (UNITED KINGDOM)

Main base and hub: London (Stansted)
Type of operation: International, regional and domestic scheduled and charter passenger
Personnel: 550

Go was created by British Airways in 1997 in an effort to tap into the rapidly growing market for low-cost and no-frills domestic and international services, now operating between four domestic and 16 European destinations. At the end of 2000 British Airways decided to sell Go.

Like other European operators of the 'low-cost and no-frills' type, Go has not been badly affected by the fall-out of the

Fleet (orders):
13 x Boeing Model 737-300

September 2001 terrorist attacks on the USA, actually gaining market share as the major airlines have lost their attraction for many travellers.

GULF AIR (BAHRAIN, OMAN, QATAR AND UNITED ARAB EMIRATES)

Main bases and hubs: Abu Dhabi, Bahrain, Doha and Muscat
Type of operation: International and regional scheduled and charter passenger and freight services
Personnel: 5,805

Gulf Airways is the flag carrier of the Persian Gulf states of Bahrain, Oman, Qatar and the United Arab Emirates. The airline can trace its origins back to 24 March 1950, when F. Bosworth, a Briton, started local services with one Avro Type 652A Anson. This operator was the Gulf Aviation Co. Ltd, and its services linked Bahrain, Doha, Dhahran and Sharjah. During its first year, the airline boosted its fleet to a strength of four aircraft by the addition of two Austers and a De Havilland D.H.86, but considerably enhanced capability arrived on 13 June 1951 with the delivery of an initial De Havilland D.H.104 Dove 1. During October 1951, the airline became a subsidiary of the British Overseas Airways Corporation, and in combination with steadily

BELOW: *Gulf Air is the flag carrier of states on the south-western side of the Persian Gulf.*

Fleet (orders):
12 x Airbus A320-200
6 x Airbus A330-200
5 x Airbus A340-300
9 x Boeing Model 767-300ER

growing capacity demand, the greater capital now available allowed the purchase of more, and also larger, aircraft in the form of four examples of the De Havilland D.H.114 Heron 1B, of which the first was received on 11 July 1956, and shortly after this, of four examples of the Douglas DC-3.

During this period, there was considerable demand for additional capacity as the world's oil companies moved in strength into the Persian Gulf, and on 6 January 1967 the airline took on strength its first turboprop-powered airliner, a Fokker F.27 Friendship Mk 600. The airline was able to satisfy its short-haul requirements with this and the Shorts Skyvan, of which the first two were delivered in November 1970, while slightly longer-haul services were provided initially by a

Hawker Siddeley Trident 1E leased from Kuwait Airways but soon by the BAC One-Eleven 432FD, of which the first was delivered in November 1969.

In April 1970, the airline started to operate to London from Abu Dhabi, Bahrain, Doha and Dubai using a Vickers VC10 leased from BOAC. Late in 1973, the airline was renamed Gulf Air, and on 1 April 1974 Bahrain, Oman, Qatar and the United Arab Emirates became equal shareholders in the newly named company. Also formed in 1974 was Doha-based Gulf Helicopters, with Gulf Air as its only shareholder. On 24 May 1981, the Gulf Air Light Aircraft Division merged with Oman International Services to create Oman Aviation Services using aircraft drawn from the pool provided by the two companies'

fleets. The major effect of this merger on Gulf Air was to leave it with only two types of aircraft with which to operate its more clearly defined tasks. These types were the Boeing Model 737-2P6, of which the first was received on 28 June 1977, for regional services to neighbouring countries in the Middle East, and the Lockheed L-1011-200 TriStar, of which the first was delivered on 16 January 1976, for longer-haul services north-westward to London, Amsterdam and Paris and eastward to Karachi and Bombay.

In 1985, Gulf Air ceased operations to Dubai, which had established Emirates Airline as its own national flag carrier, and has come to concentrate the bulk of its operations on the advanced aircraft of Airbus and Boeing.

HAINAN AIRLINES (CHINA)

Main bases and hubs: Haiku and Ningbo
Type of operation: Regional and domestic scheduled and charter passenger and cargo
Personnel: not available
Hainan Airlines was established in 1989 on the island of Hainan off southern China. In 1993, it became the first Chinese airline to be privatized. The operator now provides services between 40 Chinese destinations.

Hainan Airlines also flies a Learjet 55 for executive transport services. The airline has plans to expand its

Fleet (orders):
4 x Boeing Model 737-300
7 x Boeing Model 737-400
7 x Boeing Model 737-800
14 (5) x Fairchild Dornier
328JET
2 x Fairchild Dornier Metro 23

operations to a variety of international destinations in South-East Asia.

HAPAG-LLOYD (GERMANY)

Main base and hub: Hanover
Type of operation: International and regional scheduled and charter passenger and cargo
Personnel: not available
The Hapag-Lloyd airline was created in July 1972 and started operations in March of the following year as the scheduled and charter air operator of the German shipping line of the same name, but in 1997 became a subsidiary of Preussag. Hapag-Lloyd currently operates from 16 German, one Swiss and one Dutch airport to 37 holiday destinations around the

Fleet (orders):
4 x Airbus A310-200
2 x Airbus A310-300
5 x Boeing Model 737-400
26 (4) x Boeing Model 737-800

Mediterranean. The downturn in the package holiday business has demanded that Hapag-Lloyd trim its costs.

HAWAIIAN AIRLINES
(UNITED STATES OF AMERICA)

Main base and hub: Honolulu
Type of operation: International, regional and domestic scheduled and charter passenger
Personnel: 3,050
The operator now known as Hawaiian Airlines was created in January 1929 by the Inter-Island Steam Navigation Company as Inter-Island Airways, and adopted its present name in October 1941. The operator's initial services were, as its name suggested, between the primary islands of the Hawaiian chain, but in later years expanded to include five cities in the

Fleet (orders):
1 (12) x Boeing Model 717-200
13 x McDonnell Douglas DC-9-50
10 x McDonnell Douglas DC-10-10
5 x McDonnell Douglas DC-10-30

continental USA as its regional destinations and American Pago Pago on Samoa and Papeete on Tahiti as its two scheduled international destinations.

HEAVYLIFT CARGO AIRLINES
(UNITED KINGDOM)

Main base and hub: London (Stansted)
Type of operation: International scheduled and charter cargo
Personnel: 270

HeavyLift Cargo Airlines came into existence as a private company in October 1978 and started operations in March 1980, initially with a fleet of five ex-Royal Air Force Shorts Belfast heavy transports. The company is a specialist in the movement of large and/or heavy freight items, and after terms in the hands of Trafalgar House and Kvaerner was bought out

Fleet (orders):
2 x Airbus A300F4-200
3 x Ilyushin Il-76T
2 x Shorts Belfast

by its management in 1999. HeavyLift's three scheduled destinations are Frankfurt, Cologne and Stockholm.

HORIZON AIR
(UNITED STATES OF AMERICA)

Main bases and hubs: Seattle, Boise, Portland and Spokane
Type of operation: International, regional and domestic scheduled passenger and cargo
Personnel: 4,130

Now a wholly owned subsidiary of the group that also owns Alaska Airlines, Horizon Air was created in May 1981 and started operations in September of the same year. Soon after its beginning, the airline was able to expand by the purchase of Air

Fleet (orders):
(30) x Bombardier CRJ-700
12 x Bombardier Dash 8-100
28 x Bombardier Dash 8-200
4 (11) x Bombardier Dash
  8Q-400
22 x Fokker F.28 Fellowship Mk
  4000

Oregon, and now has an operation fully integrated with that of Alaska Airlines, with services to five Canadian and 35 American destinations, all in the west of the country.

BELOW: *Horizon is a major user of the Dash 8.*

IBERIA (SPAIN)

Main bases and hubs: Barcelona and Madrid International Airport
Type of operation: International, regional and domestic scheduled and charter passenger and cargo services
Personnel: 26,935

Iberia is the national flag carrier of Spain and is more properly known as the Líneas Aéreas de España. This operator was created in 1927 with 51 per cent owned by the Spanish government and the other 40 per cent by private interests in which the German airline Deutsche Lufthansa predominated. Deutsche Lufthansa was responsible mainly for the establishment of the airline on a sound technical basis and

Fleet (orders):
5 x Airbus A300B4-100
1 x Airbus A300B4-200
4 (5) x Airbus A319-100
44 (20) x Airbus A320-200
2 (14) x Airbus A321-200
14 (14) x Airbus A340-300
7 x Boeing Advanced Model
  727-200
3 x Boeing Model 737-400
4 x Boeing Model 747-200B
3 x Boeing Model 747-200B
  Combi
3 x Boeing Model 747-300

23 x Boeing Model 757-200
2 x Boeing Model 767-300ER
24 x McDonnell Douglas MD-87
13 x Boeing MD-88
8 x McDonnell Douglas DC-9-30

consonant with the other airlines that comprised the Germans' 'continental system' of airlines stretching to Finland, Spain and the Balkans.

Iberia's network was confined initially to Spain and the Spanish territories in North Africa, and the airline's operations came to an abrupt halt with the outbreak of the Spanish Civil War in 1936. The airline was in essence refounded in 1940, one year after the end of the civil war and again with the aid of Lufthansa, and for the duration of World War II restricted its operations to domestic services. During the war, in which Spain was a non-participant, Iberia was completely nationalized.

Expansion began in 1946, the year after that in which World War II ended, with the opening of a transatlantic service to South America using the Sud-Est SE.161 Languedoc four-engined airliner. Commercial success followed, and Iberia was gradually able to develop its network into other parts of the Spanish-speaking world, notably Cuba and Mexico, and in 1954 started a scheduled service to New York. By the middle of the 1950s Iberia's fleet comprised the Bristol Type 170, Convair CV-440 and Douglas DC-3 twin-engined transports for its short-range routes, the Douglas DC-4 four-engined airliners on its medium-haul routes, and the Lockheed L-1049 Super Constellation four-engined airliner on its long-haul routes. Turbine power made its appearance in Iberia livery during 1961 in the form of the four-engined Douglas DC-8 and two-engined Sud-Aviation Caravelle.

From this time, Iberia has increased its network and fleet quite quickly and extensively.

BELOW: *Like other major airlines, Iberia flies large numbers of Airbus and Boeing aircraft.*

ICELANDAIR (ICELAND)

Main base and hub: Reykjavik
Type of operation: International, regional and domestic scheduled and charter passenger and cargo
Personnel: 1,770

The national airline of Iceland, Icelandair came into existence during 1973 through the merger of Flugfelag Islands and Loftleidir Iceland Airlines. The airline currently links seven domestic destinations and flies scheduled services to 22 international destinations on both side of the Atlantic.

Air Iceland is a subsidiary that operates domestic services

Fleet (orders):
1 x Boeing model 737-400
8 (1) x Boeing Model 757-200
1 x Boeing Model 757-200PF
(2) x Boeing model 757-300

and also flies to a selected number of short-range overseas destinations.

INDIAN AIRLINES (INDIA)

Main bases and hubs: Bombay, Calcutta, Chennai, Delhi and Hyderabad
Type of operation: International, regional and domestic scheduled and charter passenger and cargo
Personnel: 21,990

Indian Airlines was created in August 1953 and began operations on the same day to run the services of eight private airlines. In recent times, the government of India has decided to reduce to 49 per cent its shareholding in Indian Airlines, which flies to 16 international destinations round the Indian

Fleet (orders):
6 x Airbus A300B2
4 x Airbus A300B4-200
32 x Airbus A320-200
1 x Boeing Advanced Model 737-200
4 x Fairchild Dornier 228-200

Ocean area, and also operates a network of domestic services linking 37 cities on the Indian subcontinent.

101

IRAN AIR (IRAN)

Main base and hub: Tehran
Type of operation: International, regional and domestic scheduled and charter passenger and cargo services
Personnel: not available

Iran Air, also known as Homa (an acronym of its Persian name), was created during February 1962 by the amalgamation of two existing operators, namely Iranian Airways and Persian Air Services, to become the state-owned national flag carrier.

Iranian Airways had been created as a private airline in December 1944, and began operations on 31 May 1945, with its first scheduled service launched in May 1946 to connect Tehran and Meshed. A domestic network was subsequently developed using DC-3 aircraft. The airline's route network and capacity grew steadily, allowing the establishment of regional services to Baghdad, Beirut and Cairo by the end of 1946, and of a long-haul service to Paris during April 1947.

Persian Air Services had been created in the course of 1954, and began operations the following year with a cargo service between Tehran and Geneva using Avro York four-engined transport aircraft operated under charter by Trans Mediterranean Airways. Regional and international services were then introduced, and in 1960 a Douglas DC-7C was leased from Sabena, with a Boeing Model 707, also leased

BELOW: *Iran Air flies the Model 747SP for short-haul but high-density services.*

Fleet (orders):

2 x Airbus A300-600R
4 x Airbus A300B2
1 x Airbus A310-300
(6) x Airbus A330-200
1 x Boeing Model 707-320C
2 x Boeing Model 727-100
4 x Boeing Advanced Model 727-200
1 x Boeing Advanced Model 737-200
2 x Boeing Model 737-200C
1 x Boeing Model 747-100B
2 x Boeing Model 747-200B Combi
4 x Boeing Model 747SP
5 x Fokker 100

from Sabena, following it into service.

Iran Air began operations in 1962 with the pool of aircraft inherited from its two predecessors, but acquired its own jet-powered aircraft in 1965 with the first of several Boeing Model 727-86 machines, of which the first was received on 4 July. The acquisition of more and larger aircraft allowed Air Iran to expand its route network, which soon included Frankfurt, London and Moscow. In 1964, Iran Air reached agreement with Pan American for the provision, over a three-year period, of management and technical support. This was a considerable fillip to the airline's overall capabilities and operating viability, and in March 1976 Iran Air moved into the arena of wide-body aircraft with the introduction of Boeing Model 747SP-86 aircraft, which allowed the start of services to New York.

The severing of relations with the USA, following the fall of the Shah and the introduction of a fundamentalist Islamic regime, combined with the following 10-year first Gulf War against Iraq to reduce the utility of the airline's American-supplied aircraft, for which no additional spares could be obtained on the open market, so it has been only with the introduction of European aircraft that the airline's fortunes have started to rise once more.

IRAQI AIRWAYS (IRAQ)

Main base and hub: Baghdad
Type of operation: International, regional and domestic scheduled and charter passengerand cargo
Personnel: not available

Established in 1946 as the national airline of Iraq, Iraqi Airways suffered heavily as a result of the 1991 Gulf War and the international sanctions that followed it, for it was initially prohibited from operating any form of services, this prohibition being lifted from helicopter flights in May 1991 and from a limited number of domestic services by fixed-wing aircraft in January 1992. All flights were then banned once more as a result of pressure from the United Nations, but limited domestic and, it is thought, regional services have resumed in recent years.

Fleet (orders):

(5) x Airbus A310-300
1 x Antonov An-26
1 x Ilyushin Il-76T

The known domestic destinations between which Iraqi Airlines currently operates scheduled services include only Baghdad, Basra and Mosul. Expansion in the regional and international spheres can follow only after UN sanctions on the country have been eased.

JAPAN AIR SYSTEM (JAPAN)

Main base and hub: Tokyo
Type of operation: Regional and domestic scheduled and charter passenger and cargo services
Personnel: 5,665

Japan Air System came into existence on 15 May 1971 through the merger of Japan Domestic Airlines and Toa Airways to create Toa Domestic Airlines, which name was changed to Japan Air System in 1988.

Japan Domestic Airlines itself dated from April 1964, when it had been established by a merger of the Tokyo-based Fuji Airlines, the Osaka-based Nitto Aviation and the Sapporo-based Northern Japan Airlines. Toa Airways had come into existence on 26 November 1953 to operate air services in the south-western part of the Japanese home islands.

Fleet (orders):
19 x Airbus A300-600R
7 x Airbus A300B2
8 x Airbus A300B4-200
7 x Boeing Model 777-200
17 x Boeing MD-81
8 x Boeing MD-87
16 x McDonnell Douglas DC-9-30

Japan Air System currently operates a fleet of Airbus and McDonnell Douglas turbofan-powered transports, and has created significant improvement in its capabilities with the advent of the Boeing Model 777 and additional McDonnell Douglas (Boeing) aircraft.

JAPAN AIRLINES (JAPAN)

Main base and hub: Tokyo (Narita)
Type of operation: International, regional and domestic scheduled passenger and cargo services
Personnel: 18,535

Japan Airlines was created in July 1923 by Seibei Kawanishi, a Japanese aircraft designer and manufacturer, as Japan Air Lines and operated services to the holiday resort of Beppu on Kyushu Island. On 30 October 1928, the government of Japan established the Nihon Kokuyuso Kaishiki Kaisha (Japan Air Transport Company), and in the spring of 1929 this organization engineered the merger of Tozou Teiki Kokukwai and Japan Air Lines for the operation of services within Japan. In 1938, International Airlines merged with NKKK to form the Japan Air Lines Company, and in August 1939 this was reorganized to form Greater Japan Air Lines, which began international services from Tokyo to Bangkok in June 1940. Through Japan's involvement in World War II, Greater Japan Air Lines operated as a transport adjunct of the Japanese armed forces, and ceased all operations with the surrender of Japan in August 1945.

Japanese Air Lines was the name of an operator created on 1 August 1951 by a group of private investors, and initially restricted its operations to domestic service within the Japanese home islands using aircraft and crews leased from Northwest Airlines. The first two types operated by the revived Japanese carrier were the Martin 2-0-2 and Douglas DC-4, the former a twin-engined type of which the first was received on 25 October 1951 and the latter a four-engined type of which the first was received on 2 November 1951. The airline had very ambitious plans, however, and on 18 November 1952 ordered two De Havilland Comet 2 turbojet-powered airliners, neither of which was in the event delivered. Another order was placed for five examples of the Douglas DC-6A and DC-6B, but the airline lacked adequate capital for such an expansion and financial restructuring became necessary.

On 1 October 1953, the company was therefore reorganized as Japan Air Lines, and this marked the full renaissance of the

Fleet (orders):
3 x Boeing Model 737-400
1 x Boeing Model 747-100
3 x Boeing Model 747-100B
10 x Boeing Model 747-200B
10 x Boeing Model 747-200F
13 x Boeing Model 747-300
33 (4) x Boeing Model 747-400
8 x Boeing Model 747-400 Domestic
3 x Boeing Model 767-200
18 x Boeing Model 767-300
(3) x Boeing Model 767-300ER
5 (5) x Boeing Model 777-200

(8) x Boeing Model 777-200ER
5 x Boeing Model 777-300
(8) x Boeing Model 777-300ER
10 x Boeing MD-11
13 McDonnell Douglas DC-9-40

pre-war airline as the Japanese national flag carrier, with a 50 per cent stake in the company being held by the Japanese government. Shortly before this, Japan Air Lines had received three examples of the Douglas DC-6A from Flying Tigers and Slick Airlines. The aircraft were then upgraded to DC-6B standard for the inauguration of the airline's service across the Pacific to the USA shortly after they had entered revenue-earning service on the route linking Tokyo and Sapporo on 2 October 1953.

On 19 November 1955, Japan Air Lines marked its movement into the modern turbojet-powered age with an order for the Douglas DC-8-32 four-engined airliner. The first of these aircraft was received on 16 July 1960 for use on the route linking Tokyo and San Francisco via Wake Island and Honolulu from 12 August of the same year, and, just before this, the airline's first trans-polar service on the route from Tokyo to London via Anchorage. On 1 April 1960, Japan Air Lines started a collaborative service with Air France between Tokyo and Paris over the trans-polar route with Boeing Model 707-328 four-turbofan aircraft. Soon after, on 21 July 1962 the airline received the first of another four-engined jet type, the Convair CV-880, which was used on 4 October of the same year to launch Japan Air Lines' first service to Europe via India and the Middle East. As soon as its new turbojet-powered aircraft had become established in terms of performance and reliability, Japan Air Lines transferred all its surviving piston-engined aircraft to service on its domestic network.

On 17 April 1967, a joint venture by Japan Air Lines and Aeroflot saw the inauguration of the first direct service between Tokyo and Moscow, and although this initially used the Soviet airline's Tupolev Tu-114 and later its Ilyushin Il-62 airliners, Japan Air Lines later played its part in the service with its own aircraft. Additional services to Soviet destinations were later added.

Japan Air Lines took delivery of its first wide-body transport, a Boeing Model 747-146 four-turbofan type, on 22 April 1970,

and with this, improved its service across the Pacific from 1 July of the same year; another version of the 'jumbo jet', the Model 747SR-46, was also used by Japan Air Lines, in this instance for the high-density route between Tokyo and Okinawa from October 1973. From 9 April 1976, the Model 747 was partnered by another wide-body transport, the McDonnell Douglas DC-10-40 three-turbofan type, and from this time the operator has standardized on Boeing and McDonnell Douglas aircraft.

In the 1980s, the government of Japan started to sell its shareholding in Japan Air Lines, which now trades as Japan Airlines and achieved full privatization in November 1987 as the government sold its remaining 34.5 per cent shareholding.

JAT YUGOSLAV AIRWAYS (YUGOSLAVIA)

Main base and hub: Belgrade
Type of operation: International, regional and domestic scheduled and charter passenger and cargo
Personnel: 4,445
Named Aeroput at the time of its establishment in April 1947, JAT Yugoslav Airways is the national airline of Yugoslavia and was very adversely affected by the several civil wars that attended the gaining of independence by parts of the former federal state of Yugoslavia. Serbia now controls 51 per cent of the airline, which was banned from operating many services for long periods of the 1990s. Before these bans, JAT flew domestic services as well as 104 international flights per week to 40 international destinations, but now flies between only

Fleet (orders):
6 x Boeing Advanced Model 727-200
6 x Boeing Model 737-300
5 x McDonnell Douglas DC-9-30
1 x McDonnell Douglas DC-10-30

three domestic destinations and also operates services to 38 international destinations as it starts to rebuild itself with more modern equipment and services.

RIGHT: *JAT flies the DC-9-30 on its short-haul services.*

JET AIRWAYS (INDIA)

Main bases and hubs: Bombay, Calcutta, Chennai and Delhi
Type of operation: Domestic scheduled passenger and cargo
Personnel: 5,270
Jet Airways was created in April 1992 and began operations in May 1993, initially as an air taxi operator. The airline is now India's largest privately owned airline, and currently flies a network linking 37 Indian destinations within the context of a scheduled network comprising some 200 flights per day.

Jet Airways has standardized the Model 737 as its primary

Fleet (orders):
5 x ATR 72-500
10 x Boeing Model 737-500
7 x Boeing Model 737-700
9 (9) x Boeing Model 737-800

equipment, with the ATR 72 for local services.

KELOWNA FLIGHTCRAFT AIR CHARTER (CANADA)

Main base and hub: Kelowna
Type of operation: International, regional and domestic charter passenger and cargo
Personnel: 850
Created during March 1970 and starting operations in June 1974, Kelowna Flightcraft is best known for its charter cargo flights throughout the North American continent. It also undertakes charter passenger services as well as more specialized services such as the repair, maintenance, update

Fleet (orders):
8 x Boeing Model 727-100F
4 x Boeing Advanced Model 727-200
3 x Boeing Model 727-200F
9 x Convair 580

and remanufacture of Convair CV-580 aircraft for the transport and forest firefighting roles.

KENYA AIRWAYS (KENYA)

Main bases and hubs: Nairobi and Amsterdam (Schiphol)
Type of operation: International, regional and domestic
scheduled and charter passenger and cargo
Personnel: 2,750
Kenya Airways is the national airline of Kenya, and was
established in January 1977, for the start of operations in the
following month, after the dissolution of the East Africa Airways
organization co-owned by Kenya, Tanzania and Uganda. In
1996, the airline was partially privatized, and currently flies a
domestic network linking four destinations as well as an
international network with 26 destinations.

Fleet (orders):
4 x Airbus A310-300
2 x Boeing Advanced Model
  737-200
3 x Boeing Model 737-300
(2) x Boeing Model 737-700
1 (3) x Boeing Model 767-300ER
(3) x Boeing Model 767-400ER
1 x McDonnell Douglas DC-9-30

KLM Royal Dutch Airlines has a 26 per cent shareholding
in Kenya Airways, Africa's first privately owned airline.

KLM ROYAL DUTCH AIRLINES (NETHERLANDS)

Main base and hub: Amsterdam
Type of operation: International and regional scheduled
passenger and cargo services
Personnel: 27,300
The Koninklijke Luchtvaart Maatschappij is the national flag
carrier of the Netherlands and the oldest operating airline in
the world. Generally known as KLM, this organization can trace
its origins back to 7 October 1919, when a group of banking
and business interests established the airline, which started
operations on 17 May 1920 with a service from Amsterdam to
London using a De Havilland D.H.16 transport. In the following
years, a route network was built up with destinations in
Belgium, Denmark, France, Germany and Switzerland,
generally with Fokker F.III, F.VII and F.VIIb-3m aircraft.

On 1 October 1931, KLM inaugurated a very far-sighted but
at the time adventurous route from Amsterdam to Djakarta in
the Netherlands East Indies. Here KLM had already established
the first of two colonial subsidiaries when it created KNILM
(predecessor of Garuda) in October 1928, while the second
came into existence at Curaçao in the Netherlands Antilles and
started operations on 19 January 1935 with routes through the
Caribbean to Barbados, Colombia, the Guianas, Trinidad and
Venezuela. These routes, later supplemented by services to
Cuba and Miami, operated throughout World War II at a time
when all the airline's other operations ceased.

KLM resumed European operations on 17 January 1945, and
a rapid build-up of its capabilities allowed the start of services to
New York, Curaçao and Brazil during 1946. Between 1946 and
1953, KLM's route network grew in size quite dramatically, and to
cope with the much greater demand for its service, the airline
invested in the latest types of airliner, including the Douglas DC-
6 and Lockheed Constellation four-engined types and the Convair
CV-240 and CV-340 twin-engined types. In April 1957, an
important milestone in the airline's further fleet modernization
was the introduction of the Douglas DC-7C, which was flown on
the trans-polar route linking Amsterdam and Tokyo. On 6 June of
the same year, KLM advanced into the era of turbine propulsion
with the receipt of its first turboprop-powered airliner, the Vickers

Fleet (orders):
15 x Boeing Model 737-300
14 x Boeing Model 737-400
13 x Boeing Model 737-800
(4) x Boeing Model 737-900
3 x Boeing Model 747-200B
5 x Boeing Model 747-200B Combi
2 x Boeing Model 747-200F
3 x Boeing Model 747-300 Combi
5 x Boeing Model 747-400
16 (3) x Boeing Model 747-400
  Combi

12 x Boeing Model 767-300ER
10 x Boeing MD-11

Viscount 803, for use on the airline's regional network in Europe.
Greater capacity still was provided from 15 December 1959 with
the revenue-earning debut of the larger Lockheed L-188 Electra,
which was flown mainly on the airline's Middle and Far Eastern
services.

KLM's first pure jet airliner was the Douglas DC-8, of
which the first example was delivered on 19 March 1960 for
use from 16 April of the same year on the route linking
Amsterdam and New York. As was the general practice with
long-haul operators, KLM moved into the wide-body era with
the Boeing Model 747, in this instance a Model 747-206B, of
which the first reached the airline on 16 January 1971. The
four-turbofan Model 747 and three-turbofan McDonnell
Douglas DC-10-30 (later supplemented by the upgraded MD-
11 derivative) came to comprise the bulk of KLM's longer-haul
fleet through the 1970s and 1980s, although a newer type
now in service is the Boeing Model 767-300ER.

KLM's fleet of shorter-haul jet aircraft was initially based
on the McDonnell Douglas DC-9 twin-turbofan type, which
replaced the Viscount and Electra in 1966, but this gradually
gave way to another twin-turbofan type, the Boeing Model
737 which is now flown in several variants.

In common with other major airlines, KLM is seeking to
trim operating costs and reduce capacity.

RIGHT: **KLM operates only Boeing aircraft, including the
Model 737 in four variants.**

KOREAN AIR (SOUTH KOREA)

Main base and hub: Seoul
Type of operation: Scheduled passenger and cargo services
Personnel: 14,105

The operator now known as Korean Air started life in May 1947 with the name Korean National Airlines to fly domestic services using small Stinson Voyager single-engined aircraft which were soon replaced by Douglas DC-3 twin-engined machines. The airline ceased all operations during the period of the Korean War (1950–53), but soon after its revival, the airline flew its inaugural international service to Iwakuni and Tokyo with a Douglas DC-4 leased from Civil Air Transport. The airline bought its first DC-4 in October 1953.

In August 1959, Korean National Airlines purchased one Lockheed L-749A Constellation four-engined airliner, and in June 1962 the government of South Korea reorganized the airline, which thereupon became Korean Air Lines. During the second half of the decade, the airline built up its longer-haul capability, at that time vested in the single Constellation, by the purchase of two examples of the Lockheed L-1049H Super Constellation, and these machines were used both for charter work in South-East Asia and for a three (later five) times per week service between Seoul and Osaka. During 1967, the Super Constellations were supplemented and then supplanted on this route by the Douglas DC-9-32, of which the airline received its first example on 19 July 1967.

Korean Air Lines was operating a steadily growing domestic network during this period, moreover, and this received a considerable fillip in the later part of 1963 by the introduction of the airline's first turboprop-powered type, the Fokker F.27 Friendship Mk 200, of which the first was delivered on 20 December.

In March 1969, the government of South Korea sold its controlling interest to the Han Jin Transportation Group, and the airline has been privately owned since that time. Regional and international capability was enhanced in 1969 by the airline's receipt of its first Boeing Model 720-025, arriving on 29 September, and then still further improved in 1971 by the receipt of its first Boeing Model 707-3B5C, arriving in August.

On 13 July 1972, Korean Air Lines leased its first Boeing Model 727-100 three-turbofan airliner for medium-haul

Fleet (orders):
5 x Airbus A300-600
13 x Airbus A300-600R
3 x Airbus A330-200
11 (5) x Airbus A330-300
10 (5) x Boeing Model 737-800
(16) x Boeing Model 737-900
1 x Boeing Model 747-200B
7 x Boeing Model 747-200F
1 x Boeing Model 747-300
1 x Boeing Model 747-300 Combi
25 (2) x Boeing Model 747-400
1 x Boeing Model 747-400 Combi
5 (4) x Boeing Model 747-400F
5 (1) x Boeing Model 777-200ER
2 x Boeing Model 777-300
4 x Boeing MD-11 Freighter
5 x Boeing MD-82
2 x Boeing MD-83
1 CASA/IPTN C-212-100 Aviocar
10 Fokker 100

services, and later obtained four more aircraft of the same type before it introduced the improved Model 727-200 during 1980. The first wide-body airliner to serve with Korean Air Lines was the Boeing Model 747-2B5B, a four-turbofan type, of which the first was accepted on 1 May 1973, and this pioneering transport was later followed by two other wide-body airliners, namely the McDonnell Douglas DC-10-30 three-turbofan type, of which the first was delivered on 9 February 1975, and the Airbus A300B4-2C two-turbofan type, of which the first was delivered on 1 August of the same year.

The growing numbers of these three types available to Korean Air Lines from the early part of the 1970s allowed the airline to undertake a major development in the extent and capacity of its route network into larger numbers of farther-flung destinations. With the three wide-body types, the airline has been able to expand its passenger and cargo network so that today it operates to numerous points in the Far East, Asia, the Middle East, Europe and the USA in addition to its domestic network.

Domestic services are flown by F.100 and MD-80 series machines, and longer-haul services by Models 747 and 777, MD-11 and A330 aircraft.

RIGHT: *Korean Air's fleet reflects South Korea's balance with the USA and Europe.*

KUWAIT AIRWAYS (KUWAIT)

Main base and hub: Kuwait
Type of operation: International and regional scheduled and charter passenger and cargo
Personnel: not available

Wholly owned by the government of Kuwait and also the national airline of this small state at the head of the Persian Gulf, Kuwait Airways was established in March 1954 and began operations in the same month. The airline was badly affected by the 1991 Gulf War, which was sparked by the Iraqi seizure of Kuwait, but has rebuilt itself and now flies an

Fleet (orders):
5 x Airbus A300-600R
2 x Airbus A310-300
3 x Airbus A320-200
4 x Airbus A340-300
1 x Boeing Model 747-200B Combi
1 x Boeing Model 747-400 Combi
2 x Boeing Model 777-200ER

international network extending to 41 destinations, mainly in the Middle East, Europe and Asia as well as the USA.

LANCHILE (CHILE)

Main base and hub: Santiago
Type of operation: International, regional and domestic scheduled passenger and cargo
Personnel: 7,410
In March 1929, the government of Chile established Línea Aeropostal Santiago-Larica as the national airline, and in 1932 this operator became LanChile. LanChile was privatized in 1989. In August 1995, it gained control of Ladeco (Chile's second largest airline), and in October 1998 amalgamated Fast Air with another of its holdings, Ladeco. LanChile at that time

Fleet (orders):
5 (20) x Airbus A320-200
2 (5) x Airbus A340-300
12 x Boeing Advanced Model 737-200
3 (3) x Boeing Model 767-300 Freighter
12 x Boeing Model 767-300ER

flew a route network with 17 domestic and 25 international destinations, the latter mainly in the Americas.

LAPA – LINEAS AEREAS PRIVADAS ARGENTINAS (ARGENTINA)

Main bases and hubs: Buenos Aires and Ministro Pistarini
Type of operation: International, regional and domestic scheduled and charter passenger
Personnel: not available
Created in 1976 and beginning operations two years later with charter services, supplemented by scheduled services from the following year. LAPA currently flies a network that includes 26 domestic and five international destinations. Among the international destinations are Atlanta in the USA as well as

Fleet (orders):
1 x Boeing Model 737-200
5 x Boeing Advanced Model 737-200
1 x Boeing Model 737-200C
9 (12) x Boeing Model 737-700
2 x Boeing Model 757-200
1 x Boeing Model 757-300ER

Cancún, Montevideo, Punta Cana and Punta del Este in South America.

LAUDA AIR (AUSTRIA)

Main base and hub: Vienna
Type of operation: International and regional scheduled and charter passenger and cargo
Personnel: 425
Created in April 1979 and initially flying only charter and air taxi services after it started operations in 1985, Lauda Air began scheduled services two years later and now operates a scheduled network of more than 250 flights per week linking four domestic destinations and to 33 international destinations.

Fleet (orders):
2 x Boeing Model 737-300
2 x Boeing Model 737-400
2 x Boeing Model 737-600
2 x Boeing Model 737-800
3 x Boeing Model 767-300ER
2 x Boeing Model 777-200ER
4 x Bombardier CRJ-100LR

BELOW: *The CRJ-100LR allows Lauda Air to undertake long-range regional services.*

LLOYD AÉRO BOLIVIANO (BOLIVIA)

Main base and hub: La Paz
Type of operation: International, regional and domestic scheduled passenger and cargo
Personnel: 1,740
The airline now known as Lloyd Aéro Boliviano, generally abbreviated to LAB, was created in September 1925 by Bolivian-domiciled Germans with the full support of the Bolivian government, and is thus one of the oldest airlines in the world as well as being the national airline of Bolivia. LAB was nationalized in 1941, but is currently controlled by VASP Brazilian Airlines and the government of Bolivia, with 49.0 per cent and 48.3 per cent of the equity respectively. LAB's

Fleet (orders):
1 x Airbus A310-300
2 x Boeing Model 727-100
1 x Boeing Model 727-100C
3 x Boeing Advanced Model 727-200
2 x Boeing Model 737-200
1 x Fokker F.27 Friendship Mk 200

scheduled route network embraces 12 domestic and 20 international destinations. The latter are all in other South and Central American countries, with the exception of Miami.

LOT POLISH AIRLINES (POLAND)

Main base and hub: Warsaw
Type of operation: International, regional and domestic scheduled and charter passenger services
Personnel: not available
The Polish national flag carrier, Polskie Linie Lotnicze (LOT), can trace its history back to the creation, in 1922, of two privately owned companies, namely Aero Lloyd Warschau and Aero TZ. Each of these carriers had as its initial equipment the Junkers F 13 single-engined machine which was the world's first all-metal transport aeroplane. Aero Lloyd started services on the routes linking Warsaw with Danzig and Lwów on 5 September 1922, while Aero began operations with services from Warsaw to Posen via Lodz, and to Brno in Czechoslovakia. In 1925, Polish interests bought out the German holding in Aero Lloyd, and the airline was subsequently renamed Aerolot.

On 1 January 1929, the government of Poland took over all civil airline activities in Poland to create the nationalized carrier Polskie Linie Lotnicze (LOT), whose main equipment at the time of its formation was still the F 13, complemented by the Fokker F.VIIa single-engined transport and, later in the same year, the Fokker F.VIIb-3m improved three-engined development of the F.VIIa. LOT grew steadily during the early 1930s, and by 1934 was able to start a service between Warsaw and Beirut via Lwów, Cernauti, Bucharest, Sofia, Salonika (now Thessaloniki), Athens and Tel Aviv. By mid-1939, the airline's capabilities had improved considerably as a result of the introduction of thoroughly modern equipment such as the Douglas DC-2, of which the first two had been delivered on 3 August 1935. These medium-capacity aircraft were followed in the first two months of 1936 by four examples of the Lockheed L-10A Electra small-capacity transport, which was used to launch services north-west to Copenhagen via Gdynia and also north to Helsinki via the capitals of the Baltic states. LOT also operated a fleet of German-built Ju 52/3m three-engined transports which, like the DC-2s, were powered by Polish-built Bristol Pegasus radial engines.

Fleet (orders):
2 x Boeing Model 737-300
7 x Boeing Model 737-400
9 x Boeing Model 737-500
2 x Boeing Model 737-800
2 x Boeing Model 767-200ER
3 x Boeing Model 767-300ER
6 x EMBRAER RJ-145
4 (6) x EMBRAER RJ-145ER

On 1 September 1939, Germany invaded Poland to begin World War II, and all Polish civil air operations immediately ceased: LOT's strength at that time was two DC-2 and 15 Electra and Super Electra aircraft, and of these, only one Electra did not manage to escape to the neutrality of neighbouring countries. Poland was overrun in only one month, and no civil air operations were possible.

Before the end of hostilities, however, Polish communists with the advancing Soviet forces were able, on 6 March 1945, two months before the end of the war in Europe, to re-form LOT with a fleet strength that soon rose to 20 examples of the Lisunov Li-2, the Soviet licence-built version of the Douglas DC-3. By the end of 1945, LOT was able to operate services to points as far afield as London, was re-formed and immediately acquired 20 Lisunov Li-2s, services to London resuming before the end of the year. The operator bought nine examples of the DC-3 during 1946, and during 1947 received the first three of an eventual five examples of the Sud-Est SE.161 Languedoc four-engine transport, the first of them arriving on 5 July.

More new equipment was introduced on 24 April 1949, when LOT received its first Ilyushin Il-12 two-engined transport, and three of these wholly inefficient and limited machines remained on strength to November 1959. In 1955, LOT began scheduled services to Moscow, and on 20 June of the same year took delivery of its first Ilyushin Il-14 improved twin-engined transport, which finally supplanted the Il-12. LOT also operated a more advanced Western type in the form of five examples of the Convair CV-240 twin-engined transport, of which the first was received on 2 October 1957.

111

LOT's first turboprop-powered airliner was the Ilyushin Il-18B, of which the first entered revenue-earning service on the route between Warsaw and Moscow on 25 April 1961. The growing availability of this four-engined type enabled LOT both to expand and to improve its network to the Middle East, and even to begin services into Africa. LOT also bought three examples of the Vickers Viscount 804 to complement the Il-18D on lower-density routes, and received the first of these aircraft on 11 November 1962.

In 1966, LOT received 10 examples of the twin-turboprop Antonov An-24V to take over from the Il-14 on its domestic network and some regional routes, and the first of these machines reached Warsaw on 22 March for its operational debut on the route linking Warsaw and Wroclaw on 20 April of the same year. This Soviet type rapidly became the backbone of LOT's domestic and short-haul regional network.

LOT's first jet-powered transport was the Tupolev Tu-134, of which the first two entered service during November 1968, and this short/medium-haul type was complemented from the

spring of 1972 by the altogether larger and longer-ranged Ilyushin Il-62 which entered services on routes to destinations such as London, Milan, Moscow and Paris.

By the mid-1980s, LOT was operating international services to Europe, North America, North Africa, the Middle East and Asia with aircraft such as the AN-24, Il-18, Il-62, Tu-134 and Tu-154. With the disintegration of the Soviet-dominated Eastern bloc in the late 1980s, Poland was able to exercise a greater degree of autonomy in sourcing its aircraft. It has since turned increasingly to Western manufacturers for more capable aircraft, that although more expensive in capital terms, are considerably more economical to run than their Russian counterparts. With the exception of the Tu-134 and Tu-154, LOT has been able to retire its Soviet-supplied airliners in favour of the ATR 72 (now retired in favour of the EMBRAER RJ-145) for its local and feeder services, the Boeing Model 737 for its short- and medium-haul services, and the Boeing Model 767 for its long-haul services. The introduction of more Western aircraft will further boost the airline.

LTU INTERNATIONAL AIRWAYS (GERMANY)

Main bases and hubs: Düsseldorf and Munich
Type of operation: International scheduled and charter passenger and cargo
Personnel: 5,200
Created in October 1955 to operate charter flights to the Mediterranean region, Lufttransport Union changed its name to LTU International Airways in 1956. With 49.9 per cent of its equity owned by the holding company that numbers Swissair among its other assets, LTU now flies scheduled as well as charter services not only to the Mediterranean but also to destinations in East

Fleet (orders):
2 (6) x Airbus A320-200
(7) x Airbus A330-200
6 x Airbus A330-300
3 x Boeing Model 737-700
11 x Boeing Model 757-200
6 x Boeing Model 767-300ER

Africa, the Far East and the Americas within the context of a network of scheduled flights reaching out to 73 destinations in Europe, the Americas, East Africa and the Far East.

LUFTHANSA GERMAN AIRLINES (GERMANY)

Main bases and hubs: Berlin (Tempelhof), Bremen, Düsseldorf, Frankfurt, Hamburg, Hanover, Cologne/Bonn, Munich and Stuttgart
Type of operation: International and regional scheduled and charter passenger and cargo services
Personnel: not available
Lufthansa is Germany's national flag carrier and can trace its lineage back to 1919 and the establishment in Germany, shortly after the end of World War I, of a pioneering airline named Deutsche Luftreederei that operated a primitive service between Berlin and Weimar, the former and the then current political capitals of Germany. A more immediate ancestor was Deutsche Luft Hansa, which came into existence on 6 January 1926 as a nationalized amalgamation of two other early German private operators, namely Deutsche Aero Lloyd and Junkers Luftverkehr. By 1939 and the outbreak of World War II, Deutsche Lufthansa,

Fleet (orders):
11 x Airbus A300-600
2 x Airbus A300-600R
5 x Airbus A310-300
20 x Airbus A319-100
36 x Airbus A320-200
20 x Airbus A321-100
6 x Airbus A321-200
6 x Airbus A340-200
25 (7) x Airbus A340-300
10 x Airbus A340-600
39 x Boeing Model 737-300
7 x Boeing Model 737-300QC
30 x Boeing Model 737-500

3 x Boeing Model 747-200B
4 x Boeing Model 747-200B Combi
21 (2) x Boeing Model 747-400
7 x Boeing Model 747-400 Combi

as the company had become, was the largest and most successful European airline, operating an extensive network within Europe as well as services to South America, the Middle East and the Far East as far east as Bangkok.

Moreover, in addition to its own network of routes, Lufthansa also had access to services in China and right through South America by means of a group of associated airlines established with a modest measure of German funding and greater measures of German impetus and technical expertise.

During the early part of the 1930s, the airline was involved in the clandestine training of pilots for the Luftwaffe, and by 1939 these crews had become the backbone of the German Air Force bomber squadrons. Deutsche Lufthansa continued to operate on a limited basis during World War II, but ceased flights in April 1945, and in May 1945 was banned by the victorious Allies.

On 6 January 1953, a provisional holding company was formed as Luftag, with support from the German federal railways and the state of Nordrhein-Westphalia. Soon after this the new airline was able to draw on private as well as government financing for the ordering of four examples each of the Lockheed L-1049G Super Constellation four-engined airliner and Convair CV-340 twin-engined airliner.

On 16 August 1954, Luftag changed its name to Deutsche Lufthansa, and some eight months later, on 1 April 1955, the airline flew its first domestic service with a CV-340. From this time onward, expansion was fairly rapid, and Deutsche Lufthansa soon expanded its network over most parts of the European continent, beginning with services to London, Madrid and Paris. It was on 8 June of the same year, moreover, that the operator flew its first intercontinental service, when a Super Constellation reached New York from Hamburg via Düsseldorf and Shannon.

In December 1958, Deutsche Lufthansa placed in service its first turboprop-powered airliner, namely a Vickers Viscount 814 that had been received on 5 October of the same year. Deutsche Lufthansa, or Lufthansa as it came to be called with increasing regularity, moved still further into the era of advanced-technology airliners on 3

February 1960, when it took delivery of its first Boeing Model 707-430 four-turbofan transport, and flew its first service non-stop from Frankfurt to New York on 17 March of the same year. The Model 707 was followed into Lufthansa service by another Boeing jetliner, namely the Model 727-230 three-turbofan type: the first of this important medium-haul model was received on 22 February 1964, and the type was operated mainly on the airliner's steadily growing network of European routes.

Lufthansa became the first airline to order the Boeing Model 737 twin-turbofan short-haul airliner early in 1965, and the first two of an eventual 21 of these Model 737-100 aircraft were delivered to Lufthansa on 27 December 1967. This type was also used almost without variation on the European network.

The first wide-body aircraft ordered by Lufthansa was the Boeing Model 747-130, of which the first was delivered on 10 March 1970, and with the Douglas DC-10-30, this type constituted the core of Lufthansa's long-haul fleet during the 1970s and 1980s, shorter-haul routes being entrusted to the Airbus A300 as well as two Boeing types, the Model 727 and Model 737.

Lufthansa is still a major operator of Boeing turbofan-powered transport aircraft, and also of a number of Airbus types. The airline now operates a very large route network. Its main subsidiaries are Condor Flugdienst, formed in 1961 to carry out charter and inclusive tour flights for the parent company; Lufthansa Cargo Airline, formed in 1977 for international and domestic scheduled and charter freight services; and Lufthansa CityLine, so named in March 1992 after creation in 1958 as Ostfriesische Lufttaxi for regional and domestic feeder services, then renamed Ostfriesische Lufttransport in 1970 and Deutsche Lufttransport in 1974.

BELOW: *Lufthansa uses a mix of Airbus and Boeing aircraft for its large route network.*

LUXAIR (LUXEMBOURG)

Main base and hub: Luxembourg
Type of operation: International scheduled and charter passenger and cargo
Personnel: 2,045

Luxair was created out of the previous Luxembourg Airlines in 1962, and from an initial concentration on effective air communications between a number of European capitals steadily spread its endeavours. The national airline of Luxembourg, Luxair now operates a scheduled route network connecting 30 major destinations throughout most of the

Fleet (orders):
2 x Boeing Model 737-400
2 x Boeing Model 737-500
3 (1) x EMBRAER RJ-145ER
5 x EMBRAER RJ-145LR
4 x Fokker 50

European continent, except the far north and the countries of the Balkan region.

MALAYSIA AIRLINES (MALAYSIA)

Main base and hub: Kuala Lumpur
Type of operation: International, regional and domestic scheduled and charter passenger and cargo services
Personnel: 21,685

The national flag carrier of Malaysia, Malaysian Airlines was incorporated with the name Malaysian Airlines System on 1 October 1972, although it is a descendant of Malayan Airways, itself a descendant of Wearne's Air Services. Created in 1937 by Straits Steamship, Ocean Steamship and Imperial Airways, Wearne's Air Services flew its first service on 28 June 1937 between Singapore and Penang via Kuala Lumpur and Ipoh using a De Havilland D.H.89A Dragon Rapide. Wearne's Air Services continued in operation up to 7 December 1941, when the Japanese attacked Pearl Harbor and the American and British possessions in the Far East to precipitate the Pacific War of World War II.

It was not until 1947, some 20 months after Japan's surrender, that Mansfield & Co. Ltd made plans to form Malayan Airways to resume the Malayan routes that Wearne's Air Services had pioneered. The new airline's first revenue-earning service was a charter flight on 2 April 1947 using the new operator's first equipment, an Airspeed Consul, and its first scheduled service followed on 1 May of the same year. The airline had ambitious plans for longer services with greater passenger loads, so in the period from August 1947 to March 1948 it bought five Douglas DC-3 twin-engined aircraft from British Aviation Services. The airline ended its link with British Aviation Services late in 1947, and early in 1948 the British Overseas Airways Corporation acquired a 10 per cent shareholding in Malayan Airways. In this same year a bilateral agreement with Siam Airways made it possible for Malayan Airways to started a weekly service to Bangkok from April, and over the next three years the airline began to expand fairly quickly by the standards of the day. By the end of 1951, Malayan Airways had a fleet of 11 DC-3 transports and, after the completion of further airports in Borneo, two D.H.89A Dragon Rapide aircraft were acquired from British European Airways for services to destinations in the remoter parts of this huge island.

With the emergence of the Federation of Malaya on 31 August 1957, the decision was taken to spur the growth of

Fleet (orders):
9 x Airbus A330-300
36 x Boeing Model 737-400
1 x Boeing Model 737-500
2 x Boeing Model 747-200F
1 x Boeing Model 747-300 Combi
14 (5) x Boeing Model 747-400
2 x Boeing Model 747-400 Combi
11 (6) x Boeing Model 777-200ER
5 x De Havilland Canada DHC-6
   Twin Otter Series 300
10 x Fokker 50

Malayan Airways from an essentially domestic operator into an international airline that would be the flag carrier of the new nation. To further this objective, the British Overseas Airways Corporation and Qantas each took a 32 per cent shareholding in the airline, and limited moves to rationalize the domestic network and fleet resulted in the incorporation into the airline's fleet of three De Havilland Canada DHC-2 Beaver single-engined bush transports previously operated by Federation Air Services, and the transfer of the two D.H.89A aircraft to newly created Borneo Airways. More important, however, was the leasing from Qantas during 1958 of a Douglas DC-4 four-engined transport for use on the airline's first long-haul service, in this instance to Hong Kong.

On 1 August 1959, Malayan Airways received its first turbine-powered aircraft in the form of two Vickers Viscount 760 transports. These turboprop airliners soon entered revenue-earning service, operating on the routes linking Singapore with Kuala Lumpur, Jakarta and Borneo. In March 1960, the airline leased Lockheed Super Constellation aircraft from Qantas for the service to Hong Kong, but this service ended in October for lack of adequate traffic. Malayan Airways then leased from the British Overseas Airways Corporation Bristol Britannia four-turboprop aircraft with which to operate the route from September 1961 in conjunction with Cathay Pacific Airways.

RIGHT: *Malaysia Airlines flies a schedule of domestic, regional and international services.*

In 1961, Malayan Airways decided that the time was ripe for replacement of its DC-3 aircraft, and the type selected was the Fokker F.27 Friendship Mk 200, of which five were ordered in February 1962 for delivery from May 1963. Malayan Airways' first pure jet airliner was a De Havilland Comet 4 leased from the British Overseas Airways Corporation for service from December 1962 on the service linking Singapore with Jakarta and Hong Kong.

During November 1963, the creation of Malaysia out of the Federation of Malaya resulted in a change of name, Malayan Airways thus becoming Malaysian Airways. During the later part of 1965, Malaysian Airways bought five examples of the Comet 4 from the British Overseas Airways Corporation for the first stage of a planned expansion of the airline's international route network. In 1966, the governments of Malaysia and Singapore acquired a joint controlling interest in the airline, and further change followed on 1 November 1967 when Malaysian Airways became Malaysia-Singapore Airlines. Soon after this, the airline decided to re-equip its fleet with five Boeing Model 737-112 twin-turbofan and three Boeing Model 707-312B four-turbofan airliners for its short- and long-haul services respectively. The first Model 707-312B was received on 28 May 1968 and the initial example of the Model 737-112 on 16 July 1969. On 15 December 1968, Malaysia-Singapore Airlines took delivery of two Britten-Norman BN-2A Islander twin-engined light transports for the operation of rural services in the eastern part of Malaysia. In October 1970, Malaysia-Singapore Airlines finally secured the right to operate flights to London (Heathrow).

The contract between Malaysia and Singapore for the operation of a joint airline ended in the course of December 1972 in line with the two countries' earlier decision to establish their own national flag carriers, and the Malaysian Airline System was established on 1 October 1972 with a fleet of Model 737, F.27 and Islander aircraft for services in the Malay Peninsula as well as to Sabah and Sarawak. In 1974, the operator inaugurated a service to London with Model 707 aircraft.

By the middle of the decade, the growth of the Malaysian Airline System's network and traffic made it sensible to start the acquisition of wide-body aircraft, of which the first was a McDonnell Douglas DC-10-30 three-turbofan type accepted on 2 August 1976, with two additional aircraft following in 1977 and 1981. Further expansion required still more capacity, and in 1982 the Malaysian Airline System received the first of an initial two examples of the Boeing Model 747-236B four-turbofan transports, and this type soon replaced the DC-10 on the airline's European services. The Malaysian Airline system then placed an order for five examples of the twin-turbofan Airbus A300B4, of which the first was accepted on 3 November 1979. This type was used mainly on the airline's Asian route network in conjunction with three DC-10 aircraft, with the Model 737 aircraft plying the shorter-haul regional and domestic networks, and the F.27, BN-2A and Twin Otter machines servicing feeder and local services.

In October 1987, the name of the operator was changed from Malaysian Airlines System to Malaysia Airlines, and this carrier now operates a large network.

MARTINAIR HOLLAND (NETHERLANDS)

Main base and hub: Amsterdam (Schiphol)
Type of operation: International scheduled and charter passenger and cargo
Personnel: 3,070
The airline now known as Martinair Holland was established in May 1958 as Martin's Air Charter, which was given its present name during 1971. The operator is currently owned by KLM and Nedlloyd in equal parts, and flies a scheduled international network extending to 20 destinations. These are mainly Latin American and American cities, but also include Brussels in

Fleet (orders):
2 x Boeing Model 747-200C
1 x Boeing Model 747-200F
2 x Boeing Model 757-200
6 x Boeing Model 767-300ER
4 x Boeing MD-11CF
2 x Boeing MD-11 Freighter

Belgium, Colombo in Sri Lanka and Abu Dhabi in the Middle East.

MESA AIRLINES
(UNITED STATES OF AMERICA)

Main base and hub: Phoenix
Type of operation: International, regional and domestic scheduled passenger
Personnel: not available
Mesa Airlines was established as an commuter-line operator in 1980, and since that time has grown steadily to become a major regional airline in the south-west of the USA. It has a network of 61 destinations centred on Colorado and New Mexico, but also extending to the other south-western and

Fleet (orders):
32 x Bombardier CRJ-200LR
12 x Bombardier Dash 8-200
14 (22) x EMBRAER RJ-145LR
45 Raytheon Beech Model
  1900D Airliner

midwest states as well as eastern seaboard cities of the continental USA.

MESABA AIRLINES
(UNITED STATES OF AMERICA)

Main bases and hubs: Minneapolis/St Paul, Detroit
IType of operation: International, regional and domestic scheduled passenger
Personnel: 3,370
Initially a small fixed-base operator known as Mesaba Aviation and established in 1944, this organization extended its ambitions to scheduled air services from February 1973, and is now one of the most important regional airlines in the north of the USA, with a network of scheduled services connecting

Fleet (orders):
36 x BAE Systems Avro RJ-85
23 x Saab 340A
50 x Saab 340B

five Canadian and some 95 US destinations. Northwest Airlines has a stake of almost 28 per cent in the company.

MEXICANA (MEXICO)

Main base and hub: Mexico City
Type of operation: International, regional and domestic scheduled and charter passenger and cargo
Personnel: 6,455
One of the oldest airlines in the world and the largest domestic air operator in Mexico, Mexicana was established in July 1921 as the Compañía Mexicana de Transportación Aérea, and is now a major player in the Central American air transport field, with a scheduled route network that includes 20 international destinations in the Americas as well as 31 domestic

Fleet (orders):
19 (8) x Airbus A320-200
20 x Boeing Advanced Model 727-200
6 (1) x Boeing Model 757-200
12 Fokker 100

destinations. The airline is privately owned by Cintra, which also controls Aeroméxico.

MIDDLE EAST AIRLINES (LEBANON)

Main base and hub: Beirut
Type of operation: International scheduled passenger and cargo
Personnel: 3,615
Middle East Airlines is the national airline of Lebanon, and its fortunes have fluctuated wildly in line with those of its nation when beset by internal and external strife. Middle East Airlines was established in May 1945 and began operations in January 1946, initially with the technical and administrative support of Pan American, but replaced by the British Overseas Airways Corporation between 1955 and 1959. In 1959, this operator became wholly 'independent' until 1963, when a merger with Air Leban gave Air France a 30 per cent stake; in the same year, Middle East Airlines took over Lebanese International Airways. During the worst of the conflicts in Lebanon, when the airline lost about half of its aircraft and

Fleet (orders):
3 x Airbus A310-200
2 x Airbus A310-300
2 x Airbus A320-200
2 x Airbus A321-200

also suffered important personnel losses, Middle East Airlines operated from neighbouring Cyprus. Middle East Airlines has now rebuilt itself and operates a scheduled network to 21 international destinations.

BELOW: *Re-equipping after a civil war, Middle East Airlines opted for Airbus equipment.*

MIDWAY AIRLINES
(UNITED STATES OF AMERICA)

Main base and hub: Raleigh
Type of operation: Regional and domestic scheduled
passenger and cargo
Personnel: not available
Established in November 1993 with operations beginning in
the same month, Midway Airlines is a significant regional
operator. Its commuter-line associate is Corporate Airlines,
and these two operators between them fly some 260
scheduled services per day linking some 32 destinations in

Fleet (orders):
9 (14) x Boeing Model 737-700
24 (2) x Bombardier CRJ-200ER
6 x Fokker 100

18 of the states in the eastern part of the USA. Midway Airlines
is owned by a Chicago-based investment partnership.

MIDWEST EXPRESS
(UNITED STATES OF AMERICA)

Main bases and hubs: Milwaukee, Kansas City and Omaha
Type of operation: International, regional and domestic
scheduled and charter passenger and cargo
Personnel: not available
Established in 1983 for the start of operations in June of the
following year, Midwest Express began as an offshoot of K-C
Aviation, itself created in 1969 as a more fully organized form
of the executive transport operation that the Kimberly-Clark
company had created in 1948 for the rapid transport of its own
personnel. Midway Express's primary market is still the

Fleet (orders):
6 x Boeing MD-81
3 x Boeing MD-82
2 x Boeing MD-88
8 x McDonnell Douglas
DC-9-10
16 x McDonnell Douglas
DC-9-30

business traveller, and the airline flies to some 50 destinations
in Canada and mainly in the central and eastern parts of the
USA, as well as Las Vegas and Los Angeles.

MONARCH AIRLINES (UNITED KINGDOM)

Main bases and hubs: Birmingham, London (Gatwick and
Luton) and Manchester
Type of operation: International scheduled and charter
passenger
Personnel: 2,000
A wholly owned subsidiary of the Globus Gateway Group,
Monarch Airlines was created in June 1967 to cater for the
rapidly developing British market for holiday charter flights,
and began operations in April 1968. This is still the airline's
primary market, largely to destinations in the Mediterranean,
but, under the Monarch Crown Service logo, the airline also

Fleet (orders):
4 x Airbus A300-600R
2 x Airbus A320-200
3 (5) x Airbus A321-200
2 x Airbus A330-200
7 x Boeing Model 757-200
1 x McDonnell Douglas
DC-10-30

undertakes a limited schedule of international services to
Gibraltar as well as the Spanish destinations Alicante, Malaga,
Menorca and Tenerife.

NATIONAL AIRLINES
(UNITED STATES OF AMERICA)

Main base and hub: Las Vegas
Type of operation: Regional and domestic scheduled
passenger
Personnel: not available
Created in April 1995 and beginning services in May 1999,
National Airlines was created specifically for the task of flying
first- and economy-class passengers into and out of the Las
Vegas gambling and holiday centre, and currently flies services
linking Las Vegas with eight major American cities.

Fleet (orders):
15 (2) x Boeing Model 757-200

The airline is owned by Wexford Management and a
consortium of Las Vegas-based entertainment groups.

NIPPON CARGO AIRLINES (JAPAN)

Main bases and hubs: Osaka (Kansai) and Tokyo (Narita)
Type of operation: International, regional and domestic
scheduled and charter cargo
Personnel: 655
Nippon Cargo Airlines was Japan's first specialized air freight
operator, and was established in September 1978 for the start
of operations in 1985.

Fleet (orders):
1 x Boeing Model 747-100F
9 x Boeing Model 747-200F

NORTHWEST AIRLINES (UNITED STATES OF AMERICA)

Main bases and hubs: Detroit, Minneapolis/St Paul, Memphis
and Tokyo (Narita)
Type of operation: International, regional and domestic
scheduled and charter passenger and cargo services
Personnel: 53,000
Northwest Airlines was created on 1 August 1926 as Northwest
Airways. The new airline flew its first service on 1 October of
the same year using a Curtiss Oriole to deliver a load of mail
from St Paul to Chicago. The airline flew its first passenger
service over the same route in July 1927 with a fleet of three
Stinson Detroiter aircraft. Adverse weather later meant a
suspension of services between the late autumn of 1927 and
June 1928, and in September of that year the airline acquired
more capable and better-equipped Hamilton H.47 aircraft to
provide a greater likelihood of being able to maintain services
during the winter months.

In 1931, Northwest Airways inaugurated its first
international route, to Winnipeg in Canada, and in the same
year bought two examples of the Sikorsky S-38 amphibian
flying boat for services to Duluth. During the following year, the
airline gained greater independence when the 45 per cent
shareholding in the company held in equal portions by
Transcontinental Air Transport and the Aviation Corporation of
America was bought out, and the following year the airline was
able to buy Lockheed Model 10A Electra modern twin-engined
airliners to replace the ageing Ford Tri-Motors three-engined
transports. The Electra remained in service for eight years and
proved very successful.

In 1934, the operator was renamed Northwest Airlines, and
in 1937 adopted the more capable Lockheed Model 14 Super
Electra. It was replaced by an initial seven examples of the DC-
3 aircraft, ordered in 1938 and delivered from 22 April 1939.
Northwest Airlines flew its first revenue-earning service with
the DC-3 in the same month on the route linking the Twin Cities
and Chicago. In May 1939, this route was extended west to
Seattle. The DC-3, of which the airline eventually operated 36
examples, remained in service up to 1958.

During World War II, Northwest Airlines flew transport
services from Minneapolis to Fairbanks in Alaska, undertook
pilot training for the US Army Air Forces on the Curtiss C-46
Commando twin-engined transport, and at its St Paul base
modified more than 3,000 examples of the Consolidated B-24

Fleet (orders):
21 (53) x Airbus A319-100
70 (12) x Airbus A320-200
40 x Airbus A330-300
30 x Boeing Advanced
   Model 727-200
20 x Boeing Model 747-200B
10 x Boeing Model 747-200F
14 (2) x Boeing Model 747-400
48 (5) x Boeing Model 757-200
(20) x Boeing Model 757-300
(11) x Bombardier CRJ-200LR
9 x McDonnell Douglas DC-9-10
115 x McDonnell Douglas DC-9-30

21 x McDonnell Douglas DC-9-40
35 x McDonnell Douglas DC-9-50
24 x McDonnell Douglas DC-10-30
21 x McDonnell Douglas DC-10-40

Liberator and North American B-25 Mitchell bombers.

Conventional airline operations returned in the middle of
1945, and in June of that year the airline was granted an
extension of its service from Milwaukee via Detroit to New
York. Northwest Airlines therefore placed an order for the
Douglas DC-4 four-engined airliner which entered service on
the airline's most important American routes from March 1946.
The DC-4 was soon supplemented from 1947 by the Martin
2-0-2, a twin-engined type that entered service first with
Northwest Airlines.

Northwest Airlines flew its first service to Tokyo and Manila
via Anchorage on 15 July 1947. On 29 July 1948, Northwest
Airways operated its first service to the Hawaiian Islands from
Seattle and Portland to Hawaii, and in 1947 changed its name
to Northwest Orient Airlines. In 1948, Northwest Orient Airlines
ordered 10 examples of the Boeing Model 377 Stratocruiser, as
this offered the type of economical high-altitude performance
needed for flights across the Pacific. The first of the
Stratocruiser airliners was delivered on 22 June 1949, and the
Stratocruisers were initially put into service on the Honolulu
route. They remained in service until 12 September 1960,
when Northwest Orient Airlines bought the Lockheed L-188
Electra four-turboprop airliner.

In the three-year duration of the Korean War from 1950 to
1953, Northwest Orient airlines flew more than 1,400 two-way
services across the Pacific on behalf of the military. When
Japan Air Lines was established, in August 1951, this was
made possible by Northwest Orient Airlines' provision of
technical support and aircraft, the latter comprising DC-4 and

119

Martin 2-0-2 machines, but in October 1952 Transocean Air Lines succeeded Northwest Orient Airlines in this role.

In the early 1950s, Northwest Orient Airlines decided that its growth was being hampered by the limited capacity of its DC-4 aircraft, and from September 1953 leased from Flying Tigers four examples of the Douglas DC-6A freighter which were then revised to an all-passenger configuration. The airline later took additional DC-6 aircraft, and the type served Northwest Orient Airlines with considerable success for 12 years, until 10 June 1965. In April 1953, the airline placed an order for six (later reduced to four) examples of the Lockheed L-1049G Super Constellation, and became the first operator of this type on 15 February 1955, when it supplanted the DC-4 on the operator's Far Eastern services. Northwest Orient Airlines flew the Super Constellation for only two years, until it took delivery of its first Douglas DC-7C on 28 February 1957 to replace both the Stratocruiser and the Super Constellation on its Pacific as well as longer domestic services.

Northwest Orient airlines operated only one turboprop-powered airliner, namely the Electra: the airline ordered the type in November 1958, received its first such aeroplane on 19 July 1959, and flew its first service with the type on 1 September 1959 on the route linking Minneapolis and New York via Milwaukee. On 18 May 1960, Northwest Orient Airlines received its first pure jet type in the form of the Douglas DC-8-32, which was flown on the operator's Pacific routes from 8 July 1960. Three years later, Northwest Orient Airlines replaced its DC-8 aircraft with Boeing Model 720-051B four-engined machines, of which the first two were received on 22 June 1961. The airline soon added the Boeing Model 707-351 to its fleet, and for the remainder of the 1960s this long-haul type was the mainstay of Northwest Orient Airlines' fleet, together with the Boeing Model 727 three-turbofan type which provided a medium-haul capability after the delivery of the first aeroplane on 12 November 1964.

Like other major operators, Northwest Orient Airlines adopted the Boeing Model 747 wide-body transport, and took delivery of its first Model 747-151 on 30 April 1970 for use on the airline's domestic and international services from 22 June and 1 July of the same year respectively on the route linking the Twin Cities and New York, and that between Chicago and Tokyo via Seattle. The next wide-body type to enter service with Northwest Orient Airlines was the Douglas DC-10-30, ordered in 1968 and delivered from 10 November 1972.

Northwest Orient Airlines started services from Seattle to Europe in April 1979, the first destinations being Copenhagen and Prestwick. In the 1980s, the operator ordered the Airbus A320. On 12 August 1986, Northwest Orient Airlines took over Republic Airlines. The airline is the second oldest American airline to have retained its basic identity since creation, but was reorganized in 1985 to create NWA as the holding company for the core airline, now renamed Northwest Airlines, and several subsidiaries.

LEFT: *Northwest Airlines operates a large fleet of Airbus, Boeing and Douglas aircraft, including several DC-10s.*

OLYMPIC AIRWAYS (GREECE)

Main bases and hubs: Athens and Thessaloniki
Type of operation: International, regional and domestic scheduled passenger and cargo services
Personnel: not available

The origins of Olympic Airways, the national flag carrier of Greece, can be traced back to 1951 and the establishment of TAE (Technical and Aeronautical Exploitations Co.). The new operator's services were mainly local, but the airline did not fare well as a result of the twin problems of obsolete aircraft and the lack of capital with which to procure more modern machines. After providing a measure of interim financial support, the Greek government nationalized the airline in June 1955, but this failed to improve matters, as although the airline now had the capital for a measure of technical modernization, it lacked management personnel of adequate quality. The government then put the airline into liquidation and started to sell its assets to private investors.

It was at this stage that Aristotle Onassis, the shipping magnate, offered to take over the airline, providing additional capital and management capability, to create a successful national flag carrier. The government of Greece accepted the offer, and Onassis was awarded a 50-year concession as the national flag carrier and sole operator of domestic routes. Onassis renamed Technical and Aeronautical Exploitations

Fleet (orders):
3 x Airbus A300-600R
4 x Airbus A340-300
11 x Boeing Advanced Model 737-200
1 x Boeing Model 737-300
12 x Boeing Model 737-400

Olympic Airways, and one of the first changes was the retirement of the airline's obsolete Douglas DC-4 four-engined airliners in favour of more advanced Douglas DC-6B four-engined machines leased from the French airline Union Aéromaritime de Transport as Olympic awaited the delivery of still more capable aircraft. After careful assessment of its route network, Olympic Airways opted to concentrate on its European and Mediterranean operations before developing longer-haul services.

By 1961, the airliner fleet operated by Olympic Airways had been extensively overhauled to include four examples of the jet-powered De Havilland Comet 4B leased from British European Airways, four examples of the DC-6B and two examples of the DC-4, as well as 13 examples of the venerable Douglas DC-3 for local services, with two examples of the four-jet Douglas DC-8s about to be delivered.

Growth and profitability followed, before rising fuel prices and a declining market reversed the trend, and as losses mounted, Onassis withdrew from Olympic Airways during December 1974. The airline ceased operation until a reorganization had been devised and implemented. In August 1975, Onassis and the government of Greece finally reached a settlement whereby Greece once more assumed complete ownership of Olympic Airways, which had restarted operations

ABOVE: *Financially troubled Olympic Airways flies a mix of Airbus and Boeing aircraft.*

in January of that year over a network connecting some 25 points in Africa, Asia, Australia, Europe and North America.

By 1978, the airline was again in difficulties, however, and in December an agreement with Swissair provided assistance with the management and further reorganization of the airline.

PAKISTAN INTERNATIONAL AIRLINES (PAKISTAN)

Main bases and hubs: Islamabad, Karachi, Lahore, Peshawar and Quetta

Type of operation: International and regional scheduled and charter passenger and cargo services

Personnel: not available

After a short period of independence, Pakistan decided in 1951 that it needed a national flag carrier airline, and the government of the country accordingly established Pakistan International Airlines in this role, on 25 May of the same year ordering three examples of the Lockheed L-1049C Super Constellation four-engined airliner as the new operator's initial equipment. Pakistan International Airlines flew its first service with the Super Constellation on 7 June 1954 on the route linking Karachi and Dacca (now Dhaka) which were the main cities of the country's western and eastern halves (the latter now being the separate country of Bangladesh). On 1 February 1955, there followed the operator's first international service, in this instance between Karachi and London via Cairo.

On 11 March 1955 Pakistan International Airlines formally took over the assets and routes of another Pakistani operator, Orient Airways, which had in effect been part of Pakistan International Airlines since October 1953. The consolidation of the two airlines meant that Pakistan International Airlines could enlarge its domestic network with 11 Douglas DC-3 and two Convair CV-240 aircraft, which left the Super Constellation machines wholly free for international services.

Modernization of the fleet used for domestic and regional

Fleet (orders):
9 x Airbus A300B4-200
6 x Airbus A310-300
6 x Boeing Model 737-300
4 x Boeing Model 747-200B
2 x Boeing Model 747-200B Combi
5 x Boeing Model 747-300
2 x De Havilland Canada DHC-6 Twin Otter Series 300
2 x Fokker F.27 Friendship Mk 200

operations was now a matter of high priority, and in May 1956 the airline placed an order for three examples of the Vickers Viscount 815 four-turboprop airliner, the first of which was accepted in the UK on 2 January 1959 for a debut in revenue-earning service on the service linking Karachi and Delhi on 31 January. Further enhancement came in 1961 with the debut of the Fokker F.27 Friendship twin-turboprop type, of which the first was received on 3 January 1961. The availability of the F.27 for operation on the routes linking the major Pakistani cities freed the DC-3 fleet for use on new services to the remoter parts of East Pakistan.

Pakistan International Airlines was the first Asian airline with pure jet aircraft. These were Boeing Model 707-121 machines leased from Pan American World Airways in 1960 for use from 7 March 1960 on the London service which extended to New York on 5 May of the following year. Then, on 21 December 1961, Pakistan International Airlines began to receive its own jet aircraft, when it took delivery of the first of three Boeing

Model 720-040B aircraft, whose availability permitted the operator to enlarge its international route network.

In 1963, Pakistan International Airlines called off its New York service, but on 29 April of the following year became the first non-communist airline to operate a service to the Chinese city of Shanghai with the Model 720. In 1971, East Pakistan secured its independence as Bangladesh, and Pakistan International Airlines ceased operations to that country. The airline's fleet and network were both reduced, but the service to New York was nonetheless resumed in 1972. Regional capability was now poor, and as a result, Pakistan International Airlines ordered four examples of the Hawker Siddeley HS.121 Trident, of which the first was accepted on 1 March 1966. The aircraft were later sold to the Civil Aviation Administration of China in 1970.

The first wide-body airliner used by Pakistan International Airlines was the McDonnell Douglas DC-10-30 three-turbofan type, of which the airline received its first on 1 March 1974. In April 1976, there followed a pair of Boeing Model 747-282B four-turbofan aircraft, initially leased from TAP Air Portugal) and then on 3 March 1980 the airline accepted its first Airbus A300B4-203 two-turbofan type, subsequently completed by the same manufacturer's A310-300.

The A300, A310 and Model 747 are the current core of PAI's medium- and long-haul services, with the Model 737-300 and F.27 Friendship flown on feeder and local services.

BELOW: *Mainstay of Pakistan International Airlines' long-haul services is the Model 747.*

PELITA AIR SERVICE (INDONESIA)

Main base and hub: Jakarta
Type of operation: International, regional and domestic scheduled and charter passenger and cargo
Personnel: 975
Established in 1963 but beginning operations only in January 1970, Pelita Air Service provides a wide range of air services, including executive transport and oil/gas resources exploitation support, inside and outside the Indonesian archipelago.

Fleet (orders):
1 x BAE Systems Avro RJ-85
5 x Bombardier Dash 7
1 x Fokker 70
1 x Fokker 100
2 x Fokker F.28 Fellowship Mk 4000
4 x IPTN NC-212-100
8 x IPTN C-212-200
2 x Lockheed Martin L-100-30 Hercules

PERM AIRLINES (RUSSIA)

Main base and hub: Perm
Type of operation: International, regional and domestic scheduled and charter passenger and cargo
Personnel: 1,000
Created out of the Perm Division of Aeroflot after the dissolution of the USSR into the CIS, Perm Airlines undertakes a wide range of air transport roles, including charter flights between Moscow and the Canary Islands and a single scheduled international service between Perm and Tashkent, but concentrates on its Ekaterinburg, Krasnodar, Kurgan,

Fleet (orders):
3 x Antonov An-24B
3 x Antonov An-26
4 x Tupolev Tu-134A
6 x Tupolev Tu-154B
1 (2) x Tupolev Tu-204-100

Mineralnye Vody, Moscow, Perm, Samara, Sochi and St Petersburg links.

PHILIPPINE AIRLINES (PHILIPPINES)

Main base and hub: Manila
Type of operation: International, regional and domestic scheduled passenger and cargo services
Personnel: 8,200

The national flag carrier of the Republic of the Philippines, Philippine Airlines can trace its origins back to 1931, when a Filipino named Andres Soriano and a number of Americans established the Philippine Aerial Taxi Co. (PATCO) for the operation initially of private and charter flights. In 1936, however, PATCO moved into the field of scheduled services and changed its name to the Philippine Air Transport Co. By 1938, PATCO was flying two scheduled services from Manila to Baguio and Legaspi. PATCO went bankrupt in July 1940, but was re-formed on 25 February 1941 as Philippine Air Lines with backing from American and Filipino interests, the former including Trans World Airlines, with a 25 per cent shareholding. The revised operator flew its first service on 15 March of the same year with a flight by a Beech Model 18 from Manila to Baguio.

Philippine Air Lines halted operations in December 1941 after a Japanese force invaded the islands, but got under way once more after the end of World War II with a fleet of five Douglas C-47 twin-engined transports. The first scheduled service was flown on 14 February 1946 from Manila to Legaspi. Over the next 20 years, more than 30 examples of the C-47, military version of the DC-3, saw service with Philippine Air Lines after being converted to civil use. The development of Philippine Air Lines in the years after World War II's end was extraordinarily rapid. Troop-carrying charters across the Pacific to Oakland in California began on 31 July 1946 with leased Douglas DC-4 four-engined transports, and regular passenger services to the west coast of the USA started in December 1946. Further Douglas DC-4 transports for these services were available after Philippine Air Lines had acquired Far East Air Transport on 6 May 1947.

In 1948, Philippine Air Lines bought its first four examples of the considerably more capable Douglas DC-6, the first of these aircraft being received on 14 April for initial service on the route from Manila to London, via Bangkok, Calcutta, Karachi, Cairo, Rome and Madrid, on 29 May of the same year; from London the route crossing the Atlantic and the USA to San Francisco, and thence back to Manila. In a mere two years, Philippine Air Lines had developed from a domestic operator to an airline that had a route that encircled the globe. In September 1948, Philippine Air Lines bought the financially failing Commercial Airlines, and late in 1950 acquired another Philippine airline, Trans Asiatic Airlines.

Further enlargement of the airline's route network to Italy and Switzerland was agreed shortly after this, and during 1953, Philippine Air Lines received authorization to launch a service across the Pacific to Mexico. With the exception of the Hong Kong service, however, Philippine Air Lines suspended all long-haul routes in April 1954 after the loss of a DC-6 at Rome on 14 January 1954 and decreasing passenger demand for its service

Fleet (orders):
3 x Airbus A320-200
8 x Airbus A330-300
4 x Airbus A340-300
9 x Boeing Model 737-300
3 x Boeing Model 737-400
3 x Boeing Model 747-200B
3 (4) x Boeing Model 747-400
1 x Boeing Model 747-400 Combi

to San Francisco. During the mid-1950s, the Hong Kong service was operated by Convair CV-340 twin-engined aircraft, of which the first had been delivered on 27 March 1953. The CV-340 was supplanted later in the decade by the Vickers Viscount 784, of which the first was received on 10 May 1955 for a first service on 1 June. From the start, the Viscount also operated the key domestic services to Cebu, Davao and Zamboanga.

Additional capability was provided on Philippine Air Lines' domestic routes from 1960 by the partial replacement of the C-47 by the Fokker F.27 Friendship twin-turboprop transport, of which the first was received on 23 February 1960, and from 1967 the F.27 was itself replaced by a larger twin-turboprop type, the Hawker Siddeley HS.748, of which the first was received on 20 February of that year. Throughout this period, services to more rural areas were undertaken by a number of De Havilland Canada DHC-3 Otter single-engined and Scottish Aviation Twin Pioneer Mk 2 twin-engined STOL transports.

Philippine Air Lines entered the era of jet-powered aircraft with the lease from Pan American World Airways early in 1962 of Boeing Model 707 machines, but these were replaced from 20 June of the same year by Douglas DC-8-53 machines leased from KLM. The availability of these four-jet aircraft permitted the resurrection of services across the Pacific to San Francisco. Further jet equipment began to enter service in May 1966, when the Viscount was replaced on domestic and regional services by the BAC One-Eleven twin-turbofan type, of which the first example was received on 19 April of that year. Philippine Air Lines also operated for some of its domestic services the NAMC YS-11 twin-turboprop transport, of which the first four were acquired from the bankrupt Filipinas Orient Airways in January 1974.

Wide-body equipment entered service with Philippine Air Lines to provide additional capability on long-haul services to Europe, the USA and Middle East. The first of these types was the McDonnell Douglas DC-10-30, of which an initial example was leased from KLM on 11 July 1974, and the second was the Boeing Model 747-2F6B which was bought with delivery made on 21 December 1979. These two types still constitute the main long-haul capability of the airline, which is now known as Philippine Airlines. On the short- and medium-haul routes to China, Japan and Singapore, the Airbus A300 is the operator's mainstay, the first of these aircraft having been received on 29 November 1979.

In the late 1970s, the airline decided to upgrade its medium-haul capability on lower-density routes with the

ABOVE: *The A340-300 is the largest Airbus type operated by Philippine Airlines.*

Boeing Model 727, of which the first were Model 727-2M7 machines leased from Hughes Airwest in July and August 1979 but later replaced by a pair of Model 727-134 three-turbofan aircraft bought from Transair Sweden in September and October 1981. The Model 727 aircraft were later sold, and Philippine Airlines' current capability on the short- and medium-haul routes is vested in the Fokker 50 for feeder and low-density domestic services, and the Boeing Model 737-300

for high-density domestic and regional services. The airline underwent a period of acute financial difficulty during the 1980s and 1990s, and is now seeking to re-establish itself with a larger and more capable fleet based on more Model 747 aircraft as well as three types of Airbus transports.

PIEDMONT AIRLINES (UNITED STATES OF AMERICA)

Main bases and hubs: Salisbury, Philadelphia, Charlotte, Washington (Dulles) and Pittsburgh
Type of operation: International, regional and domestic scheduled passenger
Personnel: 1,800

Fleet (orders):
43 x Bombardier Dash 8-100
18 x Bombardier Dash 8-200
3 x Bombardier Dash 8-300

Now providing services between 43 destinations in the eastern part of the USA as well as in Canada and the Bahamas, the operator known as Piedmont Airlines since 1993 began life in 1931 as Henson Aviation. Henson started scheduled services in 1962 under the Hagerstown Commuter (later Henson Airlines) logo, and then operated as Allegheny Commuter following an agreement with Allegheny Airlines, which was later known as USAir and is now US Airways. In 1983, Piedmont Aviation bought Henson, which then flew as Henson

– The Piedmont Regional Airline, until the 1987 purchase of Piedmont by the USAir group. Henson then operated as USAir Express until renamed Piedmont Airlines in 1993, then US Airways Express. The operator currently flies to five international destinations (four in the Bahamas and one in Canada) and also operates a domestic network linking 42 destinations in the eastern part of the USA.

POLAR AIR CARGO (UNITED STATES OF AMERICA)

Main bases and hubs: New York (John F. Kennedy), Anchorage and Amsterdam (Schiphol)
Type of operation: International, regional and domestic scheduled and charter cargo
Personnel: 500

Fleet (orders):
10 x Boeing Model 747-100F
8 x Boeing Model 747-200F
3 (2) x Boeing Model 747-400F

Polar Air Cargo was created in January 1993 and began scheduled freight services between Anchorage, Honolulu and New York in April of the same year. The operator's initial equipment was a pair of Boeing Model 747-100F machines,

with another pair of the same type added later in the same year. On 7 July 1994, the Federal Aviation Administration granted authorization for the operator to undertake its own maintenance at its main base in New York, and during the year, more Model 747 aircraft were added to the fleet: by the end of 1994, Polar Air Cargo had 12 Model 747 aircraft in its fleet. Together with FedEx and UPS, Polar Air Cargo is one of the fastest-expanding cargo airlines, and now offers worldwide scheduled and charter services. The airline works with cargo agencies around the world, and its scheduled services to Europe, India, Africa and the Middle East were increased by further destinations from the mid-1990s.

PULKOVO AVIATION ENTERPRISE (RUSSIA)

Main base and hub: St Petersburg
Type of operation: International, regional and domestic scheduled and charter passenger and cargo
Personnel: 7,170
Created in 1932 for the beginning of operations in June of the same year as the Leningrad Division of Aeroflot, and emerging as an entity in its own right following the dissolution of the USSR into the Commonwealth of Independent States. Pulkovo Aviation Enterprise is now one of the major Russian airlines with scheduled services on a route network that embraces 27

Fleet (orders):
8 x Ilyushin Il-86
11 x Tupolev Tu-134A
10 x Tupolev Tu-154B
10 x Tupolev Tu-154M

domestic and 20 international destinations, the latter mainly in the republics of the CIS, but also in the Middle East and Western Europe.

QANTAS AIRWAYS (AUSTRALIA)

Main base and hub: Sydney
Type of operation: International, regional and domestic scheduled passenger services
Personnel: 28,225
The national flag carrier of Australia, Qantas Airways can trace its origins back to 16 November 1920 and the establishment of the Queensland and Northern Territory Aerial Services (QANTAS). For the first two years of its existence, the company concentrated on air taxi and joyriding flights using two biplane types, namely an Avro Type 504K and a Royal Aircraft Factory B.E.2e. It was only on 1 November 1922 that QANTAS flew its first scheduled service, using an Armstrong Whitworth F.K.8 for the route linking Charleville to Cloncurry. For the rest of the 1920s and into the middle of the 1930s, QANTAS concentrated on the development of a 1,475-mile (2375-km) route network in Queensland, where it was also involved in the provision of flying doctor services. In 1931, however, QANTAS had sufficient strength and capability to co-operate with Imperial Airways in the launch of an air service on the route between the UK and Australia, and this partnership was further enhanced three years later on 18 January 1934, when the two companies formed QANTAS Empire Airways to fly the sector between Singapore and Brisbane, initially with De Havilland D.H.86 four-engined biplanes. Further long-haul capability arrived in 1938, when QANTAS took delivery of the first of an eventual six examples of the Short 'C' or 'Empire'-class flying boat designed for passenger and mail services within the context of the Empire Air Mail Service.

QANTAS cut back but did not entirely suspend its activities during World War II, and in this period the airline's most important contribution to the Allied war effort was the implementation and operation of the eastern sector of the 'Horseshoe Route' connecting the UK with Australasia via

Fleet (orders):
12 x Airbus A380-800
15 x Boeing Model 737-300
22 x Boeing Model 737-400
2 x Boeing Model 747-200B
2 x Boeing Model 747-200B Combi
6 x Boeing Model 747-300
25 x Boeing Model 747-400
2 x Boeing Model 747SP
7 x Boeing Model 767-200ER   29 x Boeing Model 767-300ER

Durban in South Africa using in the main two types of consolidated aircraft, namely the Catalina amphibian flying boat and the Liberator long-range landplane.

With the end of World War II in 1945, QANTAS was able to resume more conventional airline services. By this time, the airline was more interested in long-haul services than domestic operations, and the latter were gradually transferred to Trans-Australian Airlines from 1946 onwards. The emphasis on longer-haul routes was signalled most strongly by the nature of the aircraft ordered by QANTAS, of which the most important was the Lockheed Constellation four-engined type for which the airline contracted in October 1946.

On 3 July 1947, the government of Australia bought out QANTAS, having earlier purchased the shareholding in the company owned by the British Overseas Airways Corporation as successor to Imperial Airways, and at this time the airline became the Australian national flag carrier. On 15 May of the same year, QANTAS started a service across the Pacific to San Francisco, and in 1958 this formed the basis of a round-the-

RIGHT: *Qantas's safety record is aided by good maintenance of its Airbus and Boeing aircraft.*

globe operation as the route was extended first across the USA to New York, then across the Atlantic to London, and finally back to Australia via the Middle East and Far East. On 1 December 1947, QANTAS also inaugurated its Kangaroo Service between Sydney and London using the Constellation. Continued growth was the norm for QANTAS after this, with a link to New Zealand created across the Tasman Sea in association with Tasman Empire Air Lines, in which QANTAS was a shareholder. During 1954, its service across the Pacific was extended when QANTAS took over from British Commonwealth Pacific Airlines the route from Sydney to Vancouver via Fiji, Honolulu and San Francisco.

QANTAS entered the era of turbine-powered aircraft in 1958 with the acquisition of two such types in the form of the Boeing Model 707 four-turbojet and Lockheed L-188 Electra four-turboprop airliners, of which the former was initially operated on the route across the Pacific to North America, and the latter to launch QANTAS's own service to New Zealand. Growth continued through the 1960s, and in August 1967 the airline changed its name to Qantas Airways. The airline now flies a very substantial route network within Australia, on which the Boeing Model 737 twin-turbofan airliner is the workhorse of the fleet after Qantas's 1992 purchase of Australian Airlines, and throughout the Pacific and Far East together with other services to North America, the Middle East and Europe. It uses a small number of Airbus A300 twin-turbofan wide-body aircraft for its regional services and a substantial fleet of Boeing Model 747 four-turbofan wide-body aircraft in four variants for its longer-haul services in conjunction with Model 767 twin-turbofan wide-body airliner. Qantas was one of the first airlines to order the Airbus A380.

QATAR AIRWAYS (QATAR)

Main base and hub: Doha
Type of operation: International and regional scheduled and charter passenger and cargo
Personnel: not available
The national airline of Qatar, Qatar Airways was created in November 1993 and started operations in January of the following year. The airline was initially owned by the Qatari royal family, but was relaunched on a more 'Western' financial and administrative basis in 1997. Qatar Airways currently flies a scheduled network including some 27 international

Fleet (orders):
7 x Airbus A300-600R
5 (6) x Airbus A320-200
(5) x Airbus A330-200
(2) x Airbus A380-800

destinations, mostly in the Middle East, around the Indian Ocean and in Europe.

ROYAL AIR MAROC (MOROCCO)

Main base and hub: Casablanca
Type of operation: International, regional and domestic scheduled passenger and cargo
Personnel: not available
The operator now known as Royal Air Maroc was created in June 1953 as the Compagnie Cherifienne de Transports Aériens (an amalgamation of Société Air Atlas and Air Maroc), and started operations in the same year. Following the independence of Morocco from French rule in 1957, a majority shareholding in the airline was transferred to the government of Morocco, which renamed the airline Royal Air Maroc. This now operated a network of scheduled services extending to 14 domestic and 43 international destinations, the latter

Fleet (orders):
2 x ATR 42-200 Advanced
2 x Boeing Model 737-200C
7 x Boeing Model 737-400
6 x Boeing Model 737-600
4 (1) x Boeing Model 737-700
5 (1) x Boeing Model 737-800
1 x Boeing Model 747-200B
Combi
1 x Boeing Model 747-400   2 x Boeing Model 757-200

comprising mostly cities in the Islamic world as well as Africa, Europe and, to the extent of just two destinations, North America.

ROYAL JORDANIAN AIRLINES (JORDAN)

Main base and hub: Amman
Type of operation: International and regional scheduled passenger and cargo services
Personnel: 5,000
Royal Jordanian Airlines is the national flag carrier of the Hashemite Kingdom of Jordan, and although its current

Fleet (orders):
9 x Airbus A310-300
5 x Airbus A320-200
2 x Boeing Model 707-320C

incarnation dates back to 1963, the background of the company can be found in times as early as 1950, when Ismail Bilbeisi formed Air Jordan as a short-haul operator with a small fleet of Airspeed Consul operating from a base at Amman. It was re-equipped by an American operator, Transocean Airlines, with Douglas DC-3 twin-engined and Douglas DC-4 four-engined airliners at the start of a far-sighted or, as events were to prove, over-ambitious expansion effort. Air Jordan took over the failed Arab Airways, another Jordanian operator, and reconstituted this as Air Jordan of the Holy Land, but the revived airline became bankrupt in July 1960, and Air Jordan itself ran into major problems and ceased operations on 7 September of the same year.

On the same date, a new Jordan Airways was created as a subsidiary of Middle East Airlines, and this survived with a fleet of two Douglas DC-7C four-engined airliners until the establishment of Alia – The Royal Jordanian Airline in December 1963. The new operator soon added a domestic and regional capability in the form of two Handley Page Herald twin-turboprop airliners that remained in service up to 1965. Alia's first pure jet equipment was the Sud-Aviation Caravelle 10R, of which the first was received on 28 July 1965, and the availability of this machine allowed the airline to extend its services to Rome and Paris, while for its domestic and regional services the airline also operated leased examples of the

Vickers Viscount four-turboprop airliner from a time late in 1966 up to 31 March 1967. The Viscounts were replaced by Fokker F.27 twin-turboprop aircraft, of which the first was leased in 1967 but soon replaced by the operator's own aircraft delivered from February 1968.

Alia was now growing moderately rapidly and, to supplement and then supplant the Caravelle on its international services, Alia bought an initial two examples of the Boeing Model 707 four-jet airliner, of which the first was received on 26 January 1971. These were followed by the airline's first Boeing Model 720-030B on 30 November 1972. Another Boeing type, the Model 727-2D3, was added to the fleet from 8 July 1974 for improved capability on medium-haul routes.

Wide-body aircraft offering significantly larger capacities were now available, and Alia took delivery of its first of three such transports, a Boeing Model 747-2D3B, on 13 April 1977 for services to Western Europe and the USA. Also used on the lower-density parts of the airline's long-haul routes is the Lockheed L-1011-500 TriStar, of which the first was received on 11 September 1981.

In December 1986, the name of the airline was changed to Royal Jordanian Airlines, and this now operates three of its earlier American types (the Model 707, Model 727 and L-1011) as well as an increasing number of Airbus wide-body types such as the A310 and A320.

RYANAIR (IRELAND)

Main bases and hubs: Dublin, London (Stansted) and Glasgow
Type of operation: International, regional and domestic scheduled and charter passenger
Personnel: 1,285
Established in May 1985, Ryanair was the pioneer of 'low-cost and no-frills' type of airline operation in Europe, and has grown with considerable speed to the point at which it now operates scheduled services to five Irish and 34 international European

Fleet (orders):
21 x Boeing Model 737-200
15 (13) x Boeing Model 737-800

destinations. Ryanair has performed strongly since the airline downturn that followed the September 2001 terrorist attacks on the USA.

BELOW: *The low-cost airline Ryanair flies only Boeing Model 737 short-range aircraft.*

SABENA (BELGIUM)

Main base and hub: Brussels
Type of operation: International and regional scheduled passenger and cargo services
Personnel: 12,715

The Belgian national flag carrier, the Société Anonyme Belge d'Exploitation de la Navigation Aérienne (SABENA) was created on 23 May 1923 by business interests in Belgium and the Belgian Congo, and by the end of 1924, SABENA was operating a European route network serving Amsterdam and Basle, the latter via Strasbourg, using a mix of De Havilland types as well as Breguet Bre.14 and Farman F.60 Goliath machines.

As a significant portion of the airline's capital had been provided by elements in the Belgian Congo, SABENA soon started operations in this African territory in succession to the Ligne Aérienne de Roi Albert (LARA). Although initial consideration was given to the use of waterplanes in this extensively rivered region, SABENA finally opted for landplanes and, after the clearance of the necessary airfields, services were begun in 1926 and 1927. The longest of the services in the Belgian Congo was that covering some 1,425 miles (2295 km) between Boma and Elisabethville. This was initially operated by a De Havilland D.H.50 which was supplanted later by a Handley Page W.8f.

During the early 1930s, SABENA flew services on a network extending from Brussels to Copenhagen, Malmö and Berlin using Handley Page W.8f and W.8b as well as Westland Wessex airliners and no fewer than 16 Fokker F.VIIb-3m three-engined airliners. On the pioneering service to Leopoldville in the Belgian Congo, the airline used the Savoia-Marchetti S.73 three-engined airliner. Later that decade, SABENA adopted more modern aircraft such as the three-engined Junkers Ju 52/3m and the Savoia-Marchetti S.83, a development of the S.73, as well as the Douglas DC-3 twin-engine transport.

As the Germans surged west in May 1940 in the course of their invasion of the Low Countries and France, SABENA managed to evacuate most of its DC-3 and Savoia-Marchetti aircraft to the UK, but after two of them had been shot down opted for a further move, in this instance to North Africa, where most of the aircraft were then captured by the Germans. By this time, the part of the airline operating in the Belgian Congo with F.VII and Ju 52/3m aircraft had become in effect independent and, reinforced with numbers of Lockheed aircraft (the Model 14 Super Electra and Model 18 Lodestar), extended considerably during the course of World War II so that by 1935 its route network covered 20,000 miles (32200 km).

SABENA was revived in Europe after the war, and on 4 June 1947 launched its first transatlantic service to New York, via Shannon and Gander, with Douglas DC-4 four-engined transports, and for service on its growing European network the airline introduced the Convair CV-240 in 1949 after the receipt of the first such aeroplane on 27 February of that year. In 1956, the CV-240 was itself replaced by the improved Convair CV-340 after the receipt of the first such aeroplane on 13 June of that year.

Fleet (orders):
14 (14) x Airbus A319-100
3 (3) x Airbus A320-200
3 x Airbus A321-200
6 x Airbus A330-200
4 x Airbus A330-300
1 x Airbus A340-200
2 (4) x Airbus A340-300
2 x ATR 72-210
6 x Boeing Model 737-300
3 x Boeing Model 737-400   1 x Bombardier Dash 8-100
6 x Boeing Model 737-500   4 x Bombardier Dash 8-300
2 x Boeing MD-11

SABENA inaugurated an experimental helicopter airmail service in August 1950 with Bell Model 47D light helicopters which were later supplemented by larger and more capacious Sikorsky S-55 machines that allowed an extension of the service to Maastricht in the Netherlands as the world's first international air mail route for helicopters. On 1 September 1953, the airline inaugurated a helicopter passenger service, and this lasted to 1966, by which time the network linked 12 Belgian cities.

By this time, SABENA had moved into the jet age as the CV-440 was replaced by the Sud-Aviation Caravelle which entered service on 18 February 1961 on the route linking Brussels and Nice after an initial delivery on 20 January of the same year. SABENA's first jet-powered airliner was in fact the Boeing Model 707-329, which made its first revenue-earning service on 23 January 1960 between Brussels and New York, and the same type also launched a jet service to the Belgian Congo on 26 January of the same year. This latter service lasted only to 28 January 1961, when SABENA ceased services to the Congo after its independence from Belgium and the creation of Air Congo.

While the Caravelle and Model 707 provided adequate capability for SABENA's low-density short-haul service and long-haul service respectively, the requirements of higher-density medium-haul routes necessitated new equipment. This arrived in the form of the Boeing Model 727-29 three-turbofan airliner, of which the first was delivered on 25 April 1967 for a service debut on 15 June of the same year. Growing traffic on the long-haul routes then demanded more capacity, and the airline, now generally known just as Sabena, became an operator of the new type of wide-body transport on 19 November 1970 with the Boeing Model 747-129 four-turbofan type for its high-density services, followed on 18 September 1973 by the McDonnell Douglas DC-10-30CF three-turbofan convertible passenger and freight transport for its medium-density services. Sabena completed the first stage of the transition into its current form with the replacement of the Model 727 by the Boeing Model 737-229 which flew its first service for the airline on 15 April 1974.

Sabena then standardized on the Model 737 (originally four but now three variants), the Model 747 (three variants now out of service) and the DC-10 (one variant now out of service), later augmented by increasing numbers of five Airbus types.

SAFAIR (SOUTH AFRICA)

Main bases and hubs: Johannesburg, Cape Town, London (Heathrow) and Singapore
Type of operation: International, regional and domestic charter passenger and cargo
Personnel: not available
Established in March 1969 and beginning operations almost exactly one year later, Safair is typical of the type of small air operator found in less technically advanced areas of the world with origins in the regional and domestic charter air freight market. Safair then expanded into the maintenance and

Fleet (orders):
1 x Boeing Model 727-200F
1 x Boeing Advanced Model 727-200
3 x Lockheed Martin L-100-30 Hercules

overnight package delivery businesses, and finally the chartering and leasing aspects of air transport.

SAMARA AIRLINES (RUSSIA)

Main base and hub: Samara
Type of operation: International, regional and domestic scheduled and charter passenger and cargo
Personnel: 1,635
Samara Airlines has its origins in the Kuybyshev Aviation Enterprise, which was established in 1961 and then evolved, via 65 Squadron, into the Kuybyshev Joint Aviation Squadron, which was privatized in 1993 as Samara Airlines. The airline flies a scheduled network extending between 13 domestic destinations and to six international destinations, the latter comprising five in the Commonwealth of Independent States

Fleet (orders):
1 x Antonov An-12
9 x Tupolev Tu-134A
5 x Tupolev Tu-154B
6 (1) x Tupolev Tu-154M
3 x Yakovlev Yak-40
1 x Yakovlev Yak-40K
2 x Yakovlev Yak-42D

as well as Tel Aviv in Israel. The airline also flies charter services to Austria, Cyprus, Israel, Spain, Turkey and the United Arab Emirates.

SAUDI ARABIAN AIRLINES (SAUDI ARABIA)

Main bases and hubs: Dhahran, Jeddah and Riyadh
Type of operation: International, regional and domestic scheduled passenger and cargo services
Personnel: not available
The national flag carrier of Saudi Arabia, Saudi Arabian Airlines was established during May 1945, when a small fleet of Douglas C-47 twin-engined military transports was bought and converted for civil use. These aircraft began operations on airmail and charter services between Riyadh, Jeddah and Dhahran, and flew the airline's first scheduled service on 14 March 1947. The early services were designed in part to explore the commercial viability of airline operations in Saudi Arabia, and were sufficiently encouraging for the airline to place an order in 1948 for five examples of the Bristol Type 170 Wayfarer twin-engined transport, a high-wing type with fixed landing gear admirably suited to operations to and from semi-prepared airstrips. In 1951 Saudi Arabian Airlines moved a step along the road toward standard airline operations with an order for five examples of the Douglas C-54 Skymaster four-engined military transport revised to DC-4 civil standard. The airline received its first examples of the Wayfarer on 28 June 1949 and then the first two examples of the C-54 in June 1952.

In 1952, Saudi Arabian Airlines ordered its first three out of an eventual 10 examples of the Convair CV-340 twin-engined airliner, and accepted the first two of these on 3 June 1954.

Fleet (orders):
11 x Airbus A300-600
2 x Airbus A300B4-100
1 x Airbus A300B4-200
11 x Boeing Advanced Model 737-200
7 x Boeing Model 747-100B
1 x Boeing Model 747-200F
10 x Boeing Model 747-300
4 (1) x Boeing Model 747-400
1 x Boeing Model 747SP 21
(2) x Boeing Model 777-200ER
4 x Boeing MD-11 Freighter
29 x McDonnell Douglas DC-9-30
1 x De Havilland Canada DHC-6 Twin Otter Series 300

Gradually Saudi Arabian Airlines enlarged its domestic network, and late in 1961 launched its first international services to neighbouring countries in the Middle East as well as to Bombay, Cairo and Karachi using its first pure jet type, the Boeing Model 720-068B, of which the initial pair were received on 20 December 1961.

On 8 February 1967, Saudi Arabian Airlines accepted its first Douglas DC-9-15 twin-jet airliner as the first stage in the modernization of its high-density domestic services, on which it initially complemented and then supplanted the CV-340 on the routes linking Riyadh, Jeddah and Dhahran. Another major step in the airline's development was the inauguration of services to

London in May 1967. In the same year, Saudi Arabian Airlines contracted for two examples of the Boeing Model 707 four-turbofan airliner, and took delivery of the first of these machines on 8 January of the following year. These advanced aircraft were initially operated on a non-stop service between Riyadh and London, supplemented late in 1969 by a link with Algiers.

In 1972, Saudi Arabian Airlines changed its name to Saudia, and on 14 March of the same year took delivery of its first Boeing Model 737 twin-turbofan airliner for a further boost to its domestic route network. The delivery of additional aircraft of the same type finally permitted the retirement of the CV-340 piston-engine aircraft and the sale of the DC-9 turbine-engined

machines. By the end of the decade, Saudia was becoming well established as an operator of high-density services on long-haul routes, following the adoption of its first wide-body airliner, the Lockheed L-1011-100 TriStar three-turbofan type, of which the first was received on 25 June 1975. The continued growth of traffic on long-haul routes demanded still more capacity, however, and on 1 June 1977 the airline received two Boeing Model 747-2B4B four-turbofan airliners on lease from Middle East Airlines. The aircraft were later returned as Saudia started a programme to buy the Model 747 in moderately large numbers, and the first of the airline's own Model 747 aircraft was received on 24 April 1981.

SCANDINAVIAN AIRLINES SAS (DENMARK, NORWAY AND SWEDEN)

Main bases and hubs: Copenhagen, Oslo and Stockholm
Type of operation: International and regional scheduled passenger and cargo services
Personnel: 28,865

The 'national' flag carrier of the three Scandinavian countries of Denmark, Norway and Sweden, SAS was created on 31 July 1946 as a consortium of the leading pre-World War II airlines of Denmark, Norway and Sweden, namely Det Danske Luftfartselskap (DDL), Det Norske Luftfartselskap (DNL) and AB Aerotransport (ABA) respectively. The Danish and Norwegian were specialists in European services, but the Swedish operator had greater vision, and after the war had inaugurated a service to Tehran. DDL had started services on 7 August 1920 with the Junkers F 13 floatplane on the route linking Copenhagen with Berlin, ABA had flown its first service on 2 June 1924 with an F 13 on the route linking Stockholm and Helsinki, and DNL had made its first revenue-earning flight in April 1928.

The new consortium was divided into seven parts that were allocated in the ratio 2/2/3 to Denmark, Norway and Sweden, and its primary objective was the operation of economical services across the North Atlantic and on other long-haul routes. In this capacity, its first flight was a Douglas DC-4 service from Stockholm and Copenhagen to New York on 16 September 1946. In 1948, the three SAS partners created an SAS European Division to co-ordinate their previously separate European services, and in July of the same year the consortium was enlarged by the merger of another Swedish airline, Svensk Interkontinental Lufttrafik, with Aerotransport. It was not until 8 February 1951, however, that the three constituent airlines agreed the establishment of a single centralized management organization, with the three airlines becoming non-operating holding companies. As late as 1954, the three basic elements of the airline were still flying under their own names, however.

During the later 1940s and early 1950s, SAS launched a number of new services such as those to Buenos Aires in December 1946, Bangkok in October 1949 and Johannesburg in January 1953. By this time, SAS's most important long-haul airliner was the Douglas DC-6 four-engined type, with the Douglas DC-3 and Saab 90A twin-engined types dominating on

Fleet (orders):
(12) x Airbus A321-100
(3) x Airbus A330-300
(7) x Airbus A340-300
30 x Boeing Model 737-600
6 x Boeing Model 737-700
14 (8) x Boeing Model 737-800
13 x Boeing Model 767-300ER
20 x Boeing MD-81
28 x Boeing MD-82
2 x Boeing MD-83
18 x Boeing MD-87

8 x Boeing MD-90-30
15 x McDonnell Douglas DC-9-40

the operator's European services. SAS inaugurated the first trans-polar service between Copenhagen and Los Angeles on 15 November 1954 with DC-6B aircraft, and on 24 February 1957 added a service between Copenhagen and Tokyo with Douglas DC-7 aircraft. Two years later, moved into the pure jet age with the Sud-Aviation Caravelle, of which it received its first example on 10 April 1959 for an initial revenue-earning service from Copenhagen to Cairo on 15 May 1959.

SAS introduced the Douglas DC-8-32 four-jet airliner on its long-haul services on 1 May 1960 with a flight between Copenhagen and New York, and then pioneered the Douglas DC-9-30 and DC-9-40 twin-turbofan airliners, both developed to meet the airline's particular requirements on its short-haul services in Europe from 1968.

In common with many other airlines concerned to increase market share through the use of the latest and most economical equipment, SAS was an early customer for the wide-body airliner with a turbofan powerplant, in the form of the pioneering Boeing Model 747, which it received in February 1971. Since that time, the airline has added substantial numbers of additional short- and medium-haul twin-turbofan airliners to its fleet and now operates both the DC-9 (including five variants of the upgraded MD-80/90 series) and the Boeing Model 737 (three variants). For its longer-haul services it has standardized on the Boeing Model 767. SAS has now ordered large numbers of three Airbus types.

RIGHT: *SAS possesses the unusual distinction of being the flag carrier of three countries.*

SHANGHAI AIRLINES (CHINA)

Main bases and hubs: Shanghai (Hongqiao and Pudong)
Type of operation: International, regional and domestic scheduled passenger and cargo
Personnel: 2,300

Shanghai Airlines was created in 1985 by the municipal government of Shanghai, and began operations in the same year as China's first independently administered airline, Shanghai Airlines was initially limited to domestic services, but in September 1997 gained central government approval to launch international services, of which the first (and so far only) destination is Phnom Penh in Cambodia. Shanghai Airlines undertakes some 300 services a week on its domestic network, which links just under 40 Chinese cities. Currently,

Fleet (orders):
6 (3) x Boeing Model 737-700
(4) x Boeing Model 737-800
7 x Boeing Model 757-200
3 (1) x Boeing Model 767-300
2 (1) x Bombardier CRJ-200ER

the Shanghai municipal government holds 75 per cent of the shares, the other 25 per cent being held publicly.

BELOW: *Shanghai Airlines uses the CRJ-200ER for regional and executive services.*

SIBIR AIRLINES (RUSSIA)

Main bases and hubs: Novosibirsk and Moscow (Vnukovo)
Type of operation: International, regional and domestic scheduled and charter passenger
Personnel: 2,300

Another Russian airline whose origins can be found in the monolithic Aeroflot civil aviation organization of the USSR, in this instance its Novosibirsk Division, Sibir airlines came into existence in May 1992. Its initial incarnation was Tolmachevo State Aviation Enterprise, which was then reorganized as Sibir Airlines and has since become a major force in the development of civil aviation in Siberia. Sibir Airlines now

Fleet (orders):
1 x Antonov An-12
1 x Antonov An-24B
1 x Antonov An-32
7 x Ilyushin Il-86
16 x Tupolev Tu-154B
10 x Tupolev Tu-154M
1 x Tupolev Tu-204-100

operates a scheduled network that includes 17 domestic and nine international destinations, the latter mainly in East Asia, the Middle East and Western Europe.

SILKAIR (SINGAPORE)

Main base and hub: Singapore
Type of operation: International and regional scheduled passenger and cargo
Personnel: not available

A wholly owned subsidiary of Singapore Airlines, Tradewinds came into existence during February 1989 and started

Fleet (orders):
3 (1) x Airbus A319-100
3 (2) x Airbus A320-200

operations in the same month to provide a link between Singapore and the growing number of holiday destinations in South-East Asia. As the economy of the region began to expand, the company added regional financial and manufacturing centres, and in April 1992 the operator's name was changed to SilkAir. This now flies a scheduled network linking Singapore with 18 or more destinations in Myanmar, Cambodia, China, Indonesia, Malaysia, the Philippines and Thailand.

SICHUAN AIRLINES (CHINA)

Main bases and hubs: Chengdu, Shuanglui and Chongqing
Type of operation: Regional and domestic scheduled and charter passenger and cargo
Personnel: not available
Established in September 1986 and beginning operations in July 1988, Sichuan Airlines is typical of Chinese regional operators, and operates a scheduled network linking 20 or more Chinese cities.

During September 1997, Sichuan Airlines (wholly owned by the Sichuan provincial government) was one of six Chinese provincial airlines that collectively established the New Star Aviation Alliance. Obsolescent Chinese and Soviet aircraft are

Fleet (orders):
5 x Airbus A320-200
2 x Airbus A321-200
1 x Boeing Model 737-300
4 (1) x EMBRAER RJ-145LR
4 x Tupolev Tu-154M
1 x XAC Y 7-100

being replaced by modern Western machines.

BELOW: *Sichuan Airlines operates four Western types including the EMBRAER RJ-145.*

SINGAPORE AIRLINES (SINGAPORE)

Main base and hub: Singapore
Type of operation: International and regional scheduled passenger and cargo services
Personnel: 27,630
The national flag carrier of the island state of Singapore, Singapore Airlines came into existence on 28 January 1972 following the emergence of Singapore as a state separate from the Federation of Malaysia. This resulted in the division of the previous Malaysia-Singapore Airlines that became the national flag carriers of Malaysia and Singapore respectively. Singapore Airlines began operations on 1 October of the same year, serving the same international routes that had been the preserve of Malaysia-Singapore Airlines with the same fleet of Boeing Model

Fleet (orders):
13 x Airbus A310-300
15 (2) x Airbus A340-300
(5) x Airbus A340-500
(10) x Airbus A380-800
1 x Boeing Model 747-300
38 (1) x Boeing Model 747-400
9 (2) x Boeing Model 747-400F
13 (20) x Boeing Model
   777-200ER   5 (4) x Boeing Model 777-300

707 and Boeing Model 737 four- and two-turbofan airliners.

On 2 April 1973, Singapore Airlines began a daily service to London, and on 31 July of the same year began a major expansion in capability with the receipt of its first example of a wide-body type, in this instance the four-turbofan Boeing Model 747-212B. This was soon complemented by another wide-body transport, the three-turbofan McDonnell Douglas DC-10-30, to provide the core of the airline's long-haul fleet for high- and medium-density services. The Airbus A300B4-203 two-turbofan type, of which the first was delivered on 20 December 1980, complemented these two types of long-haul machine on

Singapore Airlines' medium- and short-haul services as a high-capacity type in concert with small numbers of the Boeing Model 727-212 three-turbofan airliner, which entered service in September 1977, as its medium-capacity counterpart.

Singapore Airlines currently flies scheduled passenger and cargo services to destinations mainly in Australia, Asia, Europe and North America with a fleet now based on the Airbus and Boeing aircraft.

SKYWEST AIRLINES
(UNITED STATES OF AMERICA)

Main bases and hubs: Portland, Los Angeles, San Francisco and Seattle
Type of operation: International, regional and domestic scheduled passenger and cargo
Personnel: 3,600

Created in 1972 and starting operations in the same year, SkyWest Airlines is the fourth-largest regional airline in the USA, and concentrates in services in the north-west of the country with offshoots into California and western Canada. The operator flies nearly 1,000 services per day, all under the Delta

Fleet (orders):
11 x Bombardier CRJ-100ER
7 (83) x Bombardier CRJ-200LR
20 x EMBRAER EMB-120
  Brasilia
72 x EMBRAER EMB-120
  Brasilia Advanced

Connection and United Express logos, and the network covers two Canadian destinations as well as 53 US cities. With 13 per cent, Delta Air Lines is the largest single shareholder.

SOUTH AFRICAN AIRWAYS
(SOUTH AFRICA)

Main bases and hubs: Cape Town, Durban and Johannesburg
Type of operation: International, regional and domestic scheduled and charter passenger and cargo services
Personnel: 9,015

The national flag carrier of South Africa, South African Airways can trace its origins back to August 1929 and the creation of Union Airways which operated De Havilland D.H.60 Gipsy Moth light planes on charter flights and then mail services from Port Elizabeth to Cape Town, Durban and Johannesburg. On 1 February 1934, the nationalized South African Railways and Harbours Administration acquired Union Airways and its five single-engined aircraft, which by now included types such as the Junkers F 13 and W 34, as the basis of South African Airways. One year later to the day, South African Airways took over South West Africa Airways, which had been operating an airmail service between Kimberley and Windhoek since 1932. With this acquisition, South African Airways began to grow as a significant domestic and African operator, with the three-engined Junkers Ju 52/3m and twin-engined Junkers Ju 86 types as its most important aircraft in the later part of the 1930s. In 1938 the airline also bought four examples of the Airspeed Envoy light transport, and these were flown on services to Durban, where passengers could board the flying boats that operated long-haul services to overseas destinations.

During World War II, South African Airways received more modern equipment in the form of the Lockheed Model 18 Lodestar, but this type was soon transferred to military service

Fleet (orders):
1 x Airbus A300B2
2 x Airbus A300B4-200
3 x Airbus A320-200
15 x Boeing Advanced
  Model 737-200
10 (11) x Boeing Model
  737-800
5 x Boeing Model 747-200B
6 x Boeing Model 747-300   3 x Boeing Model 747SP
8 x Boeing Model 747-400   2 x Boeing Model 767-200ER

until 1944, when it was used for a resumption of South African Airway's civil operations. A major step in the revival of South African Airways was the introduction of the 'Springbok Service' in co-operation with the British Overseas Airways Corporation; this route between Johannesburg and London was inaugurated on 10 November 1945 using an Avro York four-engined transport. The airline later used another seven of this interim type, all of these leased from the British Overseas Airways Corporation, up to the point in 1946 that services could be undertaken with the Douglas DC-4, of which the airline received its first example on 26 April 1946.

Another type that entered service with South African Airways in 1946 was the Douglas C-47 Dakota, an ex-military type derived from the pre-war DC-3 and in its post-war form converted for civil use. The Dakota was used by South African Airways in large numbers and remained in fruitful service up to 1970. On 15 December 1946, South African Airways received its first example of the De Havilland D.H.104 Dove Series I twin-engined transport, a second example being delivered late in 1947; these two machines were flown on the services linking Johannesburg with Lourenço Marques and Durban with Bloemfontein. Another British airliner that entered service with South African Airways in 1947 was the Vickers Viking 1B, a larger twin-engined type that was first received on 31 July of that year for use on the service linking Johannesburg and Bulawayo as replacement for the Lodestar. By the end of 1947, therefore, South African Airways had a mixed fleet of 41 aircraft.

The first pressurized airliner used by the airline was the Lockheed L-749A Constellation. The first was delivered on 24 April 1950 and entered revenue-earning service on the route linking South Africa and Europe, replacing the DC-4. It was itself superseded by more advanced aircraft only in the early 1960s. South African Airways flew its first pure jet aircraft late in 1952, in the form of a De Havilland D.H.106 Comet 1 leased from the British Overseas Airways Corporation, but this was withdrawn shortly afterwards due to technical problems. South African Airways therefore had to rely once more on piston-engined aircraft, of which one of the most successful was the Douglas DC-7B which started on the service to London on 21 April 1956 in succession to the Constellation.

South African Airways' domestic and regional services were upgraded considerably by the advent of the Vickers Viscount 813 four-turboprop airliner, of which the first two of an eventual eight were received on 26 October 1958. The Viscount remained in service up to 1972, when the seven surviving aircraft were sold to British Midland Airways as the Viscount was replaced by the Boeing Model 727 three-turbofan airliner.

On 1 October 1960, the Boeing Model 707-355 four-turbofan transport replaced the DC-7B on the route to London, and although the type was initially operated only on passenger services, it was later relegated to freight operations as more advanced equipment was taken into service. The most important of these types was the Boeing Model 747 wide-body airliner, of which the two most important early variants were the Model 747-244B and Model 747SP-44, of which the first examples were received on 22 October 1971 and 19 March 1976 respectively.

South African Airways currently operates a large fleet of Model 747 and increasing numbers of Model 767 aircraft for its longer-haul routes, while shorter-haul services are provided by the Airbus A300, Airbus A320 and Boeing Model 737 twin-turbofan aircraft which have supplanted the Boeing Model 727 and Hawker Siddeley HS.748 aircraft operated in the 1980s and early 1990s.

BELOW: *South African Airways operates a mix of obsolescent and more modern transports.*

SOUTHWEST AIRLINES
(UNITED STATES OF AMERICA)

Main bases and hubs: Albuquerque, Austin, Boise and Dallas (Love Field)
Type of operation: Regional and domestic scheduled passenger services
Personnel: 29,275

Fleet (orders):
33 x Boeing Advanced Model 737-200
193 x Boeing Model 737-300
25 x Boeing Model 737-500
96 (142) x Boeing Model 737-700

Southwest Airlines was established on 15 March 1967 as Air Southwest to provide low-fare scheduled passenger services within the state of Texas, but the name was changed to Southwest Airlines on 29 March 1971. On 18 June of the same year, the new operator began its first services between Dallas, Houston and San Antonio with a fleet of three Boeing Model 737-2H4 twin-turbofan aircraft. The airline received certification for inter-state service in December 1978, and has now expanded to considerable size with a fleet comprising only Model 737 aircraft. On 25 June 1985, Southwest Airlines took over Muse Air, which it operated for a time as a subsidiary under the name TranStar Airlines with a fleet of McDonnell Douglas DC-9-50 and upgraded MD-80 twin-turbofan aircraft.

SRILANKAN AIRLINES (SRI LANKA)

Main base and hub: Colombo
Type of operation: International and regional scheduled passenger and cargo services
Personnel: 4,690

Fleet (orders):
2 x Airbus A320-200
6 x Airbus A330-200
4 x Airbus A340-300

Air Lanka was created on 10 January 1979 to take over the services of the previous national flag carrier, Air Ceylon, which had ceased trading on 31 March 1978. The new airline's first services were undertaken with two Boeing Model 707-312 four-turbofan airliners leased from Singapore Airlines. These aircraft reached Colombo on 15 August and 25 September 1979, and the airline started regional services in November of the same year with a leased Boeing Model 737-2L9.

The Model 707 airliners were replaced on the carrier's international services by Lockheed L-10111 TriStar three-turbofan airliners, which were Air Lanka's first wide-body transports; the first of these aircraft was leased from Air

Canada from October 1980 and flew its first services on 2 November of the same year on the route linking Colombo and Paris. This type was complemented on high-density routes by a Boeing Model 747-238B four-turbofan airliner leased from Qantas from June 1984.

After that time, the airline standardized first on the TriStar and then on Airbus aircraft, starting with the A320 but then adding the A330 and A340.

SWISSAIR (SWITZERLAND)

Main bases and hubs: Basle and Zurich
Type of operation: International, regional and domestic scheduled and charter passenger and cargo services
Personnel: not available

Fleet (orders):
9 x Airbus A319-100
20 x Airbus A320-200
12 x Airbus A321-100
16 x Airbus A330-200
(11) Airbus A340-600
19 x Boeing MD-11
1 x BAE Systems 146-300

The national flag carrier of Switzerland, Swissair can trace its origins back to March 1931 and its creation from the amalgamation of Balair and Ad Astra, a pair of pioneering Swiss air transport companies. From its very start, the new airline decided to set a fast pace in its growth by the adoption of the latest equipment. In 1932, Swissair was the first European airline to operate the four-passenger Lockheed Orion, a single-engined low-wing monoplane with retractable landing gear and, as such, the fastest small air transport of its day. Also in 1932, Swissair introduced the Curtiss Condor twin-engined biplane to European service, and although this machine was slow, it was also very comfortable and carried a stewardess (for the first time in European service) to look after the 16 passengers.

By the time the outbreak of World War II in 1939 interrupted the development of air transportation throughout most of Europe, Swissair was operating a fleet of five Douglas DC-3s, three Douglas DC-2s, one De Havilland D.H.89 Dragon Rapide, one Fokker F.VIIa and one Compte AC.4 aircraft. Scheduled services were suspended during the war, but were resumed in July 1945, some two months after Germany's defeat.

By 1949, Swissair was able to inaugurate a service to New York with the Douglas DC-4 four-engined airliner. This was soon replaced by the altogether better Douglas DC-6B, which offered, among other improvements, full cabin pressurization. The availability of this longer-ranged type improved safety margins on the North Atlantic route, and also made it possible for Swissair to introduce during the first half of the 1950s new services to South America as well

as Tokyo via South-East Asia. The DC-6B was superseded on the airline's long-haul routes by the still further improved Douglas DC-7.

Even as this development of its long-haul network was being implemented, Swissair was also developing its capability in Europe and in flights to the Middle East. Destinations in all parts of Africa were added in the 1960s, and, since then, Swissair's network has expanded to include all continents except Australasia.

In the course of 1960, Swissair introduced to service its first jet-powered airliner in the form of the Sud-Aviation Caravelle III, of which Swissair operated eight examples leaded from SAS. The airline operated these French aircraft for European regional services, but kept faith with Douglas in its long-haul aircraft when it contracted for the four-engined Douglas DC-8. Early experience with the Caravelle and DC-8 confirmed to Swissair that the future lay with turbine propulsion. The airline switched as rapidly as it could to the latest airliners to create a fleet that, by 1981, had in service or on order three Boeing Model 747-200B, 11 Airbus A310, five McDonnell Douglas DC-8-62, 12 DC-9-32, one DC-9-33F, 12 DC-9-51, 15 DC-9-81 and 11 DC-10-30 aircraft for the full range of short-, medium- and long-haul passenger and freight services.

After that time, Swissair standardized on the Fokker 100 for its domestic services, the McDonnell Douglas MD-81 for its low-density short-haul services and the Airbus A310 and A320 for its high-density short/medium-haul services, and the McDonnell Douglas MD-11 and Model 747-300 for use respectively on its medium- and high-density long-haul

services. By the beginning of the 21st century, Swissair had standardized further on five Airbus and one Boeing types.

In 2001, Swissair became one of the first casualties of the airline downturn, and went out of bussiness.

SYRIANAIR (SYRIA)

Main base and hub: Damascus
Type of operation: International, regional and domestic scheduled passenger and cargo
Personnel: not available
Syrianair was established in October 1961 by the government of Syria as the national airline after its predecessor, Syrian Airways, had united with Misrair of Egypt to form United Arab Airlines. After Syria's break from the political union with Egypt as the United Arab Republic, Syrianair took back its fleet and routes, including domestic and regional routes from Damascus, and then added services to Europe from 1964 and also flew east to Karachi and Delhi. Depending on the political orientation of the government from time to time, both Western and Soviet-

Fleet (orders):
6 x Airbus A320-200
6 x Boeing Advanced Model 727-200
2x Boeing Model 747SP
1 x Ilyushin Il-76M
3 x Tupolev Tu-134B
1 x Tupolev Tu-154M

built aircraft have been operated by Syrianair, which now possesses a network of scheduled services comprising four domestic and 41 international destinations, the latter in countries of the Middle East, Africa, Far East and the Americas.

TAP AIR PORTUGAL (PORTUGAL)

Main hub and base: Lisbon
Type of operation: International and domestic scheduled passenger and cargo services
Personnel: 8,870
The national flag carrier of Portugal, Transportes Aéreos Portugueses (TAP) was created in 1944 by the civil aeronautics secretariat of the Portuguese government as a route-proving organization. The original plan of passing on the fruits of TAP's endeavours to commercial airlines, once these had been set up, was then, however, abandoned and Transportes Aéreos Portugueses was itself turned into a scheduled airline on 14

*BELOW: **TAP flies to European destinations and many other points with a fleet of mixed Airbus types.***

Fleet (orders):
5 x Airbus A310-300
17 x Airbus A319-100
6 (1) x Airbus A320-200
2 x Airbus A321-200
4 x Airbus A340-300
1 x Boeing Model 737-200

March 1945. The new operator made its first flight on 19 September 1946 with a service from Lisbon to Madrid using a Douglas DC-3 twin-engined airliner. Scheduled services deeper into the continent of Europe began in the following year, in which the airline also began flights to Lourenço Marques via Luanda, the capitals of Portugal's African colonies of

Mozambique and Angola, initially with the DC-3 but soon with the Douglas DC-4 four-engined airliner. In 1950, the service was curtailed to end at Luanda.

By 1953, the airline's costs had risen to the point at which the government of Portugal decided it was sensible to sell off Transportes Aéreos Portugueses to the private sector. On 15 July 1955, Transportes Aéreos Portugueses received its first example of the Lockheed L-1049G Super Constellation four-engined airliner, and this type entered service on the route to Luanda and Lourenço Marques as well as some longer-range European routes. In 1960, the airline leased two Douglas DC-6B four-engined airliners from the French airline UAT and, having come to the realization that it needed to make the move into turbine-powered aircraft, succeeded in making a pooling agreement with British European Airways to operate De Havilland Comet 4B turbojet- and Vickers Viscount turboprop-powered aircraft. These agreements soon lapsed, however, as Transportes Aéreos Portugueses started to receive its own turbine-powered aircraft, starting on 13 July 1962 with its first Sud-Aviation Caravelle VIR.

These arrangements provided mainly for short- and medium-haul routes, but in 1960 the airline had gained an important long-haul capability with the lease from SABENA of two examples of the Boeing Model 707-329 pending the delivery of its own Model 707 aircraft, of which the first was a Model 707-3H2B received on 18 December 1965. The availability of this advanced type allowed Transportes Aéreos

Portugueses to expand its turbine-powered operations to include from June 1966 destinations such as Rio de Janeiro, which had previously been served in association with Panair do Brasil (now Varig) with Douglas DC-7C aircraft via Ilha do Sol and Recife. In 1969, Transportes Aéreos Portugueses started a service linking Lisbon with New York, and two years later added a service to Montreal.

Further short- and medium-haul capability arrived early in 1967 with the delivery of the airline's first example of the Boeing Model 727-82 three-turbofan airliner. This type was to become the mainstay of the operator's European services routes. A superior long-haul capability arrived on 20 December 1971 with the delivery of the airline's first wide-body transports in the form of two Boeing Model 747-282B four-turbofan airliners which entered service in February of the following year. In 1982, a further exciting development was the advent of the first of five Lockheed L-1011-500 TriStar three-turbofan transport, which replaced the airline's Model 707 aircraft.

In 1975, Transportes Aéreos Portugueses was nationalized, and in March 1979 changed its name to TAP Air Portugal. In 1991, the airline became a public limited company with most of the shareholding retained by the government of Portugal. TAP Air Portugal then standardized on the Boeing Model 737 (two variants), which was gradually replaced by Airbus types for its short-haul services, and Airbus A310, A320 and A340 aircraft for its medium- and long-haul services.

TAROM ROMANIAN AIR TRANSPORT (ROMANIA)

Main base and hub: Bucharest
Type of operation: International, regional and domestic scheduled and charter passenger and cargo
Personnel: not available

Transporturile Aeriene Romana Sovietica (TARS) was established as a Romanian-Soviet airline in 1946 to succeed LARES, which had been Romania's national airline before World War II, and began operations with Soviet-supplied aircraft. Romania secured the Soviet share in the airline during 1954 and renamed the operator TAROM (Transporturile Aeriene Romane), which continued to fly Soviet aircraft until it received its first British-built BAC One-Eleven machines in

Fleet (orders):
2 x Airbus A310-300
7 (2) x ATR 42-500
1 (2) x ATR 72-500
2 x Boeing Model 707-320C
8 x Boeing Model 737-300
2 x Boeing Model 737-500
(4) x Boeing Model 737-700
(4) x Boeing Model 737-800

1968. From the early 1990s, the airline began to order larger numbers of Western aircraft, and TAROM's network of scheduled services now includes 12 domestic and 40 international destinations.

THAI AIRWAYS INTERNATIONAL (THAILAND)

Main base and hub: Bangkok
Type of operation: International, regional and domestic scheduled passenger services
Personnel: 24,150

The national flag carrier of the Kingdom of Thailand, Thai Airways International resulted from an agreement signed on 14 December 1959 between the government of Thailand and

Fleet (orders):
5 x Airbus A300-600
15 x Airbus A300-600R
12 x Airbus A330-300
2 x ATR 72-200
10 x Boeing Model 737-400
2 x Boeing Model 747-300
14 x Boeing Model 747-400
8 x Boeing Model 777-200
6 x Boeing Model 777-300

4 x McDonnell Douglas MD-11

Thai Airways has considerable ambitions, but lacks adequate resources.

Scandinavian Airlines System: 70 per cent of the shareholding was held by the government of Thailand and 30 per cent by SAS, which provided the necessary aircraft and management capability. The new airline's first two aircraft, leased from SAS on 2 April 1960, were Douglas DC-6B four-engined transports, and these entered revenue-earning service on 1 May. Thai Airways International later leased another six DC-6B aircraft, the last of which was returned on 3 April 1964.

Thai Airways International's primary route was that linking Bangkok with Tokyo, and to ensure the maximum possible load factors on this strongly competitive route, the airline leased two Convair CV-990A four-jet airliners from SAS; this type arrived on 15 May 1962 and made its operational debut on 18 May of the same year. The CV-990A was currently the fastest airliner in the world, and its operation gave Thai Airways International a decided edge over its competitors.

The DC-6B was gradually supplanted by leased Sud-Aviation Caravelle III twin-jet aircraft, of which the first was delivered on 26 December 1963 for service on the airline's shorter-haul services from 1 January 1964. By this time, South-East Asia was beginning to emerge as a major destination for the burgeoning tourist trade, and to meet the demand for additional capacity, Thai Airways International leased a pair of Douglas DC-9-41 twin-jet transports from SAS, the two aircraft reaching Thailand on 28 and 29 January 1970 for additional capacity on the airline's shorter-haul services. In April of the same year, a more advanced longer-haul capability appeared in the form of two Douglas DC-8-33 four-engined transports, and the DC-8 and DC-9 soon became

the mainstay of Thai Airways International's operations. Numerous DC-8 aircraft of different variants were added to the fleet over the following years.

The availability of these aircraft in 1970 allowed Thai Airways International to start its own inclusive tour programme under the name Royal Orchid Holidays, and a new service to Sydney via Singapore was launched in April 1971. This great expansion in the airline's first decade of operation turned Thai Airways International into the third largest regional operator in the Far East.

The majority of the airline's tourist trade arrived from Europe, so it made sound commercial sense for Thai Airways International to extend its route network to the European continent. The first such service was to Copenhagen via Moscow, and this was inaugurated on 3 June 1962 with a DC-8. On 2 November 1973, there followed a service from Bangkok to Frankfurt and London, and this link made it possible for the airline to offer a through service between London and Sydney.

Continuing growth in demand during the first half of the 1970s persuaded the airline that the time was ripe for a move into the market for wide-body aircraft, and Thai Airways International received its first such aeroplane on 30 May 1975 in the form of a McDonnell Douglas DC-10-30 three-turbofan airliner leased from UTA. This machine was soon complemented and then supplanted by the airline's own DC-10 aircraft, which became the mainstay of its longer-haul services in the later 1970s and 1980s. Additional capacity was provided on medium- and short-haul services by the purchase of Airbus A300 twin-turbofan aircraft which finally replaced the DC-8 after the delivery of the first machine on 25 October 1977. The A300 was later complemented by the Airbus A310,

141

another twin-turbofan type with small capacity.

In November 1979, an improved capability of high-density services over long-haul routes was provided by the arrival of the first of the airline's four-turbofan wide-body aircraft, a Boeing Model 747-2D7B. Thai Airways International inaugurated its initial service to the USA across the Pacific with a Douglas DC-10-30 flying the route to Seattle and Los Angeles on 30 April 1980, but on 1 November 1980 the Model 747 replaced the DC-10 on the North Pacific and European routes, thereby increasing passenger capacity to a useful degree.

Thai Airways International now operates a substantial route network with a fleet largely of Airbus and Boeing types.

THY TURKISH AIRLINES (TURKEY)

Main base and hub: Istanbul
Type of operation: International and domestic scheduled and charter passenger and cargo services
Personnel: 9,525

Türk Hava Yollari, generally known as THY Turkish Airlines, is the national flag carrier of the Turkish Republic, and can trace its origins back to 20 May 1933, when the Turkish defence ministry established Türkiye Devlet Hava Yollari (Turkish State Airlines) as replacement for the airline that had been operated by Curtiss, the US aircraft manufacturer. The first route operated by Türkiye Devlet Hava Yollari was that linking Istanbul and Ankara via Eskisehir. In 1935, the airline came under the aegis of the Turkish ministry of public works, and on 3 June 1938 was transferred to the ministry of transport.

In September 1937, the airline had received its first three examples of the De Havilland D.H.86B Express biplane airliner, and these were followed in December by a fourth machine of the same type and, in May 1936, by De Havilland D.H.89 biplanes. The availability of this fleet made it possible for Turkiye Devlet Hava Yollari to enlarge its domestic network to the point at which, in 1939, it linked Istanbul, Eskisehir, Izmir, Ankara, Adana, Kayseri and Diyarbakir.

No growth was possible during World War II, in which Turkey was neutral, as no new aircraft could be acquired, but after the end of the war in 1945, Türkiye Devlet Hava Yollari started to fly winter services using a sizeable fleet of Douglas DC-3 twin-engined airliners. The airline flew only domestic services up to 1947, when it expanded into its first international services, starting with the route to Athens. The

Fleet (orders):
6 x Airbus A310-200
7 x Airbus A310-300
7 x Airbus A340-300
3 x BAE Systems RJ-70
9 x BAE Systems RJ-100
1 x Boeing Model 727-200F
16 x Boeing Model 737-400
2 x Boeing Model 737-500
24 (2) x Boeing Model 737-800

other main type flown by Türkiye Devlet Hava Yollari, in this instance for short-haul services, was the De Havilland D.H.114 Heron 2B four-engined airliner, the first two of which were received on 15 February 1955. There followed another five of the same type, which remained in service until 1966.

On 1 March 1956, the operations of Türkiye Devlet Hava Yollari were replaced by those of Turk Hava Yollari, which had come into existence in May of the previous year as a new corporation established by the Turkish government to control national air transport. The Turkish government had a 51 per cent holding in Türk Hava Yollari, and the British Overseas Airways Corporation owned 6.5 per cent as a result of a payment that allowed the new operator to place a July 1957 order for modern equipment in the form of five Vickers Viscount 794 four-turboprop airliners. The first of these was received on 21 January 1958 with the other four following later in the year.

BELOW: *THY is one of many airlines finding it financially difficult early in the 21st century.*

The Viscounts were placed in domestic service during May of the same year, and international services, initially to Brussels but soon to a number of other European destinations, started during the summer of 1964.

On 15 January 1960, Türk Hava Yollari contracted for a total of 10 Friendship twin-turboprop airliners in the form of five Fokker F.27 and five Fairchild F-27 aircraft, the first American-built F.27 being accepted on 1 July of the same year with the first three Dutch-built F.27 aircraft following on 27 October. The availability of the full Friendship fleet allowed the replacement of the DC-3 on Türk Hava Yollari's domestic network.

More advanced turbine-powered aircraft were now clearly essential, and the first pure jet type to be used by Türk Hava Yollari was a Douglas DC-9-14 received on lease from the manufacturer on 7 August 1967, and the airline's first DC-9-32 followed on 9 July 1968. Türk Hava Yollari leased four examples of the Boeing Model 707-321 four-turbofan airliner from Pan American in 1971. The availability of these larger aircraft with their longer range permitted the airline to enlarge its route network into the Middle East, and still further expansion became possible two years later with the airline's

receipt of its first wide-body airliner, a McDonnell Douglas DC-10-10 delivered on 1 December 1972. Only slightly later, on 13 January 1973, Turk Hava Yollari accepted its first of six Fokker F.28 Fellowship twin-turbofan airliners, to allow a start on the programme to replace the F.27 on domestic services. The last of the new types to be delivered in this period of re-equipment and expansion was the Boeing Model 727-2F2 three-turbofan type, of which the first pair was received on 21 November 1974 providing a considerable boost to the airline's medium-haul capability.

The next type of aircraft to enter service was the De Havilland Canada DHC-7 Dash-7 four-turboprop airliner, the first of three such aircraft being accepted in June 1983. Turk Hava Yollari then standardized on the BAe Jetstream ATP twin-turboprop type for local services, the closely related Avro RJ-100 and BAe 146 four-turbofan types for short-haul services. It used the Boeing Model 737 (three variants) for higher-capacity short- and medium-haul services and a combination of the Airbus A310 and A340 aircraft for its high-capacity medium- and long-haul services, both of which include freight as well as passenger operations.

TRANS WORLD AIRLINES (UNITED STATES OF AMERICA)

Main bases and hubs: New York and St Louis
Type of operation: International, regional and domestic scheduled passenger services
Personnel: not available

Trans World Airlines can trace its origins back to 1926 and the creation of Western Air Express. This operator undertook airmail services in the USA, starting with the route linking Los Angeles and Salt Lake City, and during 1929 began a process of enlargement by taking over Standard Air Lines. Transcontinental Air Transport was established on 16 May 1928, and in July 1929 undertook its first transcontinental service across the USA with the Ford Tri-Motor three-engined airliner between Columbus and Los Angeles, with the sector between Texas and Los Angeles being completed by the Santa Fe Railway, which had an interest in Transcontinental Air Transport. Late in 1929, the airline bought Maddux Airlines for the acquisition of its services in the San Francisco and San Diego areas.

On 16 July 1930, Western Air Express merged with Transcontinental Air Transport to create a major operator initially known as Transcontinental and Western Air, but in 1934 the original Western Air Express element of Transcontinental and Western Air was bought out and became the basis of Western Airlines. Transcontinental and Western Air was renamed Trans World Airlines on 17 May 1950, retaining the acronym TWA generally used for this long-established operator.

During the early 1930s, the airline approached Douglas to build the aeroplane that would revolutionize the air travel industry all over the world. This was the DC-1 – which paved the way for the very good DC-2 that itself led to the classic DC-3 – which entered service with Transcontinental and Western

Fleet (orders):
(25) x Airbus A318
(20) x Airbus A319-100
17 (33) x Boeing Model 717-200
27 x Boeing Model 757-200
7 x Boeing Model 767-200ER
9 x Boeing Model 767-300ER
40 x Boeing MD-82
64 x Boeing MD-83
27 x McDonnell Douglas DC-9-30

Air in June 1937. The importance attached by the airline to the use of the latest equipment was next reflected in its adoption of the world's first pressurized airliner, the Boeing Model 307 Stratoliner four-engined machine, during July 1940, and this important type entered service on the airline's route between Chicago and Los Angeles. Further development was effectively halted during the USA's involvement in World War II between 1941 and 1945, and in this period the airline undertook transport, training and modification work for the US military.

With World War II over and a semblance of normality returning to the airline business as air transport became increasingly commonplace, Transcontinental and Western Air started its first international service on 5 February 1946, using a Lockheed L-049 Constellation four-engined airliner for the route between New York and Paris. On 19 October 1953, some 30 months after it had become Trans World Airlines, the airline inaugurated a non-stop coast-to-coast service across the USA with the Lockheed L-1049A Super Constellation.

Further progress along the high-technology road followed on 20 March 1959, when the airline introduced the Boeing Model 707-131 four-turbojet airliner on the route between New

York and Los Angeles, then on 31 December 1969 when it received its first Boeing Model 747-131 four-turbofan airliner, the pioneer of the wide-body type of air transport, and finally on 9 May 1972, when it took delivery of its first Lockheed L-1011 TriStar three-turbofan airliner. The Model 747 and L-1011 became the mainstays of Trans World Airlines' long-haul operations for high- and medium-density services respectively.

Despite a number of financial and administrative vicissitudes in more recent times, Trans World Airlines had emerged as a major force in American and world air transport, and currently operates large numbers of modern aircraft to maintain its capability and market share. Trans World Airlines has been one of the US carriers worst affected by the post-September 2001 airline slump.

TRANSBRASIL (BRAZIL)

Main base and hub: São Paulo
Type of operation: International, regional and domestic scheduled and charter passenger and cargo
Personnel: 3,580

The Brazilian meat company Sadia started flight operations as Sadia S.A. Transportes Aéreos in January 1955, primarily to transport freight from Concordia to São Paulo, but advanced into the passenger-carrying business in March 1956 and then developed services into the south-eastern region of Brazil. Co-operation with REAL and Transportes Aéreos Salvador began in 1957, the latter being taken over by Sadia in 1962 after the collapse of REAL, and the enlarged company expanded into the north-eastern part Brazil. Sadia changed its name to Transbrasil in June 1972, and divided its scheduled and charter routes with

Fleet (orders):
12 x Boeing Model 737-300
1 x Boeing Model 737-400
3 x Boeing Model 767-200
2 x Boeing Model 767-300ER

Varig. Transbrasil is now the third largest airline in Brazil, and operates a network of scheduled services that comprises 23 domestic and five international destinations, the latter including three in the USA as well as Buenos Aires in Argentina and Lisbon in Portugal. The major shareholders are the Fontana family and the airline's employees.

TUNISAIR (TUNISIA)

Main base and hub: Tunis
Type of operation: International, regional and domestic scheduled and charter passenger
Personnel: 7,260

Tunisair was created in 1948 as a subsidiary of Air France under the terms of an agreement with the Tunisian government, and began operations in 1949. By 1957, the government of Tunis had acquired a controlling 51 per cent interest, and Air France's shareholding had been gradually reduced. Tunisair currently operates a network of scheduled services that comprises seven domestic and 49 international destinations, the latter in Africa, Europe and the Middle East.

Fleet (orders):
2 x Airbus A300-600R
1 x Airbus A300F4-200
2 (1) x Airbus A319-100
11 (1) x Airbus A320-200
4 x Boeing Advanced Model 727-200
3 x Boeing Advanced Model 737-200
4 x Boeing Model 737-500   6 (1) x Boeing Model 737-600

BELOW: *Tunisair combines Airbus and Boeing aircraft in its schedule of services.*

UNITED AIRLINES
(UNITED STATES OF AMERICA)

Main bases and hubs: Chicago (O'Hare), Denver, San Francisco and Washington (Dulles)
Type of operation: International, regional and domestic scheduled passenger services
Personnel: 100,000

United Airlines was formed by Henry Ford, to act as an airmail operator that undertook its initial service on 3 April 1925 between Detroit and Chicago. One year later, on 6 April 1926, Walter T. Varney started mail services in the north-west area of the USA, and on 12 May, National Air Transport started mail services between Chicago and Dallas, operating 10 Curtiss Carrier Pigeons. On 31 July of the same year, Bill Stout also began airmail and passenger services between Detroit and Grand Rapids. Another airline, Pacific Air Transport, started its first service from Los Angeles to Seattle on 15 September 1926.

All these airlines became involved in the creation of United Airlines, but the operator's most direct ancestor was Boeing Air Transport, which flew its first service on 1 July 1927 between Chicago and San Francisco, with one of the 24 Boeing Model 40A biplane transports that were this operator's primary equipment. On 1 January 1928, Boeing Air Transport took over control of Pacific Air Transport's operations, and on 17 December of the same year, the two companies effected a complete merger. The United Aircraft and Transport Corporation was formed on 1 February 1929, and on 30 June of the same year, UATC bought Stout Air Services and Ford, and on 7 May of the following year, UATC assumed control of National Air Transport, while on 30 June 1931 Varney Air Lines became a subsidiary.

On 1 July 1931, therefore, all of these pioneering airlines were part of UATC, and the new operator now possessed a route network spanning the USA between New York in the east and California in the west as well as Chicago in the north and Dallas in the south, although UATC gave up the route between Chicago and Dallas during 1934. UATC was the first customer for the Boeing Model 247, which was the first of what may be described as the 'modern airliners', as it was of all-metal construction with a cantilever low-set wing, enclosed accommodation for the crew and passengers, and retractable main landing gear units. The type made its maiden flight on 8 February 1933 and entered service with UATC, making its first revenue-earning flight on 30 March of the same year. By the end of June 1933, UATC had 30 Model 247 aircraft in service, but discovered that the aeroplane had poor performance at high-altitude airports; this problem was solved by the introduction of a variable-pitch propeller designed by Hamilton Standard, and this created the more effective Model 247D. UATC eventually operated 70 of the 75 Model 247 aircraft.

On 1 May 1934, the airline became United Airlines, which absorbed Pennsylvania Central Airline. In January 1940, United Airlines started to operate the Douglas DC-3. In July of the previous year, however, United Airlines had ordered six examples of the conceptually very advanced Douglas DC-4 (later DC-4E) four-engined airliner, and placed the prototype in

Fleet (orders):
36 (33) x Airbus A319-100
70 (38) x Airbus A320-200
75 x Boeing Advanced Model 727-200
24 x Boeing Advanced Model 737-200
101 x Boeing Model 737-300
57 x Boeing Model 737-500
44 x Boeing Model 747-400
98 x Boeing Model 757-200
11 x Boeing Model 767-200
8 x Boeing Model 767-200ER
35 (2) x Boeing Model 767-300ER

16 x Boeing Model 777-200
34 (11) x Boeing Model 777-200ER
1 x McDonnell Douglas DC-10-30F

limited experimental service on 1 June 1939. The type had too many advanced features for adequate reliability, however, and therefore did not enter production.

Late in 1940, United Airlines received a contract to train military personnel at the Oakland Training Center. The airline included a service from 15 May 1942 between Fairfield in Ohio and Anchorage in Alaska, and from 27 June of the same year a service from Salt Lake City to Anchorage. On 23 September 1942, United Airlines started to fly Douglas C-54 Skymaster four-engined transport aircraft on routes out into the Pacific theatre, a service that lasted to 31 March 1945. In January 1942, the airline was contracted to modify Boeing B-17 Flying Fortress bombers for photographic work.

On 11 September 1944, United Airlines ordered the Douglas DC-4 four-engined civil version of the C-54 but cancelled this contract in October 1945 when the US government released a large number of the C-54 model, and the type entered service in March 1946 linking Chicago and Washington, DC, followed by the service between California and Hawaii on 1 May 1947. On 24 November 1946, United Airlines took delivery of its first Douglas DC-6 four-engined transport, followed on 11 April 1951 by the improved DC-6B. Pending the delivery of an adequate number of the DC-4 and then the DC-6 series, United Airlines operated most of its services with a civilianized variant of the Douglas C-47 Skytrain/Dakota twin-engine military transport, itself a derivative of the DC-3, and in 1946 United Airlines was operating 77 of this type including 21 leased aircraft. United Airlines operated the C-47/DC-3 up to 1949.

On 20 February 1951, United Airlines placed an order for 30 examples of a considerably more advanced twin-engined type, the Convair CV-340, for its shorter-haul services, and took delivery of the first of these machines on 12 May of the same year. By this time, United Airlines had become aware of a technology gap in its long-haul fleet and ordered the Douglas DC-7 and, as an interim measure until this advanced type could be delivered, flew the Boeing Model 377 Stratocruiser, which entered service on 1 December 1953. With the arrival of the DC-7, United Airlines sold its whole Stratocruiser fleet to British Overseas Airways Corporation. The airline accepted its

145

ABOVE: *UAL's fleet includes large numbers of machines from the Airbus and Boeing stables.*

first DC-7 on 10 April 1954 for service from 1 June of the same year.

The DC-7 was United Airlines' long-haul mainstay throughout most of the 1950s, but towards the end of the decade, the airline required more advanced aircraft and ordered the DC-8-11 (later -12 and finally -22) four-jet airliner. United Airlines received its first DC-8 on 29 May 1959 into operational service from 18 September of the same year. The airline complemented the long-haul DC-8 with the medium-haul Model 720-022 which entered service on 5 July 1960 on the route linking Chicago and Los Angeles via Denver.

On 1 June 1961, United Airlines bought Capital Airlines, this being at the time the largest merger in US airline history. The combined airlines operated to 116 cities with a fleet of 267 aircraft, many of the shorter-haul services in the eastern and central USA being operated by a total of 20 Sud-Aviation Caravelle VIR twin-jet airliners imported from France.

In the first half of the 1960s, United Airlines needed to revive its medium-haul fleet, and opted for the Boeing Model 727-22 three-turbofan transport which entered service on 6 February 1964 between San Francisco and Denver. United Airlines eventually took very large numbers of the Model 727 in steadily improved models, and the ultimate Model 727-200 variant is still in large-scale use. The airline was the first American airline to order the Boeing Model 737, the twin-turbofan short-haul partner to the Model 727, and the first of this type was delivered on 29 December 1967. Like the Model 727, the Model 737 is still in service with United Airlines in three advanced variants. These two Boeing aircraft eventually replaced the Caravelle and the Vickers Viscount, the latter having entered service with United Airlines as a result of the merger with Capital.

United Airlines then bought the Boeing Model 747-122 wide-body transport for long-haul operations, and the first of these aircraft reached United Airlines on 30 June 1970. The airline still flies the Model 747 in three variants, together with substantial numbers of another wide-body transport, the McDonnell Douglas DC-10 three-turbofan airliner (two variants), which entered service in its original DC-10-10 form on 14 August 1971 on the route linking San Francisco and Washington, DC. Later wide-body types in United Airlines' current fleet include three Airbus twin-turbofan type for shorter-haul services and three longer-haul Boeing types – the Model 757, Model 767 and Model 777. United Airlines' current route network reached its present level with the 1985 purchase of the failing Pan American airline's Pacific division.

UPS (UNITED STATES OF AMERICA)

Main bases and hubs: Louisville, Hamilton, Miami and Taipei
Type of operation: International, regional and domestic scheduled and charter passenger and cargo
Personnel: not available
United Parcel Service was established in 1907, and is currently the world's largest company of its type. In 1953, the company set up its two-day 'UPS-Air' service, and in 1982 entered the overnight small package delivery market. UPS now provides services to more US destinations than any other carrier. It was only in 1987 that UPS established its own flight operations, however, up to that time contracting with airlines for its point-to-point deliveries. The company flies more than 1,000 domestic and 500 international services per day, these serving

Fleet (orders):
9 (81) x Airbus A300-600F
(13) x Boeing MD-11SF
45 x Boeing Model 727-100C
8 x Boeing Model 727-200F
12 x Boeing Model 747-100F
1 x Boeing Model 747-200B
6 x Boeing Model 747-200F
75 x Boeing Model 757-200PF
30 Boeing Model 767-300
  Freighter
49 x McDonnell Douglas DC-8-70

some 400 domestic and 220 international destinations, the latter in every continent of the world.

UZBEKISTAN AIRWAYS (UZBEKISTAN)

Main base and hub: Tashkent
Type of operation: International, regional and domestic scheduled and charter passenger and cargo
Personnel: not available
In 1992, the government of Uzbekistan, newly independent, created Uzbekistan Airways out of the aircraft and administration of the previous Tashkent Directorate of Aeroflot. This operator now flies a network of scheduled services linking 10 domestic designations and extending to 41 international destinations in Asia, Europe and the Middle East.

BELOW: *Uzbekistan Airways matches its CIS aircraft with growing numbers of Western types.*

Fleet (orders):
3 x Airbus A310-300
2 x Antonov An-12
1 x Antonov An-24
6 x Antonov An-24B
3 x Antonov An-24RV
3 x BAE Systems Avro RJ-85
3 x Boeing Model 757-200
2 x Boeing Model 767-300ER
1 x Ilyushin Il-62
4 x Ilyushin Il-62M
9 x Ilyushin Il-76T
4 x Ilyushin Il-86
4 (4) x Ilyushin Il-114
(10) x Ilyushin Il-114-100

12 x Tupolev Tu-154B
2 x Tupolev Tu-154M
14 x Yakovlev Yak-40

US AIRWAYS
(UNITED STATES OF AMERICA)

Main bases and hubs: Charlotte, Philadelphia, Baltimore and Pittsburgh
Type of operation: International, regional and domestic scheduled and charter passenger and cargo services
Personnel: 43,030
USAir came into existence in its present form as recently as 1979 but can trace its origins back to 5 March 1937 and the creation of All American Aviation to operate a semi-experimental airmail service, using the airborne pick-up technique, to cover 58 communities in Delaware, Maryland, Ohio, Pennsylvania and West Virginia. In March 1949, All American Aviation became All American Airways when it received permission to operate passenger services with Douglas DC-3 twin-engined airliners, and on 1 January 1953 this operator was renamed Allegheny Airlines. The airline grew steadily during the 1950s, and used its first turbine-powered aircraft, albeit briefly, in the course of 1962 as it flew

Fleet (orders):
57 (5) x Airbus A319-100
16 (26) x Airbus A320-200
6 (28) x Airbus A321-200
9 (1) x Airbus A330-300
45 x Boeing Advanced Model 737-200
84 x Boeing Model 737-300
54 x Boeing Model 737-400
34 x Boeing Model 757-200
12 x Boeing Model 767-200ER
19 x Boeing MD-81

10 x Boeing MD-82
40 x Fokker 100
20 x McDonnell Douglas DC-9-30

the Convair CV-540 turboprop-powered conversion of the CV-340 piston-engined airliner.

In the middle of the decade, Allegheny Airlines decided that the time was ripe for a transfer to advanced jet-powered aircraft, and the equipment it picked was the Douglas DC-9-14, of which the first leased example was received on 29 July

147

1966. In 1967, the relaxation of the regulations governing air transport operations in the USA allowed the airline to start a programme of considerable development and expansion, and by the end of 1967, Allegheny Airlines had extended its sphere of operation to the whole of the north-eastern part of the USA through the creation of Allegheny Commuter Lines which brought together a number of smaller operators to provide feeder services for Allegheny Airlines.

Further growth followed Allegheny Airlines' purchase of Lake Central Airlines on 14 March 1968 and of Mohawk Airlines on 14 December 1971. The additional routes and aircraft resulting from these acquisitions turned Allegheny Airlines from a local into a major regional operator, and on 28 October 1979 the continued expansion of Allegheny Airlines into an operator soon covering virtually the whole of the USA was signalled by a change of name to USAir. By this time, the capabilities of the airline had been enhanced by the continued purchase of DC-9 aircraft for its shorter-haul services as well as the larger Boeing Model 727 three-turbofan airliner for its

longer-haul services. Still more capability came with USAir's adoption of the Boeing Model 737 twin-turbofan airliner in the form of the Model 737-2B7 (first received on 18 November 1982) and Model 737-4B7 (first delivered on 28 November 1984), and also of the BAC One-Eleven.

USAir merged Piedmont Airlines and Pacific Southwest Airlines into its operations during 1988 and 1989 respectively, and is now a major factor in US domestic air operations, with its fleet of Boeing Model 737, Fokker 100 and McDonnell Douglas DC-9 and Boeing MD-80 series twin-turbofan aircraft augmented by its growing fleet of Airbus and Boeing Model 757 and Model 767 twin-turbofan aircraft for longer-haul services that now include a growing international element.

US Airways is currently ranked the sixth-largest passenger airline in the USA, and sees its future as resting in an agreed merger with United Airlines.

RIGHT: *Like other US airlines, US Airways sees merits in European as well as US aircraft.*

VARIG (BRAZIL)

Main bases and hubs: Rio de Janeiro and São Paulo
Type of operation: International, regional and domestic scheduled passenger and cargo services
Personnel: 15,605

Varig is the national flag carrier of Brazil, and is more formally known as Viação Aérea Rio-Grandense, or VARIG as it was at first rendered. This was established in Brazil on 7 May 1927 by an expatriate German, Dr Otto Ernst Meyer, with assistance from the German-backed Condor Syndikat, and began its first services on 15 June of the same year with a Dornier Wal flying boat, initially on the route linking Rio de Janeiro with Porto Alegre. There followed a period of modest growth as many services were added to the route network, but in 1931 the airline temporarily ceased operations because of the unsuitability of its Dornier Merkur and Wal seaplanes for continued services within the Rio Grande do Sul region, VARIG's primary operating area.

In April 1932, the airline resumed operations with two Junkers F 13 landplanes, the availability of this type allowing daily flights to some of the most popular destinations in Brazil, and further expansion of the route network became possible in 1938 with the delivery of larger airliners in the form of two Junkers Ju 52/3m three-engined transports. On 5 August 1942, a De Havilland D.H.89A Rapide was used on the airline's first international service on the route linking Porto Alegre and Montevideo in neighbouring Uruguay. By this time, World War II was occupying the attentions of most of the world's aircraft-manufacturing nations, and even though the airline took delivery of seven Lockheed Model 10A Electra twin-engined light transports, continued expansion of service was generally made impossible by lack of adequate aircraft. A freight service between Porto Alegre and Petotas was started in 1943 with F 13 and Model 10A aircraft.

In 1946, the first five of an eventually large fleet of Douglas

Fleet (orders):
2 x Boeing Model 727-100F
2 x Boeing Model 727-200F
13 x Boeing Advanced Model 737-200
34 x Boeing Model 737-300
4 x Boeing Model 737-400
5 (4) x Boeing Model 737-700
(10) x Boeing Model 737-800
5 x Boeing Model 767-200ER
6 (6) x Boeing Model 767-300ER
(6) x Boeing Model 777-200ER
12 x Boeing MD-11

3 x Boeing MD-11ER
2 x McDonnell Douglas DC-10-30F

DC-3 twin-engined airliners were delivered, these being followed in the late 1940s and early 1950s by numbers of the civilianized version of the larger Curtiss C-46 Commando twin-engined military transport, of which the first was received on 10 May 1948.

In 1953, VARIG was granted authorization to fly the route to New York, and for this service ordered three examples of the Lockheed L-1049G Super Constellation, of which the first was received on 3 May 1955 for the operation of the first service on 2 August of the same year. At the same time, VARIG reached agreement with Pan American World Airways for the purchase of five of the latter's Convair CV-240 twin-engined airliners, of which the first was accepted on 23 September 1954, for use on the Brazilian airline's domestic services. By the middle of the 1950s, VARIG had come to the conclusion that jet-powered equipment was required for the maintenance of its position on the New York service, and in October 1957 it ordered from France two examples of the Sud-Aviation Caravelle I, of which the first was received on 16 September 1959 for an operational debut on 19 December 1959 on the route between Buenos Aires

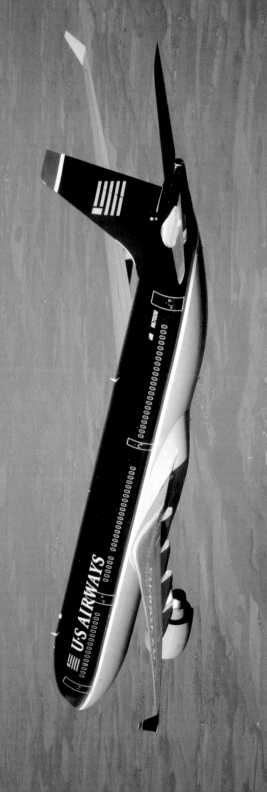

and New York via Montevideo, São Paulo, Rio de Janeiro, Belém, Port of Spain and Nassau. The Caravelle had too short a range for effective use on this service, however, and was soon superseded by the Boeing Model 707-441 four-turbofan airliner, of which the first two were received in June 1960 for first service on 2 July 1960.

VASP BRAZILIAN AIRLINES (BRAZIL)

Main bases and hubs: São Paulo (Congonhas and Guarulhas)
Type of operation: International, regional and domestic scheduled passenger and cargo
Personnel: 7,840

Viação Aérea São Paulo was created in November 1933 by the regional government of São Paulo and the municipal bank, and began operations in April 145. In 1939, the operator took over the Brazilian-German Aerolloyd Iguaçú, which added many more routes. In 1962, VASP took over two more airlines, Loide Aero Nacional and Navegação Aérea Brasileiro. Through a process of steady modernization and sensible growth, VASP became Brazil's second largest airline, and in this capacity started to add the Boeing Model 737 to its fleet in July 1969.

In the late 1990s, VASP bought into Ecuatoriana and Lloyd

Fleet (orders):
3 x Airbus A300B2
3 x Boeing Model 727-200F
6 x Boeing Model 737-200
13 x Boeing Advanced Model
  737-200
2 x Boeing Model 737-200C
1 x Boeing Model 737-300

Aereo Boliviano, but then fell into financial problems during 2000 and reorganized itself along smaller lines without a European component to its route network

VASP currently flies a network of scheduled services to 32 domestic and four international destinations, the latter comprising Miami and New York in the USA, Buenos Aires in Argentina, and Toronto in Canada.

VIRGIN ATLANTIC AIRWAYS (UNITED KINGDOM)

Main bases and hubs: London (Gatwick) and London (Heathrow)
Type of operation: International, regional and domestic scheduled passenger services
Personnel: 7,900

Virgin Atlantic Airways can trace its origins to British Atlantic Airways, which was created in 1982 but then failed to win a Civil Aviation Authority licence. Richard Branson then established Virgin Atlantic through his Virgin Group during 1984, the object being the provision of low-cost scheduled passenger services across the North Atlantic. The model for the new airline was the collapsed Laker Airways, a pioneer of the concept of 'cheap' services from London. Virgin Atlantic began services in June 1984 between London and New York (Newark), from November of the same year adding a connecting service between London and Maastricht in the Netherlands with BAC One-Eleven aircraft, later replaced by Vickers Viscount aircraft until the link was terminated in 1990.

Despite the fact that it offered no optional 'frills', Virgin Atlantic was able to capitalize on imaginative advertising to win a larger slice of the market hitherto dominated by British Airways. The airline continued to add Boeing Model 747 'wide-body' transports to its fleet, and this allowed an expansion of the American destinations to include Miami and New York (John F. Kennedy International) as well as Tokyo via Moscow. Late in 1993 Virgin Atlantic added the Airbus A340 to its fleet for services to Hong Kong and Australia, while an Airbus A320 flying a feeder service to Athens was later succeeded by an Airbus A321. In 1996, Virgin Atlantic bought a Belgian operator, EuroBelgian Airlines, as the

Fleet (orders):
1 x Airbus A321-200
10 x Airbus A340-300
(10) x Airbus A340-600
(6) x Airbus A380-800
11 x Boeing Model 747-200B
6 (7) x Boeing Model 747-400

basis for its new European network operating under the Virgin Express logo. In 2001, Virgin Express was flying seven Boeing Model 737-300 and four Model 737-400 aircraft on a scheduled network connecting nine European cities.

In 1996, Virgin Express also added Johannesburg in South Africa to its route network, and two years later received authorization to transport military personnel between London and Washington. Further expansion came in 1999 with the establishment of the Manchester-based Virgin Sun as a charter operator with three A320-200 and one A321-200 aircraft. Other subsidiaries are Virgin Express (Ireland), created in 1998 and now flying five Model 737-300 and two Model 737-400 aircraft, and Virgin Express France, created in 1995 as Air Provence Charter and adopting its present name in 1998. Plans for a similarly conceived low-cost Australian airline began to mature in mid-2000 with the creation of Virgin Blue Airlines, operating a fleet of five Model 737-400 aircraft supplemented by nine Model 737-700 machines.

RIGHT: *The current mainstay of Virgin's long-range capability is the Boeing 747.*

GLOSSARY

ABA	AB Aerotransport
ABH	Airlines of Britain Holdings
An	Antonov
ANA	All Nippon Airways
ANZ	Air New Zealand
APR	Automatic Performance Reserve
APU	Auxiliary Power Unit
ARIA	Aeroflot – Russian International Airlines
BEA	British European Airways
BOAC	British Overseas Airways Corporation
BWIA	British West Indian Airways
CAAC	Civil Aviation Administration of China
CF	Consolidated Freightways
CGTA	Compagnie Générale de Transports Aériens
CIDNA	Compagnie Internationale de Navigation Aérienne
CIS	Commonwealth of Independent States
CLS	Ceskoslovenská Letecká Spolecnost
CRJ	Canadair Regional Jet
CSA	Ceskoslovenské Státní Aerolinie
DDL	Det Danske Luftfartselskap
DHC	De Havilland Canada
DNL	Det Norske Luftfartselskap
Do	Dornier
DST	Douglas Sleeper Transport
EFIS	Electronic Flight Instrumentation System
HUD	Head-Up Display
Il	Ilyushin
JAL	Japan Airlines
JHATC	Japan Helicopter and Airplane Transport Company
KLM	Koninklijke Luchtvaart Maatschappij
KNILM	Koninklijke Nederlandsche Indische Luchtvaart
LAB	Lloyd Aéro Boliviano
LAI	Linee Aree Italiane
LAMSA	Líneas Aéreas Mexicanas SA
LAPA	Líneas Aéreas Privadas Argentinas
LARA	Ligne Aérienne de Roi Albert
LAT	Lignes Aériennes de Latecoere
LOT	Polskie Linie Lotnicze
LTU	(originally) Lufttransport Union
MD	McDonnell Douglas
NATO	North Atlantic Treaty Organization
NKK	Nihon Kinkyori Airways
NKKK	Nihon Kokuyuso Kaishiki Kaisha (Japan Air Transport Company)
NRT	Neue Rumpf Technologien
NVS	Noise and Vibration System
NWA	(holding company for) Northwest Orient Airlines
NZNAC	New Zealand National Airways Corporation
PATCO	Philippine Aerial Taxi Co.
PIA	Pakistan International Airlines
PIP	Performance Improvement Package; Performance Improvement Program
PW	Pratt & Whitney
QANTAS	Queensland and Northern Territory Aerial Service
RAM	Royal Air Maroc
RJ	Regional Jetliner
Sabena	Société Anonyme Belge d'Exploitation de la Navigation Aérienne
SAS	Scandinavian Airlines System
SKOGA	People's Aviation Corporation of China
STOL	Short Take-Off and Landing
TAE	Technical and Aeronautical Exploitations Co.
TAP	Transportes Aéreos Portugueses
TAROM	Transporturile Aeriere Romane
TCA	Trans-Canada Air Lines
TARS	Transporturite Aerienne Romana Sovietica
TEAL	Tasman Empire Airways Ltd
THY	Türk Hava Yollari
Tu	Tupolev
TWA	Trans World Airlines (formerly Transcontinental and Western Air)
UATC	United Aircraft and Transport Corporation
UK	United Kingdom
UPS	United Parcel Service
USA	United States of America
USSR	Union of Soviet Socialist Republics
Varig	Viação Aérea Rio-Grandense
VASP	Viação Aérea São Paulo

INDEX

PICTURE ACKNOWLEDGEMENTS

The Publishers wish to thank Teddy Nevill from TRH Pictures for researching the pictures listed below:

TRH Pictures 9, 22, 73, 88, 96, 120, /Aermacchi 33, /Aerospatiale 16 /Air France 56, /Air Photographic International 14, 42, 43, 45, 92, 117 /Airbus 6, 11, 89, 98, 109, 113, 115, 125, 137,139, 141, 147, 149 /American Airlines 67, /ATR 15, /Boeing 21, 23, 24, 25, 27, /Bombardier 28, 29, 30, 58, 110, /Austin J. Brown/The Aviation Picture Library 18, 51, 91, /CASA 13, /Daimler Chrysler 10,100, /EADS 8, 12, /Embraer 32, 135, /Eva Air front cover centre, 93,/ Fairchild Dornier 34, 35, /Fokker 36, 37, /Robert Hewson 134, /E Nevill 85, 97, 127, /Ewan Partridge 7, 17, 19, 20, 31, 41, 47, 49, 52, 53, 55, 57, 60, 63, 65, 70, 75, 76, 78, 81, 83, 86, 87, 95, 101, 102, 105, 107, 122, 123, 129, 133, 142, 144, 151, /Raytheon 40, /Tim Senior 26, /Colin Smedley 44, 80 /United Airlines 146, /Dave Willis 39

Executive Editor: Trevor Davies
Editor: Rachel Lawrence
Executive Art Editor: Geoff Fennell
Designer: Line + Line
Picture Research: Teddy Nevill and Liz Fowler
Production Controller: Edward Carter

Tailfins: Line + Line
Line Artwork: Mark Rolfe